ADDICTION BY PR

Doctor
Lovuge

Addiction by Prescription

One Woman's Triumph and Fight for Change

Joan E. Gadsby

KEY PORTER BOOKS

Canadian Cataloguing in Publication Data

Gadsby, Joan E.
    Addiction by prescription : one woman's triumph and fight for change

ISBN 1-55263-156-7

1. Medication abuse. 2. Tranquilizing drugs. 3. Gadsby, Joan – Health.
4. Medication abusers – Canada – Biography. I. Title.

RM146.5.G32   2000   362.29'9   C99-933068-3

The Canada Council | Le Conseil des Arts
for the Arts | du Canada
since 1957 | depuis 1957

The publisher gratefully acknowledges the support of the Canada Council for the Arts and the Ontario Arts Council for its publishing program.

We acknowledge the financial support of the Government of Canada through the Book Publishing Industry Development Program (BPIDP) for our publishing activities.

Key Porter Books Limited
70 The Esplanade
Toronto, Ontario
Canada M5E 1R2
www.keyporter.com

To obtain a video cassette copy of the 1998 television documentary Our Pill Epidemic: The Shocking Story of a Society Hooked on Drugs *(tranquilizers and sleeping pills), call 1-800-471-5628 (Canada and the United States.) For international formats, call (780) 412-8944 or fax (403) 474-0418. Or write Crown Video at P.O. Box 1108, Edmonton, Alberta, Canada, T5J 2M1. E-mail: sales@crownvideo.com.*

Electronic formatting: Kim Monteforte, Heidy Lawrance Associates
Design: Peter Maher

Printed and bound in Canada

00 01 02 03 04 6 5 4 3 2 1

To my beloved children,
who have given, and continue to give,
purpose and meaning to my life:

DEBRA LYN
born September 3, 1961; died May 1, 1999, of breast cancer

DEREK SCOTT
born September 21, 1962; died December 25, 1966,
of a brain tumor

CARRIE DARLENE
born June 28, 1970, who is my ongoing source of strength,
inspiration, and love

Acknowledgments

On February 2, 1990, I almost died following an unintentional overdose of tranquilizers and sleeping pills—both of which were prescribed by a trusted family physician for over twenty years after the death of my son Derek of a brain tumor. I have spent the last decade rebuilding my life, my health and my family. It has been a long, lonely, devastating experience for me and all of those closest to me.

My two beloved daughters, Deb and Carrie, have been ongoing sources of strength, inspiration and love. Although Deb tragically died on May 1, 1999, following a battle with breast cancer, I know that she is still with me—providing guidance, wisdom and love, and encouraging me to be strong and to live each day to its fullest. During the horrors of withdrawal, Bryan Adams's song "Everything I Do, I Do It for You" became the focus of my thoughts about my daughters and our love for each other. I knew I would become the mother they always deserved.

My sister, Pat, and brothers, Bill and Bob, were also right there for me. Along with my son-in-law, Martin, they continue to provide love, meaning and purpose to my life.

It's also important to say that, although our marriage ended in 1977, I have a positive friendship with my former husband, Alan. He is very supportive of all my efforts to raise awareness of the insidious effects of prescription drugs, my fight for justice, compensation and systemic change. The details I've revealed about our dysfunctional home life and our relationship when I was on pills were not disclosed to discredit or criticize him. Alan and I were very young when we married, and we were faced with the most intense emotional challenges imaginable, beginning with the death of our son in 1966. Although we have chosen to live separate lives, today we enjoy a mutually caring relationship free of the anger, resentment and turmoil that once characterized our lives together.

I continue to cherish my friends Anita, Miriam, Cathy, Madeleine, Kay, Donna and Una, as well as my friendship with Dan[1]; my former love relationship of five years. Dan was there for me during the early stages of withdrawal, and he gave me the book of poetry in which I found the original title for this book—*Out of Tune.*

For the past three years, my vision and passion for this book has been shared and encouraged by Suzanne Zeviar. She collaborated closely on the proposal and assisted in writing the first draft. Her patience in keeping me focused and her commitment to this project are very much appreciated. I also received assistance with the rewrites from two other writers, Michael Carroll and Ric Bearisto. In addition, I would like to acknowledge Ina Hart's dedicated computer work on the final revisions. I am also very grateful to Key Porter Books for their courage and commitment to this project, which I see as an important follow-up to Barbara Gordon's book, *I'm Dancing As Fast As I Can*, written two decades ago.

I would particularly like to thank four of my health care professionals—Dr. Susan West, Dr. Ursula Wild, Dr. Raymond Parkinson and Dr. Mary Stewart-Moore—for their recognition of my past "addiction by prescription" and for their unending support during my horrifying protracted withdrawal and efforts to rebuild my health and my life. Regrettably, they are in the minority. I can only hope that others within the medical community and health care system will become "tuned in" and replace ignorance, apathy and denial with openness, honesty and caring concern for their patients.

My international research over the past decade has included interviews with hundreds of patients, benzodiazepine action/survivor groups, doctors, health care professionals, researchers, pharmaceutical representatives, government bodies, politicians, and medical and legal professionals.

All provided valuable knowledge and direction in shaping this book, and I am most grateful for their input.

I have been free of tranquilizers and sleeping pills for ten years now, and the quality of my life has improved tenfold. I believe God kept me alive to carry my vital message of triumph over prescription drugs and to carry on the fight for justice and systemic change. For this, too, I am thankful.

Contents

The world is too much with us; late and soon,
Getting and spending, we lay waste our powers:
Little we see in Nature that is ours;
We have given our hearts away, a sordid boon!
This Sea that bares her bosom to the moon;
The winds that will be howling at all hours,
And are up-gathered now like sleeping flowers;
For this, for everything, we are out of tune …

—WILLIAM WORDSWORTH, "Sonnet XXXIII: The World Is Too Much with Us"

Preface

Regrettably and tragically, while I was writing and revising this book over the past year and a half, my older daughter, Deb, was diagnosed with and treated for breast cancer; she died on May 1, 1999, at age thirty-seven, after a courageous and stoic battle with this insidious disease.

She was a remarkable young woman—one of the best and brightest. She had been very happily married for eighteen years, and throughout her life had dedicated herself to helping others and trying to make the world a better place, one day and one person at a time. She was an executive working in a health-related field, and this June after her death she was recognized in the British Columbia Legislature by the Minister of Labour and the Opposition for her energy and spirit, and her ongoing commitment and service to the workers and employers of the Province—"a model of dedication who impressed everyone she met." A great humanitarian, and an accomplished athlete, Deb participated enthusiastically and passionately in whatever she was involved with, in work or in play. Her smile was infectious and her motto was "Go hard or go home." Her zest for life, her love of nature, people, adventure, sports (golf in particular), her love of music and cars was unmatched. Despite our dysfunctional home life when she was growing up making her early death even the more tragic, she survived to live a meaningful and productive life.

In the nine years since overcoming a debilitating addiction to the drugs prescribed for me for more than twenty years, I have struggled to rebuild my life and my family. I continue to grieve over my beloved daughter's death. It is cruelly unfair that she is not here to experience and share life with us.

I had no need of pills to cope with the fear and uncertainty that Deb's disease created, nor did I need them to cope with grief over the loss of my beloved daughter. But once more I have to ask: Why does one so young have to die? I have lost two of my children to cancer. My son, Derek, died of the disease when he was only four years old. The pain of losing them both will never leave me, but I realize that I must carry on with my mission to help others, and continue to work toward making the world a better place. I know Deb would want that. One of her final messages for me, conveyed through her husband, Martin, after she died, was to get my book out. I love her dearly and miss her very much, but I still have her with me all the time, running beside me every day and encouraging me to do my very best. She was and still is my rock.

ON FEBRUARY 2, 1990, I unintentionally overdosed on drugs prescribed for me. If the ambulance had arrived just two minutes later, I would, in all likelihood, have died.

Four months later, I was lying on the couch at home, trying to read Barbara Gordon's *I'm Dancing as Fast as I Can*, which had been a best-seller when it was published in 1979.[1] I was struggling: the words jumbled before my eyes, and the lines of text ran together; I read and reread the words, unable to grasp their meaning. This inability to focus was symptomatic, I would later realize, of cognitive damage. The symptoms alarmed me, but I was intensely interested in the subject matter, so I persevered, and little by little I managed to read Gordon's account of her similar problems with prescribed tranquilizers, her drug-induced nervous breakdown, and her bizarre and harrowing experiences during withdrawal. Her story brought back, with frightening intensity, all the memories of my own terrible past. It also described, in powerful terms, the confusion, panic, and pervasive emotional disturbances I was experiencing as I read it.

Six weeks earlier, without medical supervision, I had begun the gradual process of discontinuing my use of the tranquilizers and sleeping pills that had been prescribed for me continuously for twenty-three years by Roderick MacGillivray, my formerly much-trusted family doctor. All the pills I had taken were benzodiazepines, manufactured under a variety of trade names, including Librium, Valium, Dalmane, Restoril, Serax, and Ativan. They differ little, except in strength, but they represent a serious hidden epidemic that is affecting millions of unsuspecting individuals from all walks of life, worldwide. According to the World Health Organization, benzodiazepines are among the most frequently prescribed drugs on the planet. I was given the first of these medications shortly after my son, Derek, died at the age of four of a brain tumor on Christmas Day 1966.

When I stopped taking the pills, I thought things would only get better, that the turmoil and unpredictability I had endured for so many years would end. But the months that followed were, without question, the most terrifying and uncertain period of my life. It has taken years for me to regain my physical, mental, and emotional health.

During withdrawal, I lost more than twenty pounds. I lived on milk and bananas almost exclusively for two months, because I was scarcely able to swallow. I also endured severe paranoia, hallucinations, visual distortions, depersonalization, derealization, panic attacks, headaches, and painful flashbacks to my son's death twenty-four years earlier. I slowly came to believe that the pills had suppressed my vision, touch, smell, hearing, and emotions more and more every year, and that my intellectual functioning had been impaired not only when I was on the pills, but during withdrawal and for many years afterward.

It is amazing to me now to think back and realize that I managed, against all the odds, to have a successful professional and political career despite my unknowing addiction. I had worked for four of Canada's largest companies—Colgate-Palmolive, Scott Paper, Kelly Douglas & Co., and the Southland Corporation (owner of the 7-Eleven chain)—in senior-level marketing management, strategic corporate planning, public affairs, government relations, and property planning and development. I had also served as an elected councillor in my community for thirteen years. Somehow, I was able to function despite the formidable difficulties created by my ever-worsening addiction. Withdrawal, however, was another matter altogether.

Throughout my withdrawal, I lived alone. For months I was crippled by feelings of dread and slept for as little as an hour a night. Scarcely a day passed that I didn't think I was going to die. Simply getting dressed and leaving the house was a huge undertaking. Although withdrawal gave me no choice but to take indefinite leave from my job, I forced myself to keep active and I attended a few business luncheons and events, desperate to keep up appearances with former colleagues. I recorded my thoughts on tape every day; I had informed my daughters Deb (Debra) and Carrie that, if I died, they were to retrieve the tapes and listen to them so they could understand what had happened to me. I was filled with fear and uncertainty about the future: Was I going to get better? What was to become of me? How was I going to cope financially? These weren't thoughts I ever expected to have, and it was a shock to feel so vulnerable and lost. I was reduced to feeling like a frightened child.

To make matters worse, I had to go through this harrowing time without professional support or guidance. There was virtually no medical help or information available. In fact, there was widespread denial among the medical profession that the problem of prescription-drug addiction existed. For many doctors, the solution was increased dosages or a change to another type of tranquilizer. Dr. MacGillivray, who had given me the prescriptions for all those years, discouraged me from attempting to withdraw. He was convinced I needed those pills.

As the detoxification process continued and my level of awareness improved, I had to face many painful memories. During my years of addiction, I had frequently flown into rages, often landing in either jail or hospital. I was a public figure in my community, and my escapades hit the newspapers more than once, causing me and my family extraordinary humiliation. Recollections of these episodes surfaced during withdrawal, like pieces of a shattered funhouse mirror.

I was also haunted by my numerous unintentional overdoses. I had everything to live for, and never consciously wished to take my own life, yet on many occasions I swallowed dozens of pills, sometimes washing them down with alcohol, never once realizing the significance of my behavior or making the link between my actions and the drugs' paradoxical side effects.

Yet I also experienced great joy during the period of my withdrawal. As the weeks passed, and I slowly regained my senses, I was overwhelmed by the intricacy and beauty I saw in everyday things. For the first time in many years, I was aware of the detail in clouds, the pistils and stamens in flowers, the vivid oranges and reds of the sunset, and the sea of brilliant stars in the night sky. And the visual and auditory revelations kept coming. I live high up, in a neighborhood nestled beneath the famous Grouse Mountain Sky Ride in North Vancouver, British Columbia. Driving down toward Vancouver from my home one day shortly after discontinuing the pills, I saw the beauty of the city's skyline with a sharpened perception I hadn't known in years. It was this excitement at seeing a whole new world emerging that kept me going during that horrendous time. I experienced intense feelings of regret and sadness for all the years I had lost, but I also felt reborn.

Today, I feel as though I've started my life over again. I'm full of energy, enthusiasm, and purpose. I take care of my health—get lots of fresh air, eat good food, and take a daily run along the West Vancouver seawall, rain or shine—and have cultivated a support system of family, friends, and associates who have been instrumental in my recovery. Despite the ongoing obstacles I face (legal battles, struggles with insurance companies, uncertain financial security, and the general indifference of a system that doesn't work), I derive considerable satisfaction from the belief that what I'm doing with this book and my other initiatives will help people in similar circumstances, and effect the systemic change required.

The effects of prescribed benzodiazepines have been misdiagnosed as schizophrenia, manic-depression, cyclothymia, borderline psychosis, agitated depression, hysteria, and just plain neurosis. Like Barbara Gordon's, my outbursts, rages, and unpredictable states were attributed to an alleged psychiatric illness or emotional problems. During my twenty-three years on drugs, even though I managed to maintain a successful career in both politics and business, I was, on several occasions, arrested; put in restraints; sedated; jailed; and labeled bipolar, alcoholic, and psychotic. Not once in those years did a psychiatrist, physician, or any other medical professional deal with what I believe to be the real root of the problem—a rapidly growing chemical dependency on highly addictive prescription drugs with known serious side effects. In fact, they all did their best to convince me that the drugs would relieve my problems, keep me calm, and allow me to sleep at night.

In the late 1960s, the entire medical system bought into the pharma-ceutical companies' vigorous campaigns to market and promote tranquil-izers and sleeping pills. During that time, and later, those who confided and trusted in physicians after a crisis such as the death of a loved one, a divorce, or the loss of a job were particularly vulnerable. Drugs were touted as the answer to everything, including the normal emotional reactions to life's everyday challenges.

As my awareness increased, so did my anger at and disillusionment with the medical system that had facilitated my deterioration. I was deter-mined to learn the truth about the drugs and what they had done to me physically, mentally, and emotionally. I needed to know more about the residual effects, how long I could expect to continue in this state, and what the future might hold for me. Given my extensive business experi-ence and skills in strategic marketing, research, and politics, it was nat-ural for me to apply my knowledge in these areas to an investigation of the history and medical facts surrounding benzodiazepines. My only regret is that I did not do this much sooner, and that I had blindly trusted my family doctor. My quest for information began in my own North Shore community, then extended throughout British Columbia, across Canada and the United States, and around the world. What I discovered shocked and incensed me.

The deleterious and paradoxical effects of benzodiazepines, prescribed short- and long-term, had been researched and discussed for *decades*. It seemed incredible to me that, despite the substantial amount of infor-mation available to doctors as far back as the 1960s, a lack of insight among medical professionals concerning the dire side effects of highly addictive prescription drugs and the often severe withdrawal people suf-fer when they try to stop were so commonplace. Enormous attention is paid to the use of illegal drugs (heroin, cocaine, and marijuana) in our society today; publicly and privately, money is allocated to facilities and resources to help people overcome addiction and drug withdrawal, but the prescription-drug problem is barely acknowledged, and no real assis-tance is offered to those who want to cease long-term use of tranquilizers and sleeping pills.

Why has nothing been done to address this serious and entirely preventable health problem? Why is the medical community, even today, unwilling to correct it? Worldwide, millions of prescriptions for old and new types of tranquilizers, sleeping pills, and antidepressants are being written for vulnerable patients who blindly trust their doctors to "do no harm."[2] It's my hope that, by telling the story of my own long nightmare with prescribed drugs, I can help some of those people avoid some of the painful consequences of involuntary addiction and also act as a catalyst for change in the medical community.

The second half of this book details my investigation of international documented research and the systemic denial within the medical profession, pharmaceutical industry, and political system. It also serves as a comprehensive call to action to address this serious health issue.

Over the past nine years, I have interviewed thousands of people: consumers (patients), doctors, health-care professionals, pharmaceutical-company representatives, academic researchers, pharmacists, and government officials. My contacts with many other men and women who have been similarly affected led to my forming the Benzodiazepine Call to Action Group in 1995, which is now in regular contact with the international Victims of Tranquilizers (VOT) group in the United Kingdom, and similar organizations in Great Britain, Continental Europe, Australia, South Africa, and the United States, including Action for Benzodiazepine Awareness, the Council for Involuntary Tranquilizer Addiction, Survivors of Psychiatry, Patients Rights Advocacy, Tranx, Tranquilizer Users Recovery Network, and the International Center for the Study of Psychiatry and Psychology, to name only a few of an expanding worldwide network of groups dedicated to the responsible prescribing and use of these drugs. Recently, we also formed Benzodiazepine Awareness Network International (BAN).

Above all, the Benzodiazepine Call to Action Group is committed to improving the quality of life of thousands of people who innocently trusted their doctors and to saving millions of dollars within the health care system. Our objectives are to create a high level of awareness of the problem, and to advocate for systemic and legislative change that will hold physicians, drug manufacturers, pharmacists, health authorities, and political decision makers to a higher standard of ethics and accountability.

In April 1997, in Ottawa, I made a presentation to Canada's House of Commons Standing Committee on Health, outlining the prescription-drug crisis, and am still pressing for Senate hearings and a full-scale public inquiry on this subject. BAN is planning an international conference in Boston in the spring of 2001. With Jack McGaw (former executive producer of CTV's "W5" investigative reports), I co–executive-produced a television documentary, *Our Pill Epidemic: The Shocking Story of a Society Hooked on Drugs,* which took two and a half years from concept to completion and was broadcast twice nationally on Canada's CTV network in 1998 and is now available in video format worldwide. As a result of its airing, we received hundreds of phone calls and letters from across the country.

In addition to assembling a library of more than 2,000 research papers, abstracts, and books on the subject of benzodiazepines published since the late 1960s worldwide, I have located seven other books written by victims/survivors of benzodiazepines since Barbara Gordon's *I'm Dancing as Fast as I Can,* in 1979: *Life without Tranquilizers* (1985, Vernon Coleman), *Alive and Kicking* (1989, Peter Ritson), *Prisoner on Prescription* (1990, Heather Jones), *Back to Life* (1992, Pam Armstrong), *Benzo Junkie* (1993, Beatrice Faust), *The Accidental Addict* (1994, Di Porritt and Di Russell), and *The Judas Window* (1996, Felicity Bielovich).

In essence, the medical establishment's pharmacological approach to normal fluctuations of mood, mind, and emotion is seriously "out of tune" (to borrow a phrase from William Wordsworth's well-known sonnet "The World Is Too Much with Us"). The pursuit of bottom-line profits by drug companies, and the unfortunate complicity of doctors who, through their ignorance, collective denial, and neglect, foster chemical dependency in their patients, have created an epidemic of "accidental addicts." And I was one of them.

During the past drug-free decade, I have come to understand more fully that all the money in the world means nothing if you don't have your health. My experience with prescription pills has already cost me more than a million dollars in lost income, assets, and legal fees. My fight for justice in the courts in a lawsuit against Dr. MacGillivray—which is mirrored by more than 5,000 similar actions initiated through Victims of Tranquillizers in the United Kingdom—put my personal life under a public microscope, complete with sensational headlines and news reports covering the trial's proceedings. However, I am determined to continue speaking out about this issue, in order to effect much overdue systemic changes, to enlighten those who are ignorant or may be judgmental, and to explain what actually happens to people and their lives under the influence of these legally prescribed drugs.

I sincerely believe God kept me alive through many close calls, and my last unintentional overdose in 1990, to carry the message to others about the dangers of benzodiazepines. These drugs can, and do, cause far more problems than they alleviate, and accepting them as ongoing treatment is often the first step in a downward spiral that can result in ruined lives and careers, alienated families, financial devastation, lost years, and even death. If through sharing my experience I can spare others the damage and heartbreak that my family has undergone, I will accomplish something very meaningful. Sadly, my children Deb and Carrie grew up with a mother they didn't know. In fact, I was on drugs for Carrie's entire childhood and teenage years; she was twenty years old when I finally freed myself from addiction. On the Mother's Day card she gave me in 1990, when I had just come off the pills, she wrote, "You are so different. Give me time. ..." When I read that message, I cried, thinking about all the years we had lost. My determination to get well has been fueled by my love for my two very special daughters, and a desire to be the kind of mother I always wanted to be, and could have been— the mother my children always deserved.

Prologue

WHEN DAN ARRIVED FOR dinner at my North Vancouver home, I couldn't help greeting him at the door with the usual warm, lingering kiss, even though I had asked him over so I could break off our five-year relationship. After we ate, we made love, then sat on the sofa in the living room, listening to romantic pop songs on the stereo, enjoying the hiss and crackle of the fire, drinking the remaining bottle of Chablis.

It was a cold, rainy day in February 1990. Outside the French doors, a particularly savage gust of wind knocked something over on the deck. I knew that if I was going to do it, now was the time. "We can't go on like this, you know."

He sighed. "So now we get to what's really bugging you. Joan, we've got something pretty good. Don't spoil it."

"You mean you've got something pretty good. A wife and children to go home to and another woman on the side."

"You want me to get a divorce and marry you? Is that what you're saying? We've already discussed that and agreed it's not what either of us wants."

"I need someone all the time, Dan. I've told you that many times. This just doesn't work anymore for me. It's too lonely when you leave."

"That's crap! It's my heart condition, isn't it? That's what scares you more than anything."

I took another sip of wine, trying to remember how much Serax I'd taken that day. "Dan, I just can't——"

"So you make a terrific salmon dinner, we have sex, play some Lionel Richie and Barbra Streisand, then: Boom! It's over."

He stood, snatched up his coat, and walked to the door, with me following him.

"You can't go now!" I cried as he opened the door.

"Didn't you just say we're finished? Make up your mind!"

Suddenly I was filled with an inexplicable rage; before I knew what I was doing, I reached over, pulled his tie, and screamed, "I'll tell your wife everything."

He went completely white and grabbed my neck as if to choke me. I was so startled that I released my grip on his tie and tried to step back. Realizing what he was doing, he let me go, spun around, and headed out into the pouring rain. My heart pounding, I slammed the door, afraid he might come back. I had never before seen such a look of pure hatred and raw fear in anyone's eyes. And yet part of me wanted to run out into the rain after him. This was the man I thought I loved.

For a full minute, maybe longer, I just stood there, listening as his car drove off and the rain pelted down relentlessly. Then I went into the bathroom in search of more Serax. When I opened the medicine cabinet, all I could see was a maze of plastic pill containers. There were capsules, caplets, and tablets for everything. Where was the Serax? Maybe I'm out of them, I thought with mounting panic. But hadn't I just filled a new prescription? Finally, I spotted it. I took the pill bottle into the kitchen, where I fetched a glass and took a Coors Light beer and a can of Diet Sprite out of the refrigerator. I mixed the beer with some of the soda, popped one of the yellow Serax pills into my mouth, and washed it down with my "cocktail." I began to feel anxious. What had I done? Would I ever see Dan again? I loved him, didn't I?

A little unsteady on my feet, I wandered out of the kitchen and into the dining room, my glass of beer and Sprite clutched in my hand. I went over to the French doors, opened them, walked out onto the deck, and looked at the towering fir trees in the backyard. They were taking a beating from the wind, which whipped rain onto the wooden decking. Behind me the cedar logs in the fireplace were still crackling, and, as if mocking me, Engelbert Humperdinck sang "Are You Lonesome Tonight?" through the stereo speakers. I turned and went back into the living room, wandering over to a photo montage I had made after Derek died. My eyes focused on a picture of my son and daughter, Deb and Derek, when they were small, holding hands and smiling happily at each other.

And suddenly all my grief at Derek's early death came rushing back, with full force.

"You were only four years old," I cried. "It isn't fair. No one should die so young!"

Twenty-four years after Derek's death, my body was again racked with anguish, and I sobbed as if I had never cried for him before. When I'd exhausted myself, I gulped down the rest of my drink and went back to the kitchen to refill my glass. Now my grief was replaced with crushing guilt. Deb and Carrie, my two daughters, were alive, but I'd lost them, too, thanks to all the pills and alcohol I'd consumed over the years, all the crazy things I'd done. Their photographs also swam before my eyes: graduation pictures, vacation snapshots, Christmas, birthdays. … I wandered through the house, looking at all the memories. The pain and guilt that tormented me seemed unbearable. Suddenly, I knew I had to talk to someone.

I made my way uncertainly out of the living room and into the kitchen, and snatched the cordless phone off the counter. I punched in Dan's number. His answering machine came on, but I hung up before the message was finished. I took another two Serax pills, washing them down with more beer. After that I phoned everybody I could think of, including my brothers and sister back east, Deb, Carrie, friends. … Some of them answered. I was crying, rambling. Incoherently, I spilled out all the grief, guilt, pain, anger, and anguish that was consuming me. I called and called. If I got answering machines, I left long, emotional messages, hysterical recriminations, babbling nonsense.

Eventually I took the whole bottle of Serax. At some point, as my mood became ever bleaker, I phoned Carrie. She answered immediately, reminded me that I had already called her several times that night, and told me to go to bed. I cried and tried to tell her how sorry I was for everything I had done. Then a wave of nausea and dizziness washed over me.

The receiver slipped from my hand, and I fell to the floor. I lay staring up at a distant, blurring ceiling, and from somewhere far off a voice sang about regret, lost love, years gone by. Time, I thought. Memories. So many … Darkness.

CHAPTER ONE

Early Promise

THE VINEYARDS AND ORCHARDS of Niagara served as a backdrop for most of my formative years in the 1940s and 1950s. Our home, Hi-Ho Camp, a former inn and ten country cabins located on a scenic highway, sat on five acres across from an enormous natural pond that became a gathering place for skating parties every winter. I was raised here with my brother Bill, who is two years older than I am. My sister, Pat, and my brother Bob—thirteen and twelve years older respectively—were already living away from home when I was still quite young.

Our big semicircular driveway was framed by rosebushes and hollyhocks that blossomed crimson, yellow, and pink each spring, and the willow trees on the huge lawn provided shady places to sit on hot afternoons. I used to sit high up in one of the big cherry trees, and from that vantage point I would observe the comings and goings of the many world travelers who stayed with us. Most of them were educated and interesting, and I think the experience contributed much to my ongoing curiosity about life and the world.

The fruit farming in the area was also the source of my first entrepreneurial pursuits. In the spring I earned money tying grapes, and in the summer and fall I picked other fruit—strawberries, cherries, peaches—at the neighboring orchards, and sold it in baskets at the side of the highway in front of our property. I saved the money I earned to buy clothing and gifts, or a new bike. It always gave me great satisfaction to pay for these things myself with the money I had worked for. The value of a buck, and of earning my own money, were very clear to me at an early stage.

My father, Reuben, helped out with repairs and errands around the business, but it was my mother, Eva, a woman considerably ahead of her time, who really ran the place. A hard-working French woman born in Midland, Ontario, she had been an assistant to a member of Ontario's legislature for some years prior to getting married. She oversaw every aspect of the family enterprise. A consummate hostess with a vivacious personality, she had high standards, and a natural talent for public relations. Despite her accomplishments and abilities, however, Mom always had an air of unfulfilled potential. I probably inherited a lot of my ambition and drive from her.

Mom was a devout Roman Catholic, but Dad was a United Churcher. My mother put great stock in attending church, and visits of priests were a common feature of my childhood. Although we had a kind of feast-or-famine existence, buffeted by the continual fluctuations in the tourist business, my mother always came up with the Church's share of whatever money we had.

It was Mom who created the warm, welcoming atmosphere in our home. My friends loved to visit and often referred to Mom as "The Duchess." She enjoyed entertaining our guests by playing the piano and singing. Young and old, rich and poor, were treated with the utmost graciousness. Mom had a strong sense of style, always dressed impeccably, and kept her hair neatly coiffed. She made sure that I, too, looked my best, and on special occasions carefully laid out my dresses for me, sometimes complete with layered crinolines and accessories. She doted on me, and I loved her dearly.

When I was about ten years old, my mother developed high blood pressure and heart problems, and had to take several types of pills, including digitalis, daily. Often she had to stay in bed to rest, and on those occasions, when I sat with her, I would look across at all the pill bottles lined up on her nightstand. Many years later, it occurred to me that some of those bottles might have contained sleeping pills or barbiturates, drugs that were commonly prescribed in the 1940s and early 1950s.

Dad was from a well-off German family that had settled in Kincardine, Ontario, where I was born in 1940. When I was just a baby, Dad owned a dance pavilion right on the shore of Lake Huron. He was quite flamboyant in his earlier years, wearing dapper white suits and driving fancy cars. He loved to dance. I was told he was quite the ladies' man in his time, very showy and accustomed to the finer things in life.

I was a late child—my parents were gray-haired and in their mid-forties when I was born—and, by the time I came along, it seemed that Dad had lost his flair for high living. He projected a sense that life had passed him by, causing him to retreat into a lonely aloofness, perhaps in part because of Mom's dominating, capable presence. Everything just sort of flowed around and past my father; in good weather he would sit for hours in a chair outside, under the willows, absorbed in his own thoughts, sometimes with a drink in his hand. I don't think Dad ever really learned to motivate himself, but he was a very sensitive and intelligent man with a strong spiritual side. Often I would see him on his knees, clutching a Bible and praying beside his bed before going to sleep at night. As a child, I don't remember much intimacy between my parents, and they seldom slept together. There were times, though, when they could be quite tender, and I believe they loved each other, despite all the bickering.

I attended a small country school, called Fairview, about a mile away from our home, for grades one through eight. I was always motivated to do well in school. I completed the second and third grade in one year and was an avid reader. And like my mother, who played the piano, I had a passion for music. I took piano lessons for nine years, sang, and led the rhythm band at school. I loved sports and competition as well, and won the cup in track-and-field every year throughout elementary school. Among other sports, I played hockey with the boys on the pond across from our house in the winter, often as the goalie, which could be particularly perilous. One year I conducted the band at the Lincoln County Music Festival in St. Catharines with a whopping black eye, the result of a bat thrown at a softball game the day before.

When I started high school, I had to take the school bus every morning, which wound through the country roads and the fruit farms for nearly an hour before arriving at St. Catharines Collegiate. I was a bit shy at first and was teased a lot about being "from the sticks." However, I soon adapted to my new surroundings and poured full effort into everything I did. I was determined to be somebody, to accomplish meaningful goals in my life. There had never been any question in my mind that I would attend university, even though it wasn't all that common for girls to do so in those days. I became quite interested in pursuing a career in medicine, especially after dating a boy whose father was a doctor, and who was himself planning a medical career. Our many interesting conversations on the subject piqued my interest in this field, and I geared my studies accordingly.

Although maintaining top grades was always a priority for me, I continued with many extracurricular activities throughout high school and was awarded the school honor letter in grade thirteen. I loved to perform and, in addition to my piano and singing, I got involved in ballroom dancing, speaking competitions, theater, and, eventually, beauty pageants. In the tenth grade, after winning a number of local titles, I competed in the Niagara District Blossom Queen event, which was the forerunner of the Miss Canada pageant. My mother loved this sort of thing, with all its pomp and ceremony, and always made a big fuss on competition nights. My picture appeared in the newspaper when I won various titles, and she saved all the clippings in a scrapbook.

In addition to my school and extracurricular activities, I worked at Eaton's part-time as a sales clerk and for four years wrote a weekly column called "Collegiate Corner" (about school events and students' concerns) for the Standard, the St. Catharines daily newspaper. At eighteen, with my earnings from these two jobs, I saved enough money for a down payment on my first car—a shiny, tree-green 1954 Ford convertible. I definitely inherited my dad's love for nice cars, particularly convertibles. In fact, I still own three of them today, two of them classics.

The summer after graduation from high school, I continued to work at the Standard as a reporter and features writer, then later as fashion and beauty editor. My snowballing involvement in journalism, my grades, and my public-presentation accomplishments earned me a scholarship to study honors journalism at the University of Western Ontario (UWO), in London, which I began attending in September 1958. By then I had decided against medical school, although I had taken the maximum number of mathematics and science courses in preparation for it. My various interests and experiences seemed to be guiding me in a different direction. In addition to having a professional life, I wanted to marry and

E A R L Y   P R O M I S E   31

have children, something I thought would be more difficult to accomplish as a doctor. I wanted it all, and there was no reason to think I couldn't have it. A successful career was clearly feasible, and I certainly had plenty of energy and drive.

Many of my peers were from wealthy Ontario families, and although I didn't have money to throw around, I usually managed to earn for myself what many of them were given by their parents. I put myself through university with income I earned, as well as with scholarships, bursaries, and student loans. With money I saved from my various jobs, I eventually bought my second car—a sky-blue 1956 Ford convertible with a Thunderbird engine. I loved to go for long drives over the rural roads, taking in the country sights and smells, with fresh air blowing through my hair.

In the summer of 1959, after I had finished my first year at UWO, my dad became seriously ill. He was having trouble swallowing, was losing weight, and was eventually diagnosed with cancer of the esophagus. His sudden life-threatening illness was devastating to the whole family. It was horrible to see him at St. Michael's Hospital in Toronto, wasting away, unable to eat, being fed through a tube. We knew that his illness was terminal, but it was difficult to accept. We all felt powerless. Whenever we happened to eat in front of him, I would feel a terrible guilt. Life was still carrying on around Dad, only now he wasn't just aloof and distant.

Day after day, I listened to him try to speak through his pain, and I constantly checked the various tubes going into his body to make sure they were working properly. When he appeared to be in even greater pain, I rushed out into the corridor to find a nurse to give him another morphine injection. But most of the time I just sat with him quietly, holding his hand.

At one point, when he was drifting in and out of consciousness, I was in the hospital room alone with him, trying to talk to him whenever he opened his eyes. He didn't say much, but he did glance up at me affectionately. I think he knew he was dying. It was tough seeing him that way, and I couldn't stop my tears. I had just begun to know him. It wasn't fair.

"Dad," I whispered, "if only you could talk. If only we could. ...There's so much to say. I love you, Dad."

He squeezed my hand hard, and I thought I detected a smile brushing his dry lips. I wanted to believe he was smiling.

Not long after that, in September 1959, Dad died, at age sixty-one. His death crushed me; it was the first time anyone close to me had died, and I felt terribly cheated.

CHAPTER TWO

Married Life

AFTER MY FATHER'S DEATH, I decided not to return for a second year at Western; I wanted to live at home with my mother and brother. But I didn't give up on my studies. I attended night school through McMaster University in Hamilton, where I completed my second year on schedule, and, during the day, I worked full-time as fashion and beauty editor at the *Standard*. It was there, in January 1960, that I met my future husband, Alan Gadsby, who was working as a reporter.

Alan and I had attended the same high school, but had never met, since he was five years older than me. As fashion editor, I had an office off to one side of the newsroom, where the "Women's Section" was located. Occasionally Alan would pass by, and I couldn't help noticing him. He had a great walk. He was tall, slim, good-looking, and had a thick head of light brown hair, already touched with gray even though he was only in his mid-twenties. Well-dressed, reserved, and very much the gentleman, he was the opposite of the kind of big-man-on-campus types I usually dated.

At the time, actually, I was seeing two other men—Ian, a *Standard* photographer, and Marvin, who was studying engineering at Queen's University. Ian, who had long, curly black hair, had been educated at the Ealing School of Art in Britain, was somewhat arty and bohemian, and drove an Austin-Healey sports car. He was the son of the assistant headmaster at Ridley College—a private boys' school in St. Catharines. Marvin was six foot one and slim with short brown hair; he hailed from a well-off family, had a black belt in judo, and owned a Porsche. The rebel in me was attracted to Ian, while my more traditional side liked Marvin, although he, too, had a certain dash about him. And we got along well. It was a mad whirl; some nights I even went out with both of them.

But I couldn't get Alan out of my thoughts. It's true that, in some respects, he reminded me of my father. Like Dad, he was introspective and not particularly aggressive, but he also seemed very mature, with a strong value system. The career-oriented part of me was drawn by the fact that he had worked as a program clearance manager for CBC-TV in Vancouver prior to taking the job at the *Standard*. At that time, I was contemplating a career in television work as a researcher/on-camera interviewer.

Whenever I encountered Alan in the newsroom, I shamelessly flirted with him, but he didn't seem to get the message. At first I figured he was playing hard to get, but as I got to know him I realized he was quite bashful. No matter what I did, I couldn't get him to ask me out. I got so frustrated that I even enlisted the aid of Alan's cousin Judy, who also worked at the paper. Nothing worked. Finally, about a month after we met, I invited him to join me for a cup of coffee.

"Ah, Alan, I was wondering if you'd like to go out sometime?" I ventured, taking a hurried gulp of the worst coffee this side of Hamilton's smelters. "You know, a movie, a play, something like that."

He looked at me a for a moment, seemingly in deep contemplation. "Yeah, let's do that sometime."

I had hoped he might suggest something more definite, but I could see that wasn't going to happen. "How about *Porgy and Bess*?" I blurted. "It's playing at the Royal Alex in Toronto."

"Sure, okay," he mumbled, and that's how it all began.

Not long after that, we settled on a night for the opera, and before I knew it Alan was picking me up with another couple at Hi-Ho Camp and whisking me off to the big city. We both enjoyed George Gershwin's tragic tale, and after such a special evening, and with my growing attraction to him, I assumed Alan would take the initiative and ask me out again. But he didn't. When two weeks had passed, I knew I had to make the next move once more. This time I invited him to dinner at home, at the tourist camp. We had more dates, finally at his initiative (at least some of the time), and I continued to see Ian and Marvin. But at the end of the summer in 1960, everything changed. I went back to my last year at Western. Ian went back to England to continue university, and Alan left the *Standard* to rejoin CBC-TV in Vancouver. That's when I knew Alan was the man for me. I missed him terribly, and judging by the dozen red roses he sent me every two weeks and his passionate love letters, our separation was hard on him, too.

During the Thanksgiving long weekend, I flew out to see him on the West Coast, where I had never been before. It was a gloriously romantic four days, though, of course, everything was prim and proper. I stayed in a hotel, and Alan was a perfect gentleman. One afternoon we were walking along Granville Street downtown and a photographer with a Polaroid buttonholed us. He snapped us arm in arm—a picture I still have. We were young, we were in love, and anything seemed possible.

Two months later, Alan moved back to Ontario and landed a job with CBC-TV in Toronto as a coordinating producer. We were still apart, since I was finishing my third year of university at Western in London, but at least we were closer. In fact, the first weekend Alan was back we spent the second night in a hotel in Hamilton and finally made love. We continued to see each other regularly and planned to get married after I graduated from UWO.

Early in the new year, I called Alan and told him we needed to talk. As soon as we could, we got together at a restaurant in downtown St. Catharines. I guess the look on my face must have alarmed him, and I thought he might easily guess what I had to tell him, but he only asked, "Are you okay?"

I laughed nervously. "Well, that depends on what you mean by okay. … I'm pregnant."

He was silent for a moment, then said, "Let's get married."

"Just like that? I can't. I've got to finish my degree. I can't just——"

"Why not? Let's get married right now. This instant. Let's go find a justice of the peace."

"Alan, let's think about this, okay?"

He was silent again, then, in a very serious tone of voice, he finally said, "You know, Joan, I have love enough for both of us." My heart melted.

That year, 1961, was a time of many changes in my life. My mother's health had deteriorated dramatically. At age sixty-five, she had developed a heart condition and high blood pressure, complicated by a muscle disorder. She sold Hi-Ho Camp and went to live in St. John's Convalescent Home, north of Toronto, for several months. The sale of our family home upset me a great deal, since I had long dreamed of redeveloping and renovating it, and I loved living in the country.

Mother was unable to attend my graduation from Western and so, sadly, neither of my parents would be there for me on this very important day, which I had worked toward for so long. I had also planned to take my mom on a trip to visit the Vatican. Now I had a feeling that this would never happen.

I had kept my pregnancy secret—other than Alan, the only other person who knew was my sister, Pat—and I was still determined to find a job as soon as I had my degree in psychology, English, and journalism. My extracurricular work with the *University Gazette* as associate editor and writing a weekly column—"Timely Topics" about fashions, fads, and facts—led to my being offered a unique position with *Chatelaine* magazine as assistant to the fashion and beauty editors. However, I decided to take a better-paying job as a feature writer/reporter with the *Toronto Telegram* newspaper (now defunct).

A few weeks before the graduation ceremony, Alan and I moved into an apartment together in an old house near the university in Toronto, and shortly after that we were married one lunch hour by a priest who made us promise we would baptize our children as Roman Catholics. The next day, I told Mother that we had been married when I was in Vancouver and that I was pregnant. She said, "Thank God. It's about time." I hadn't been fooling her about the pregnancy either.

At first it was a strange sort of love and bond Alan and I shared. Although there was no doubt I wanted my baby, I didn't like the fact that I had to get married and make a lifetime commitment. I didn't feel I was ready. Even when we were getting married I wondered how difficult it would be to get out of the marriage, and thought that perhaps I should raise my child alone. But by the time my beautiful, healthy, brown-eyed baby daughter Debra Lyn was born on September 3, 1961, weighing eight pounds, four ounces, I was ecstatic. I had settled in with Alan, and we had moved again to a spacious garden apartment near my sister's home, which I spent hours decorating. And now there were three of us.

In those days maternity leave had not yet even been thought of, and the *Telegram* didn't hold my job for me. So, when I was ready to work again, I set about looking for another writing position. Alan was doing well as a coordinating producer at CBC-TV, and soon I was hired as assistant product manager at Colgate-Palmolive. This was a real coup. The job carried a substantial salary and it provided me with great training and experience in the marketing of consumer packaged goods. Colgate was one of the most progressive companies in Canada, but I was only the second woman their marketing department had ever hired. My duties included consumer research and analysis, and assisting on multimillion-dollar marketing plans that took new products from concept to completion.

Eventually I was assigned some of my own brands. I also worked closely with Colgate Palmolive's four advertising agencies, providing creative input for television and radio commercials. Don Brown, the company's vice president of advertising, took me under his wing and encouraged me greatly. He believed I had the smarts to move ahead, and told me I had one of the brightest minds he had ever seen in marketing.

With a beautiful new baby at home, whom I adored, and a challenging new job, it was an exciting, busy time. Alan and I were earning good money, considerably above average, and were grateful that we could afford to hire a top-notch nanny/housekeeper to take care of Deb during the daytime and keep things running smoothly on the home front.

When I became pregnant again in January 1962, I continued working right through to my ninth month. This time the labor was slightly shorter than it had been with Deb—eighteen rather than twenty hours—but I had some trouble breathing. My obstetrician said it wasn't anything to worry about, and when I first saw my healthy, strapping ten-pound, blond baby boy on September 21, I put aside my concerns. I called him Derek, which means silent strength and power. Four weeks after Derek was born and a few days after I turned twenty-two, I went back to work at Colgate-Palmolive. During the day, our nanny/housekeeper, Barbara, continued to look after Deb and now Derek. It was hectic, happy time.

Early in 1963 Alan was offered an exciting opportunity to head up the program-clearance department at CBC-TV in Vancouver, where he had worked before. It was a big break for him and us as a family and, after some discussion, we decided to move. I had some regret about leaving

Colgate, but was confident that I would find work in British Columbia. I had impressive references, diverse experience and knowledge despite my youth, and enthusiasm to burn. My plan was to approach Nabob Foods and Scott Paper, two of the largest companies on the West Coast. I knew my marketing training and experience in packaged goods could be applicable at either firm.

Leaving my mother and the rest of my family was my biggest concern. When I told Mom we were moving so far away, she took it hard at first. However, I assured her we would have her out for visits as much as possible. I continued, though, to wrestle with my doubts and fears about being lonely so far away from familiar surroundings and people.

In April of that year, we bundled Deb and Derek, both still under two, onto a plane and flew to Vancouver to our new life. I knew exactly the type of home I wanted to live in—I had even dreamed about it ahead of time—and found it on Capilano Road in North Vancouver, nestled below the mountains. The three-bedroom rancher we rented sat on a beautiful treed lot blazing with rhododendrons, hydrangeas, and azaleas in full spring bloom, and boasted an idyllic playhouse and sandbox for the children in the backyard. How fortunate we were as a family I thought, and I thanked God for such an opportunity.

I was completely overwhelmed with the beauty of Vancouver. The mountains, the numerous islands off the coast, the ferry ride to Victoria, the big skies, the ocean, the trees and flowers were spectacular. Most of our spare time was spent exploring. Alan and I often took the children to Stanley Park and Ambleside Beach in West Vancouver, and up the chair lift to the peak of Grouse Mountain, where it seemed all of the world was laid out for us to see.

I was eager to find a challenging new job and save toward owning our first family home. Colgate-Palmolive had been at the leading edge of progressive marketing strategies in the packaged-goods industry, and my training there had been first-class. After aggressively lobbying a few key companies for four months, I finally landed a great job with Scott Paper, initially as assistant to the director of marketing and later as manager of marketing research and new-product development. I soon came to realize that the laid-back attitude and work ethic in Vancouver were quite different from what I was used to in Toronto, and for a while I missed the diversity and sophistication of the business world back east. However, I eventually came to appreciate the Vancouver lifestyle, where people "didn't live to work, but worked to live."

I was the first woman on the marketing team at Scott Paper. In the early 1960s, business was mostly a man's world; there were very few women in key executive positions anywhere. When I attended meetings at the University Club (later the Vancouver Club), our marketing management group had to reserve a board room separate from the main meeting areas because of my gender. Eventually the Vancouver Club opened its membership to women, but not until much later. Once, I was invited to participate in a business meeting at the Terminal City Club, which was the *nouveau* counterpart to the "establishment" Vancouver Club, but I was turned away at the door when they discovered I was a woman. My invitation was addressed with my initials only.

Within Scott Paper itself, I was expected to dress in a fashion that disguised my femininity; I had to compete hard, keep up with the boys and then some, and I also had to deal with the sometimes flagrant harassment that came my way. At a Scott Paper sales conference dinner in Montreal, one of the male executives grabbed me as I passed by and plunked me on his lap. Somehow I extricated myself without ruffling his feathers. But I could not expect an apology. That was the way the game was played back then.

At home Alan and I needed someone truly exceptional to take care of the children while we worked. I interviewed many women and eventually found a warm, loving, motherly, compassionate person, Mrs. Manson, who treated Deb and Derek as if they were her own children. She cooked wholesome meals, took them for long walks to a nearby park, and read to them; Deb and Derek loved her greatly and called her "Auntie." She quickly became like one of the family.

We spent our first western Christmas with Alan's father, who lived in Victoria. The winter ferry ride through the Gulf Islands was breathtaking, and we had a marvelous time. I couldn't get over the fact that the roses were blooming at Christmas in Victoria; to an Easterner, it was little short of miraculous.

Derek proved to be quite a handful; there was no stopping him. He grew rapidly and was soon almost as big as Deb. Many people thought they were twins. Derek was a bundle of energy, but he was sometimes clumsy. One day we took the two of them up the Grouse Mountain chairlift for lunch at the restaurant on top. Derek walked straight into the corner of a table, which frightened us, but—amazingly—didn't hurt him. At the time Alan and I thought he just wasn't paying attention to where he was going. But there were other instances of odd clumsiness, and I eventually took him to see our pediatrician, Dr. Padwick. Derek passed his checkup with flying colors.

In the spring of 1964, we packed up our big maroon Ford Galaxy, rigged the back seat with a mattress for the children to sleep on, and set out on a month-long road trip across the continent. Our hearts filled with a sense of adventure, we drove through the United States— Washington, Idaho, Montana, North Dakota, Minnesota, Wisconsin, Illinois, Indiana, Ohio, Pennsylvania, New York—and crossed back into Canada at Niagara Falls.

All in all, despite the uncertain beginning, those early years of marriage were some of the happiest and most satisfying times of my life. Alan and I had a good relationship, two beautiful children, and great jobs. Life was full of promise, and I felt that "the world was my oyster."

CHAPTER THREE

Our Silent Strength

O NE AFTERNOON, IN JULY 1964, I received a phone call at my office at Scott Paper that was to change my life forever.

"Joan, it's Auntie. I didn't want to bother you needlessly at work, but I'm so worried. It's Derek——"

"Is he okay? What happened?"

"I don't know for sure, but his left arm has gone limp."

"Did he fall?"

"I don't think so. It just … it just went limp."

"I'm on my way."

I hung up, called Alan, and headed home, driving fast, telling myself that he was a toddler, just under two years of age, who now and again took a tumble. That's all it would turn out to be. Some little mishap, something easily fixed. But my heart wasn't listening to my mind. It pounded harder and harder the closer I got to our home.

Derek was sitting quietly beside Deb in our living room when I arrived. Auntie hovered nervously around him, seemingly afraid to touch him. I took a quick look at my son's limp arm, then called Dr. Padwick, hoping to book an immediate appointment. He couldn't see us until early the next morning.

That evening was tough, but when I woke up the next day, after tossing and turning all night, the situation seemed even worse. By that time, Derek's whole left side appeared to be affected, and he was dragging his leg. Alan and I called our offices to say we wouldn't be coming in. Both of us now knew something was seriously wrong. Frightened and upset, we drove Derek to the pediatrician's office, which was only about ten minutes from home. Auntie stayed with Deb.

Dr. Padwick, who had treated Derek since birth, examined him carefully, checking all vital signs, maneuvering and prodding his limbs, inspecting his eyes. I watched the doctor intently as he did all this, searching his face for some hint that would tell me what was happening.

Both Alan and I were afraid to say anything, especially with Derek in the room. We didn't want to alarm him any more than he already was. But the silence was unbearable. I had to know what was going on. The doctor's fleshy face revealed nothing, however; nor did he say anything for some time.

"Yes," he finally said, looking at me somewhat forebodingly, "Derek does have general paralysis on his left side and his eyes seem to indicate internal pressure in his head."

"What do you mean, 'internal pressure'?" I asked with much apprehension.

"I think you should get Derek dressed, then I'd like to talk to you both in the next room," he said, his eyes now avoiding mine.

By the time we sat down across from Dr. Padwick in the adjoining room, I was very edgy. I held Derek on my lap and waited. Alan coughed and shifted restlessly in his chair. The doctor straightened some papers on his desk.

"Mr. and Mrs. Gadsby, Derek's situation could be very serious. We'll have to run some tests of course, but his symptoms seem to indicate the possibility of meningitis, perhaps even a brain tumor. We need to get him into the Children's Health Centre at Vancouver General Hospital right away. Can you drive him over?"

It suddenly seemed as if the doctor was talking from very far away. I felt myself slipping into a state of disbelief. *Meningitis? Brain tumor? ... Cancer?*

A few minutes later we were in our car driving over the Lions Gate Bridge. I glanced out the window at sunlight sparkling on the smooth-as-glass waters of Burrard Inlet. Giant freighters glided slowly out to sea. Big, fluffy cumulus clouds capped the North Shore mountain peaks behind us.

"Alan, what does it mean?" I whispered, stroking Derek's thick blond hair as he sat quietly in my lap.

"Let's see what the doctors at the hospital say," he said as we came off the bridge and into Stanley Park.

Traffic slowed to a crawl, and my nerves were stretched to the limit. Then the tears started to flow.

"Oh, my God, why is this happening Alan?" I said, sobbing. It was a hot summer day, but I felt chilled all over.

"Calm down, Joan. Everything will be okay. Derek's going to get the best of care. Besides, we don't know anything for sure yet."

I glanced at him in between shudders. Outwardly he seemed composed, as always, but I could see that his face was drawn and tense. Derek tugged at my arm, and I looked down into his huge brown eyes. "I love you, Mommy," he said softly. "Don't cry."

We spent the rest of the day at Vancouver General Hospital waiting anxiously as Derek underwent a seemingly endless battery of tests— X-rays, a CAT scan, an electroencephalogram, a spinal tap. Doctors, nurses, and orderlies rushed here and there while other patients, with their parents, came and went. At last we were told that the test results wouldn't be ready until the next morning.

Alan and I went into Derek's room to stay with him for a while. When he saw us, he started to cry. We sat beside his bed and tried to soothe him, telling him what a brave boy he was. He fell asleep, but a little later, when we got up to leave, he awakened and began to cry again.

"Mommy, don't leave me," he sobbed.

I told him a story about a little prince that always settled him down when I put him to bed, then I tucked him in. "Mommy and Daddy will be back in the morning, Derek. You need to stay here tonight. There are a lot of nice people here who'll take good care of you."

As we left the room, I looked back at our son. He seemed so tiny and vulnerable in the big hospital bed. It broke my heart to leave him there alone.

We were back at the hospital early the next morning. When Derek saw us come into the room, his eyes lit up and he smiled faintly, but the pain he was experiencing was obvious in his face.

We sat beside his bed, and held his little hands. Nobody on the staff said much to us, although they were in and out of the room, checking this and that, doing more tests, nodding at us noncommittally. At the end of the day one of the doctors we had met the day before came to speak to us. Dr.

Frank Turnbull was a thin man in his early sixties, with receding gray hair and glasses. He was, at the time, president of the Canadian Medical Association, and we had been told that he was one of the country's best neurosurgeons.

The news he brought us was terrifying. "Mr. and Mrs. Gadsby, there's no other way to put this. I'm sorry, but I'm afraid your son does have a brain tumor."

I started to tremble. It wasn't a bad dream. It was all too real.

"But you can operate and take it out, can't you?" Alan asked.

"I'll be straight with you. Derek's situation is very grave. As far as we can tell, with a tumor like the one he has, it's likely he won't live. But we can't know for sure until we actually get inside and take a look. Yes, things look bad, but I never give up hope. We'll do everything in our power to make your son well again. Believe me."

"When will you operate?" I stammered.

"As soon as we can—probably tomorrow. I'll be doing it."

The next twenty-four hours were sheer agony. All I could do was repeat one prayer in my mind over and over: *Please, God, let Derek live. Let him be okay.*

The day of the operation passed with excruciating slowness. A nurse shaved Derek's beautiful blond hair, and he was wheeled down to the operating room, leaving us with nothing but more time on our hands. I drank innumerable cups of tea and paced many miles. When Dr. Turnbull finally met with us after the operation, he looked tired and haggard, his seamed face once more unusually solemn.

"Oh, my God!" I cried. "He's all right, isn't he?"

"I couldn't remove the tumor," he began quietly. "It's deeply embedded in the occipital lobe of his brain. What's more, there was a large cyst sitting on top of the tumor. I was able to drain it and that should bring down some of the swelling and pressure."

"Will it spread—the tumor, I mean?" Alan asked, his voice faltering.

"No, as far as we can tell, the tumor … won't likely spread to other parts of his body. But, as I said, we can't remove it. Our best option now is cobalt treatment. That should help shrink the tumor."

The reduced pressure on Derek's brain had immediate results, and his condition seemed to improve, giving us new hope. Cobalt-60 radiation therapy, the "cobalt bomb," had been developed in Canada in the early 1950s under the direction of Dr. Harold Johns. At the time, it was a major breakthrough in the treatment of cancer, particularly since it was safer, and 300 times more powerful, than radium therapy.

Each day Derek was treated at the nearby B.C. Cancer Agency. He was placed on a stretcher and his head was moved into the cobalt unit to be exposed to the radiation. The sessions fatigued and confused him, probably because of the heavy sedation he received beforehand, but otherwise he didn't seem to suffer any significant side effects, something I had been worried about.

After several weeks of radiation, the tumor had shrunk a bit, encouraging us even more. With daily physiotherapy, Derek was able to move his left arm and leg a little more and with purpose, but the partial facial paralysis gave him a little sideways smile that never altered. His left-eye peripheral vision was completely gone as well, and we were told it would never return. But we could live with that.

Derek was hospitalized for two months following the surgery. Alan eventually went back to his job at CBC-TV and I arranged to work mornings only at Scott Paper. My colleagues there showed a lot of support and understanding toward me and my need, as a mother, to be with my son. At around lunchtime every day, I went straight to the Children's Health Centre to spend the afternoon with Derek. I would read his favorite Dr. Seuss books to him—*The Cat in the Hat* and *Are You My Mother?*—and sing little songs. He particularly loved "I'm a Little Teapot" and the way I acted it out with great gusto.

"Mommy funny," he would say as I pretended to be a "teapot short and stout."

"Is that so, Georgie Porgie?" I'd reply, tickling him so that he giggled, his big brown eyes filled with mischief.

Several times each day we walked the hospital corridors—"doing our rounds," we called it. There were many toys and stuffed animals available for the children to play with, and the nurses were exceptionally warm and empathetic. Derek liked to visit with other children in the ward and became friendly with several of them. And every evening, Alan brought Deb to see her little brother. She was too young to fully understand much of what was going on, except that Derek was very sick and couldn't come home yet. She loved him very much, and Derek's eyes always lit up when his sister appeared. She would hug him every time she came into the room and kiss him goodbye tenderly. We ate our dinner together in the hospital cafeteria nearly every evening and stayed with Derek for several hours afterward.

The doctors allowed us to take Derek home for a day trip about six weeks after his surgery. We were ecstatic. It wasn't easy, though. Derek had been slowed down a bit, but he was still a little boy with an amazing amount of energy. Alan and I hovered protectively around him all day, trying to anticipate his every move. We taught him to compensate for his vision problems by turning his head to the left to see, but he was still constantly at risk of accidents, and more than once that day my heart nearly stopped as I watched him try to navigate a roomful of everyday obstacles.

Finally, two months after his operation, Derek was allowed to come home from the hospital. We were all so happy that this day had finally arrived, and Deb was overjoyed at having her brother home to play and cuddle with again. Although the doctors were cautious in terms of their expectations for him, we made the decision to live each day to its fullest. Alan and I never gave up hope, and each day I prayed for a miracle that would let my son live a complete life.

Having Derek back home was wonderful, but it did take a while for us to adjust. His impaired peripheral vision continued to be a problem for him, and we couldn't let him play outside without an adult to supervise him, which wasn't always possible. He would look out the window and see the comings and goings of neighborhood children and wonder why we wouldn't let him run about freely in the yard like the other kids and Deb did. When we did go out with him we had to be always on guard, afraid that he might fall and hurt his head. We lived from day to day, never knowing what would happen next.

And there were the seizures, during which Derek would become extremely pale, his eyes vacant, his breath shallow, and his whole body rigid. I found these episodes terrifying. In order to control the seizures, we gave him a daily dose of phenobarbital, as prescribed by our pediatrician.

Eventually I left my job at Scott Paper altogether and opted to take some afternoon courses at the University of British Columbia toward a master's degree in business administration. I was still able to spend mornings with Derek, and I attended classes in the afternoons when he was often having a nap. I needed a focus outside my intense personal circumstances, and going to school part-time was easier than trying to cope with a demanding job. Although I was often preoccupied with thoughts of Derek, I did very well at university and was awarded a graduate scholarship for having the highest marks in marketing and industrial relations in my class. I was also one of the first two women ever admitted to that program.

Derek's third birthday party, in September 1965, was a bittersweet occasion. Although we never said it aloud, Alan and I certainly wondered deep down if our son would be around for his fourth. I made a big fuss about him turning three and let him help me bake his birthday cake. He loved doing things like that, and after we were done, he hurried down the hall to tell Deb all about it, still licking icing from a spoon in his hand. I loved being home with the children for occasions like this, and took lots of pictures of the children enjoying Derek's special day.

If Derek acted up at all, he was treated with great tolerance. None of us really had the heart to discipline him. The whole family spoiled him a little, since his condition was always a source of frustration for him. Sometimes he would flare up and pinch Deb or get a little rough with her when they were playing. Yet, despite these incidents, she loved him very much and was always watching out for him. This was a blessing, of course, since she could have reacted quite differently to all the attention her brother was getting. But somehow she sensed the bigger picture, the gravity of the situation, and it was actually quite painful for me to see that she had to experience this burden of worry at such a young age.

Throughout Derek's illness, I made numerous phone calls to medical facilities, specialists, and research centers in other parts of the world to find out if there was more that could be done for him. Each inquiry brought a ray of hope, which was inevitably followed by profound disappointment. There was a time when we thought we might take him to the Mayo Clinic in Rochester, Minnesota, but we decided against it when doctors there told us they had nothing different to offer in Derek's case. I also went on a tour of the cancer-research facility at UBC. The staff there assured me that British Columbia was in the forefront of this area of study and treatment, but that there was really nothing else we could do to help our son. His fate was in God's hands, and so we prayed. To this day, I still follow news of research developments concerning the treatment of brain tumors.

Although Derek continued to experience pain and have periodic seizures, we tried our best to provide a normal routine for Deb. In September 1966, she started kindergarten at the little neighborhood school a few blocks down the road from our home. However, she attended her new kindergarten for only two days before disaster struck once more. In the morning, I went into the room that Deb and Derek shared and found him barely conscious and horribly pale.

"Derek!" I called, shaking his arm. "Wake up!"

Finally he roused slightly and looked at me, but his eyes were vacant and he couldn't seem to speak. Quickly I lifted him out of his bed and carried him to mine. But when I put him down, he went rigid again and began to moan softly. I was terrified. I called Alan, then Dr. Padwick and Dr. Turnbull, who both advised me to take Derek directly to the hospital. I was convinced he would stop breathing at any moment, so I called Pat Fortin, our neighbor, and asked her to come over. We made sure Derek was still breathing and tried to make him as comfortable as we could. When Alan pulled up in our car, I left the house and scrambled into the passenger side of the vehicle with Derek in my arms. Alan drove to the hospital as fast as safety would allow. I cuddled and soothed Derek, but I couldn't hold back the tears any longer.

Later that day Dr. Turnbull met with us again.

"I wish I had better news for you," he said, fidgeting with his glasses. "The tumor's grown and there's nothing we can do about it."

"Can't we give him more cobalt treatments?" I asked.

"I wish it were as easy as that, but Derek's already had the maximum number of treatments allowable."

"But there must be something you can do," I insisted, feeling helpless, frustrated, and fearful.

"The only hope now is that the cancer goes into remission, but I have to tell you that's extremely unlikely. All we can really do is make him as comfortable as possible."

On the way back home, Alan began to cry; it was one of the very few times I saw him do so, throughout the agony of our son's illness.

From that day on, Derek's condition steadily deteriorated. I dropped out of my MBA classes to spend every day with my son, from morning till night. He stopped talking altogether, but still showed a little spark whenever we came into his hospital room. The pressure on his brain was affecting many of his bodily functions and he was wasting away to nothing. He was kept on pain-killing medication. All I could do was hold him on my lap and rock him and sing to him quietly, while his beautiful big brown eyes looked up at me from his once lively face. One day I brought in a huge montage of different cutout animals and put it on a wall where he could see it. Although he couldn't speak or laugh, his eyes twinkled a little when I pointed at the pictures and imitated the sounds of the cats, cows, horses, sheep, and roosters.

Every evening before I left the hospital, I wrote out detailed instructions for the nurses about precisely how and when to turn Derek so that certain pressure points on his body wouldn't get chafed, and I bought lamb's wool to put under him to help prevent bed sores. Every night, I collapsed into bed exhausted and overwhelmed by terrible sadness. The burden we shared took its toll on my relationship with Alan. A normal life of any kind was impossible. Nothing was a comfort, and we were each lost in our own world, trying in our own ways to cope with Derek's devastating illness. Alan seemed to grow only more distant as the days slipped by. One night we were at home after a particularly harrowing time with Derek and I said, "Alan, talk to me. I need to talk to you."

He was sitting in a chair near the fireplace, reading a newspaper.

"Look at me, Alan!" I shouted. "Our son's dying and all you do is read newspapers."

He shot a bitter glance at me, but continued reading.

Enraged, I strode over to his chair and snatched the paper out of his hands. "Don't you feel anything? Talk to me, damn it!"

Alan still wouldn't speak to me. He struggled out of his chair, went to the hall closet to get his coat, and left the house without saying a word. On nights like that, he would take long walks until he thought I was finally asleep, then return home and go to bed.

The days grew colder and darker through November and early December. By that time, Derek was being fed through a tube. We discussed the possibility of taking him home for the last weeks of his life, but the doctors wouldn't let us. I continued to pray every day and was riddled with a sense of unexplained guilt. Why had this happened to my son? Was there any way I could have prevented it? I remembered how I had had difficulty breathing when he was born and wondered if that had been a factor. Then one day, as if I wasn't wrestling with enough torment, a Roman Catholic priest, whom I didn't know, came into Derek's room while I was there.

"I've been told you're a Catholic, Mrs. Gadsby, and I thought I'd pay you and Derek a visit. Perhaps we could pray together."

"Uh, I don't——"

"God always has a reason for the bad things that occur in our lives. So you must look into your heart and recall what you did to cause this terrible thing to happen to your son."

I was dumbfounded. "Get the hell out of here!" I yelled. "And don't ever come back."

He retreated in a huff and I never saw him again.

I read many books on the subject of death and dying in an attempt to understand what I was going through. When I was ten years old, a Protestant missionary who stayed at the Hi-Ho Camp had taught me passages from the Bible, and one verse in particular had made a lasting impression on me. It was from the Gospel of St. John 3:16: "For God so loved the world, that he gave his only begotten Son, that whosoever believeth in him should not perish, but have everlasting life." Now, as Derek drifted ever closer to death, those words provided some comfort for me.

On Christmas Eve, we hung Derek's stocking up at the foot of his bed and stayed with him for a long time before we went home. The house was decorated and the tree twinkled with lights, but our spirits were heavy. Although we tried our best to be cheerful for Deb, it was futile. There was no escaping the sadness. In the morning, we opened our presents and had a little breakfast before we set out for the hospital again.

That morning Derek looked very bad. He had been having frequent seizures, and when we arrived at the hospital, he lay motionless, his eyes glazed, his pupils dilated. His presents lay untouched, as did his Christmas stocking. We kept him company all day, until we had to take Deb home and put her to bed. When we left at around 7:45 that evening, we told the doctors and nurses to call us if anything happened or changed, no matter what time it was.

A few hours later, at approximately 11:40 p.m., the phone rang. I answered. It was the hospital. The doctor asked to speak to Alan. I handed him the phone and watched intently for some sign of what he was hearing. Slowly, as he listened, all the color drained out of his face. When he hung up, he began to weep. Derek had died.

CHAPTER FOUR

Aftermath

THE DAYS AND WEEKS following Derek's death were arduous and confusing. The grief that Alan and I were experiencing was made surreal by the mood of the Christmas season. While everyone else seemed to be enjoying their families, celebrating, and making plans for the new year, we were making arrangements to bury our son. Alan retreated deeply into himself during those terrible days. He was not able to be of much comfort to me, nor I to him.

For Derek's burial, I had his body dressed in his favorite pajamas, and covered with an ivory wool blanket that my old school friend Sara had sent when he was born. I wanted to lay his body to rest as though he were sleeping. After a simple memorial service at Highlands United Church, he was buried at Capilano View Cemetery, in West Vancouver, very near to our home on Capilano Road. The sight of Derek's gravestone, embossed with a cross and the words I had chosen—"Our Silent Strength"—hit me hard. I just couldn't believe that he was truly gone.

I realized it was important to try to keep up a strong front for Deb, but it was nearly impossible. We bought her a kitten, which she named "Gigsy," and that seemed to help her somewhat. She loved her new pet, cuddling and rocking him for hours on end. We told her that Derek had gone to live with God, and she seemed to accept that, although she asked many questions. How do you explain to a five-year-old child that her brother will never come home again?

One thing I did right away was put together two huge photo montages of Derek's life from birth. Although Alan and I were in some of the pictures, most were of Deb and Derek together, smiling and playing—filled with love for each other. Assembling the montages was a painful process, but it meant a great deal to me. I framed the two collections and placed one in our living room, and the other in our bedroom. I wanted a prominent, visual record of Derek's life to be displayed in our home.

I decided not to continue with the MBA program at UBC the following semester, even though the university had kept my scholarship for me. At that point, it just didn't seem important to continue, and I wanted to go back to work. Alan had returned to his job at CBC, and I felt that I needed to do the same, and move forward with my life. Within a month I had a job with the federal Department of Manpower and Immigration as a job analyst; I was responsible for collecting and analyzing data for a dictionary of occupations. The work entailed interviewing the employees of various large organizations, studying the jobs they performed, then preparing detailed reports and analyses based on this information. My new position did indeed provide me with a focus, and helped to relieve, at least for several hours each day, my terrible sadness. There can't be anything more difficult than losing a child, but nobody that I worked with really knew the battle I was fighting on the inside, or the grief that kept overwhelming me.

I spent many hours trying to rationalize my working in the business world, where money seemed to be the only thing that mattered to most people. I began thinking that I should have gone into research work myself, as I had always had a real leaning toward the field of medicine. I wanted to do something that would absorb all my energy and make me feel that I was contributing to the fight against cancer, something that would also help me to move through my grief a little. I decided to offer to work with the Canadian Cancer Society as a volunteer. As it turned out, my timing couldn't have been better. The April fundraising campaign was just a few weeks away, and the society was having difficulty finding someone to take on the job of campaign chairman in North Vancouver. While I realized it would be a big commitment, I felt that I had found a way that I could help, and readily accepted the responsibility.

I was soon coordinating an aggressive fundraising campaign—organizing door-to-door canvassers, mapping out zones, assigning zone chairpersons, designing and ordering promotional materials, and holding orientation meetings in my home. My neighbor Miriam Brownlow had also volunteered, and almost every night for weeks, after Deb had gone to bed, Miriam and I worked until around midnight, organizing a campaign that proved to be a success far beyond our expectations. It was a very satisfying experience; its significance to me was deeply philosophical. Involving myself with others in an effort to achieve humanitarian ends gave me a sense of inner peace, and I came to a greater understanding of what was truly important in my life.

My main reason for becoming involved with the Society was summed up by something Deb had said to me just after Derek died: "You must thank the doctor for letting Derek live longer." She was right, and so wise and intuitive at such a young age.

Things at home were moving along somewhat mechanically. I got Deb off to school in the morning, and Auntie was there to pick her up in the afternoon. Alan and I, however, were still not relating to each other very well. He said very little, seeming to keep all of his feelings deeply buried. He went through the motions from day to day, but he was not himself. I, on the other hand, found that the busier I was, the easier it was. Long spells of free time were not good for me. Only weekends were unstructured, and they brought on the inevitable pain and sadness, and left me feeling increasingly alienated from Alan.

I began to have a few drinks on the weekends, although certainly not regularly. Before that time, I had rarely ever had more than one drink on any given day, and even that was unusual. Although I thought at the time that drinking eased my tension a little, it really didn't help. A couple of times I overdid it and became weepy and emotional, thinking about Derek and reliving the night he died. Three-day weekends were particularly troublesome, the most likely time for me to indulge in alcohol.

I was also having trouble sleeping and was still feeling quite down. Several months earlier, given the strain we were under when Derek was so gravely ill, our family physician, Dr. MacGillivray, had referred Alan and me to a psychiatrist for counseling, but we hadn't continued with it for long. The root cause of all our problems, as far as we were concerned, could not be alleviated by anything anyone could say or do. The brutal reality of Derek's serious illness was not going to go away. Records show that Dr. MacGillivray also issued me a couple of prescriptions for barbiturates during that period, but I don't have any recollection of taking them.[1]

Whenever I saw Dr. MacGillivray, he always asked how I was doing in general. As a result, I confided in him about my grief, the problems in my marriage, and my occasional bouts with alcohol. During one of these visits, he gave me a prescription for something he said would help me get some sleep.[2]

By late spring, Alan and I were pretty well living separate lives. My schedule was very busy, and he was quite removed from everything I was involved with. In the past he had always taken an interest in my career and activities, but now there was little communication between us. In addition to the grief and frustration I was feeling, I began to feel resentful toward Alan. He seemed uncaring, impervious to my need for emotional support, and resistant to any efforts I made to bring about a greater emotional connection between us.

He did spend considerable quality time with Deb, reading to her and playing with her, but beyond that he didn't seem to care much about anything. He began to work late at his office on many weeknights, and even sometimes on weekends. He was also taking long walks in the evenings by himself. He seemed agitated and unhappy, and I became genuinely concerned about him. I thought he might be nearing some sort of breakdown.

One evening when Alan was out walking for a very long time, I became more and more worried. Terrible things were running through my mind. Why was he gone so long? Perhaps something awful had happened. I finally walked out onto our driveway and looked around, wondering if I should get in the car to go searching for him. He had been gone for hours and could be miles away for all I knew. As I walked out toward the road, I looked down the street and saw a red sports car pull over about a half a block away. Something told me to stop where I was. I stepped back into the shadows and watched, and a moment later the passenger door of the car opened, and Alan stepped out. I could not see clearly who was driving, but I could certainly see that it was a woman. Then, to my utter dismay, Alan circled the car, leaned in the window, and kissed the woman.

I couldn't believe my eyes. I hurried back to the house and went inside, my heart pounding. How could he do such a thing? I tried to tell myself there must be some innocent explanation, something that would prevent the catastrophic explanation of an affair from crashing down on me. I quickly sat in front of the fireplace, and struggled to compose myself as best I could, but when Alan walked through the door I found it extremely difficult. My adrenaline was soaring.

"Where were you? I was worried about you," I managed, without looking at him.

Alan's reply told me that he must have seen me outside, and that he, too, was agitated. "Oh, I ran into a fellow from work. He just dropped me off."

It didn't seem possible, and yet my anger actually increased at that moment. He was obviously gambling that I had been able to see the car but not who was driving. Incredibly, on top of it all, he was now lying to me!

"It wasn't any 'fellow!'" I seethed, barely able to control myself. "It was a woman! I saw her! Who is she?"

Alan lapsed immediately into silence. When he turned and left the room, I was after him in an instant, a tigress in pursuit of her prey.

But Alan would have none of it. He admitted that the driver was a woman, but insisted that she was just "a friend." The situation was indeed entirely innocent, he claimed. But I was not about to be deterred. I didn't believe for a moment that she was just a friend, and I demanded to know her name. He continued to be cagey and evasive, refusing to answer. The evening came to an end with us sleeping in separate bedrooms, and me feeling more hurt and betrayed than I would ever have believed possible.

Before we went to bed I had told Alan that I wanted to know in the morning who the woman was, so next morning, in a moment when Deb was not in the kitchen, I cornered him.

"Okay, who is she? What's her name?"

"Look," Alan began, a tense and weary edge to his voice, "I will tell you, but first I want to speak to her."

Once both Alan and Deb had left the house, I called my office to say I would not be coming in until late morning. I was still intensely angry and upset, and I was determined to get to the truth, at that point not much caring how I had to do it.

Within hours, I found myself sitting on the couch in her apartment, feeling like a reluctant actor in a bad movie. She and Alan had arrived before me, and had clearly had a chance to rehearse their story: they were not having an affair, they were simply "good friends." Alan had been confiding in her. She even had the audacity to claim that, on those occasions when she had seen me arrive with Deb to pick Alan up after work, she had admired, even envied, our "perfect family."

Their denial only fed the flames of my anger. I felt insulted by their claims. "You can't expect me to believe this," I said to Alan. "I'm not stupid."

"It's the truth," Alan said, and shrugged.

The stress of the situation was soon too much for her. She abruptly stood and left the room, rushing back in a moment later with, rather absurdly, the hook of a wire coat hanger held to her throat.

"I'll kill myself! I'll kill myself if that's what you want!" she cried in near hysteria.

Alan struggled to calm her, but I was more surprised that Alan could be involved with this woman. Yes, she was young and attractive, and seemed relatively bright, but just as obviously she was immature and fairly unstable.

The entire bizarre encounter ended within an hour, with Alan agreeing to stop seeing her.

In the ensuing days, I remember an ongoing feeling of profound hurt, and the clear sense that our marriage had been significantly, perhaps permanently, damaged. I would not have believed that things could get any worse for me, but they had. I got up every morning and set out for work with even greater determination. Other than my love for Deb and being with her, my career was the only thing that seemed to make any sense in my life at that point.

I had been at my government job for only about six months when I was assigned to do an analysis at Kelly Douglas & Co.—a subsidiary of George Weston, and Western Canada's largest manufacturer, wholesaler, and retailer of food products. The project led to a job offer from the president of Kelly Douglas at the time, Victor MacLean, who was impressed with my background in marketing and industrial relations.

I was offered the position of staff assistant to the president. It was a tremendous opportunity, well suited to my specific training and experience, and the job came with a salary considerably higher than I had been earning, plus profit sharing. At the time, I was hoping we would be able to buy a house soon, and the extra money was very attractive to me. I accepted the offer. It was not terribly difficult to leave my old job, as I had begun to be quite frustrated with the bureaucratic tangles involved in working for the government, and with what I considered to be strait-jacketed thinking.

My position with Kelly Douglas began to expand and diversify almost immediately after I began there, and I had little time to dwell on my troubles with Alan. My work included research, economic analysis, marketing, and government relations, and I was involved in nearly all aspects of the organization's many divisions, subsidiary companies, and outside affiliations. I found that I had to deal with occasional comments and insinuations from some male colleagues who were quite skeptical of a young woman (I was only twenty-seven) holding such an influential position, so close to the president, but I didn't let it bother me. I soon came to feel very comfortable working with the senior management of the company, and they with me. It was a great learning experience.

My new job gave me an opportunity to fly back east regularly to make presentations and attend conferences, which I appreciated because I was able to see my family more often. My public persona was becoming further and further removed from the private emotional pain I held inside, and I missed my family terribly at times. I had virtually no trust in Alan any more, and we were arguing often. I was racked with doubts about my marriage, but I just wasn't ready to give up. My Roman Catholic upbringing had done nothing to prepare me for the concept of divorce. And I was not a personality type that could easily quit anything, much less a supposedly lifelong commitment. All that I had ever gained in life had been as the result of hard work, determination, and persistence, and so I took the same approach toward our strained relationship. I hoped that time would heal the rift.

In September 1967, Dr. MacGillivray referred Alan and me to Dr. Norman Hirt, a psychiatrist who saw us, both separately and together, on many occasions. Dr. Hirt's role with us, as defined by him, was "to determine if the marriage could be made to work by attempting to overcome personality and emotional differences, to help us to work through the pain of the loss of Derek, and to try and help Alan to open himself to greater emotional warmth and support than he was showing at the time."[3] During our many sessions, Dr. Hirt gave me genuine support by confirming that my anguish with Alan was warranted. He recognized that Alan was rather withdrawn, and that his extramarital relationship had hurt me tremendously. Yet, for all that, I was the one Dr. Hirt began treating with psychotropic drugs. As I would find out much later, these were the very same drugs that would adversely affect my ability to cope or clearly evaluate my situation.

At some point during our first few sessions, Dr. Hirt issued me a prescription for Dalmane, which he described in later reports as "a very mild sleeping pill which is nonaddictive nor habituating."[4] I only used them occasionally, when I was having a particularly bad night and couldn't sleep.

Soon after that, however, Dr. Hirt also began issuing me prescriptions for Librium, a tranquilizing medication in the same class as Dalmane— a benzodiazepine—to use in the daytime, as needed. Unfortunately for me and countless others, Dr. Hirt's prescription was—I found out much later—just what pharmaceutical companies were encouraging at that time. In reviewing ads placed in the medical journals of the day, I found one print promotion for Librium that claimed "where there is anxiety— either as a complicating factor or as a cause of illness itself—there is a place for Librium ... whatever the diagnosis ... Librium."[5]

So, by the summer of 1967, I had been prescribed two different tranquilizing drugs, one to take as a "sleeping pill" and the other to take during the day. I certainly never understood that they would impede my mental, emotional, and physical abilities in any way. I started taking them regularly, as prescribed, and carried on with my busy life.

As winter closed in that first year after Derek's death, it brought with it some very painful reminders. Christmas lights and decorations began appearing, and I felt more and more anguished by the day. I could barely tolerate a short visit to a shopping mall, with Santa Claus, baubles, and lights everywhere. On one occasion, as I entered a shopping center I immediately encountered a small boy about the age Derek would have been had he lived, in the company of his mother. I was instantly grief-stricken and had to rush out of the center.

During my routine annual checkup with Dr. MacGillivray that December, I told him about the distress the approaching Christmas season was causing me, coinciding, as it did, with the anniversary of Derek's death, and that my stomach was in knots at times. Other than that, I felt physically well, and had no specific health concerns. I came out of the doctor's office that day with a prescription for Stelazine, which Dr. MacGillivray told me was for my stomach.[6] Perhaps the pharmaceutical sales force had something to do with this prescription as well, given the drug's advertising slogan at the time: "You've tried, you've listened ... but here she is again. Looks like chronic anxiety—looks like a case for Stelazine."[7]

I did not know it then, but Stelazine is a very strong drug—also called an "antipsychotic" or "neuroleptic"—that was likely to affect my ability to work, drive a car, and concentrate fully on anything. In his book *Toxic Psychiatry*, Dr. Peter Breggin describes how neuroleptic drugs produce an effect that he likens to a "chemical lobotomy." He goes on to say that, "while the neuroleptics are toxic to most brain functions, disrupting nearly all of them, they have an especially well-documented impact on the dopamine neurotransmitter system ... [which affects] ... the major nerve pathways from the deeper brain to the frontal lobes and limbic system—the very same areas struck by surgical lobotomy."[8] Nevertheless, off I went that day with my third prescription, and attempted to carry on with my busy life. The Stelazine and Dalmane were to be used short-term, but the Librium was to be taken continuously. I trusted my doctors, and took these tranquilizers regularly as prescribed, in the same way I took birth control pills. I didn't think about their side effects, but I presumed they were helping me to relax and sleep better.

In remembrance of Derek, I bought a large Bible and donated it to the church that Christmas. I also had a beautiful wreath made for the altar, which Alan, Deb, and I took to Derek's grave after the Christmas Day service. Other than that, we did very little by way of recognizing Christmas that year. If it hadn't been for Deb, I would have rather done nothing at all. To this day, Christmas remains a very melancholy time for me; only in recent years, since I have been off the pills, have I been able to celebrate it with much enthusiasm.

I moved into the new year with a sense of relief that the holidays were over, and continued to occupy myself with my many business and community activities. Although things were far from perfect between Alan and me, and I still struggled with issues of trust, I sensed that the worst of the crisis in our marriage had likely passed. He began to express what seemed to be a genuine desire to work toward strengthening our marriage, and I thought we were finally making some progress in our sessions with Dr. Hirt. I also recognized that what we had been through in losing Derek was probably the most emotionally challenging experience we would ever face, and that different people react to grief and stress in very different ways. Seen in that context, Alan's infidelity was something I knew I could never forget, but I felt I should try to overcome and move past. I also had Deb's happiness to consider.

Early in 1968, we started looking to buy our first home, and I was also becoming quite keen on having another baby. Alan and I had always agreed that we would have another child at some point, but it was important to me that we own a home first. We were both earning substantial salaries, and for the first time we were in a good financial position to buy a house. We began spending our weekends checking out the local real estate market, and after several months we found a jewel of a place nearby, tucked into a secluded corner, with a beautiful parklike backyard. We both fell in love with the place, and made an offer on it right away. I was thrilled that we had found such a beautiful house, and thought that buying it would bring a needed change to our lives, perhaps even mark the beginning of happier times for our family.

However, soon after the deal for the house was signed, I began experiencing some intense, unexpected emotions. As I faced the reality of packing up and moving, I realized that it was going to be painful for me to leave the home that Derek had lived in. That house was filled with happy memories of his life; I could still see him running about, digging in the sandbox, watering the plants, and playing with the neighbor's dog in the yard. I somehow felt as though I would be abandoning him by leaving there. In fact, my reaction was so profound that I was unable to go through with the move. Although Alan seemed a little surprised and disappointed by my sudden change of heart, he didn't say much, and we agreed to postpone our move. We ended up renting out our new house for over a year before I could come to terms with what I had to do.

We finally moved into our new home in the fall of 1969, and I became pregnant again shortly afterwards. Although we had agreed to have another child, Alan seemed a little tentative about the news at first. To some extent, I could understand his feelings. We had, after all, lost our son, and the full realization that we were having another child triggered many conflicting emotions in both of us. But we were very young, and we had our whole lives ahead of us. I had begun to realize I could actually go on to be happy again, that life does indeed keep moving forward, and I felt that Alan would come around. The new life stirring within me gave me hope and a renewed sense of faith.

About the same time as I became pregnant, I was assigned to head up the biggest consumer study on grocery shopping ever conducted in the province. It involved thirty-three cities and towns and would take many months to complete. My position with Kelly Douglas had really launched me into the forefront of consumer research and strategic marketing, and provided me ample opportunity to put my training into action. The work was very complex and challenging, and I was required to do some traveling around the province. Once again, my professional life was moving ahead full steam, despite the uncertainties in my personal life.

Alan was still a little emotionally distant, and at times he was showing some rather questionable judgment, which made me uneasy. For one thing, he had been spending quite a lot of money. We had just purchased a new home and had a baby on the way, and in my estimation it was no time to be extravagant in our spending. Nevertheless, he was dressing better than he ever had—buying fine-quality suits and shoes—and indulging in rather pricey hobbies. He took flying lessons and bought an expensive camera. He was an amateur marksman, belonged to a local gun club, and had bought two guns. I was the one doing the books for our family, and when I started becoming more watchful than usual because of Alan's excessive spending, I discovered a number of bank withdrawals that seemed unwarranted. Alan didn't seem to have any plausible explanation for them, and I became increasingly suspicious.

One afternoon, when I was four-and-a-half months pregnant, my world collapsed around me yet again. I was particularly upset with him that day, and deliberately went through his jacket pockets. I found something, and my stomach clenched into a tight knot as I stared down at the receipt in my hand—expensive flowers, which I had certainly not received.

I couldn't believe it was happening again. I confronted him, and again he denied an affair. But I wasn't buying it, and decided to do some investigating. Pretending to be his secretary, I phoned the flower shop that had issued the receipt and stated that I needed to know, "for accounting purposes," to whom the flowers had been sent. I was given a name, and I was informed that there had been many orders for flowers, all pink baby sweetheart roses. I was devastated. I was going to have a baby in just a few months and my marriage was in ruins.

When Alan returned home that night, I demanded that he leave the house. He quietly gathered up a few things and moved to a motel not far away. Once he was gone, I found myself feeling just as furious and disgusted with Alan as ever, and very confused. Was I also to blame for the state of our marriage? Could I have done things differently and prevented some of our problems? I didn't know. None of it made any sense to me.

The next morning, I visited a lawyer, a woman. I was intent upon initiating divorce proceedings, but when she saw me, already beginning to swell at the midriff, her advice to me was to "wait until after the baby is born." "You're going to look kind of funny in court," she added. "Not at your most persuasive."

And so I struggled on, making a special effort to appear composed and confident at work, and actually succeeding fairly well. Although I was very distracted at times, I had Deb to consider, another baby on the way, and it looked as if I was on my own. I had always been ambitious, but at that point, I felt it was essential for me to really excel in the business world. Perhaps I was also using my work to escape from the pain of my faltering marriage, but I felt that Deb, my new baby, and everything in my world were dependent on my hard work and success.

I was seeing Dr. Hirt regularly during this time of crisis, and he kept me supplied with tranquilizers. I had grown to trust him completely; he had seen me through some terrible times and had shown me a great deal of understanding and support. I was well into my pregnancy and he was fully aware of the emotional turmoil I was in, tending to Deb's needs and maintaining a high-profile career. I though that the medication he prescribed was entirely harmless to me and the developing baby, and was advised to keep taking it to ensure that I got enough rest, and that I remained calm and relaxed enough to carry on effectively. No concern or doubt was raised by Dr. Hirt about the safety of the drugs, nor was I warned by him of any potential side effects. I certainly never understood that this medication might damage my mental, emotional, or physical abilities in any way. On the contrary, I understood that Librium was prescribed to alleviate the distress I felt, precisely so that my mental, emotional, and physical health would *not* be adversely affected. Yet at the time, as I found out later, the *Compendium of Pharmaceuticals and Specialties* (*CPS*), a publication often referred to as the doctors' drug bible, stated that patients treated with Librium "should be cautioned about engaging in activities requiring mental alertness, judgment, and physical co-ordination. ..."[9]

The shopping study I was assigned to develop was a huge undertaking. Throughout my entire pregnancy I struggled to focus on my work, producing extensive, detailed reports based on my research, complete with complex cross-correlations and analyses. It was an arduous process, but I got through it, and went on to make major presentations to the senior executive personnel of the many divisions and subsidiaries of Kelly Douglas, receiving a tremendous response for the work I had done. In fact, that study eventually became a model for students of marketing at Simon Fraser University (SFU). However, as I became more visibly pregnant I was asked to postpone one major presentation until after I had my baby—another interesting sign of the times.

The fact that I had taken off my wedding ring also did not go unnoticed. Victor MacLean asked me about it, one day when I was in his office. Flustered, I chose not to confide the truth about my personal situation, and instead told him that the ring was "giving me a rash." Clearly I was very conflicted about my marriage. And as my due date loomed closer, I became even more distressed by my predicament. I was very confused, and although I now realize that it flew in the face of all logic, I finally allowed Alan to come home again.

On June 28, 1970, after a very long labor, I gave birth to a beautiful baby girl who weighed in at ten pounds, four ounces. There was some difficulty with her birth, which nobody really explained to me at the time, and the doctors were considering a caesarean section at one point because my contractions were not progressing normally. They used the term "uterine apathy" to describe the problem.

Despite the robust size of my new daughter, she had to be placed in what was then called a "strong-arm box" for observation because her responses after birth were a little on the slow side. I never understood that this phenomenon was connected with the drugs I was taking during my pregnancy, but I now realize that it probably was. Although it may seem odd today, this was in 1970, and people were not nearly as aware of the potential dangers of medicines on the fetus. Nevertheless, as I found out later, the *Compendium of Pharmaceuticals and Specialties* at the time, cautioned against treating women "of child-bearing potential" with benzodiazepine drugs at all. A later report of the effects of benzodiazepines used during pregnancy and labor, published in the *British Medical Journal* in 1978, discussed newborn baby "syndrome," which included "shallow, inadequate respirations, floppiness, subnormal temperature, and poor sucking. …"[10] The same journal report went on to say that "the depressant effects of other drugs given during labor would be made worse" in a woman on benzodiazepines, which would certainly explain my weak contractions.

When Alan came to see the baby and me in the hospital the next morning, he brought me a single rose in a cracked vase. I couldn't help thinking that there were no pricey bouquets of baby sweetheart roses for me on this occasion, and my anger soon grew. When I asked him about a name for the baby, he seemed entirely uninterested, didn't have a single suggestion. All this was too much for me, and our exchange soon erupted into a terrible row.

I brought my daughter, whom I named Carrie, home from the hospital a few days later. I tried suggesting to Alan that I wanted to stay home with her for a year, but he wasn't at all supportive of the idea. Instead we brought Auntie back and I returned to work within six weeks. It was a tremendously stressful time for me, and I kept right on taking my tranquilizers three times a day, as prescribed.

It is clear to me today that it was very unhealthy to have stayed in my marriage at that point. Perhaps if my emotions and senses had not been flattened with drugs that also affected my ability to cope and make sound judgments, I would have acted quite differently. *It's Just Your Nerves*, a guidebook published by Health and Welfare Canada in 1981, discussed this backward psychiatric trend directly in saying that "tranquillizers are often used to help individuals adapt to conflicts generated by intolerable behaviour in a spouse. ..."[11] In an article published in the *Ontario Medical Review* in 1982, which I read many years too late, Dr. Mark Berner wrote: "To merely prescribe drugs for the relief of stress-related symptoms ... constitutes an abrogation of responsibility on the part of the physician, reinforcing the patient's belief that something is intrinsically and/or organically wrong with him. A process is set in motion which may result in a chronically 'ill' patient receiving repeat prescriptions for years on end."[12]

Although I was unaware of it back in 1970, I, too, was being guided down a very dangerous path, a path that would ultimately threaten every aspect of my life.

CHAPTER FIVE

Front-Page News

THE WEEKS AND MONTHS following Carrie's birth were confusing and emotionally tumultuous. Although I certainly didn't feel the same about Alan as I once had, having another child in the family renewed my determination to try to hold our marriage together, for the sake of the children as much as anything else. And I could not overlook the fact that, for the most part, Alan was a very good father. He loved Deb and Carrie very much, and they him. Deb adored her new baby sister and spent many moments lovingly holding her, playing with her, and watching her with great pride as she grew bigger and responded more to everything and everyone around her.

Alan, however, continued to show little enthusiasm about our home, or concern for our quality of life or our future. My commitment to the marriage was still much greater than his. I was the primary decision maker in regard to our finances, holidays—everything. Any recognition of special occasions, such as birthdays, was left entirely up to me.

Although, to the best of my knowledge, Alan never had another affair after Carrie was born, my frustration with the situation always lurked just beneath the surface, and our relationship soon descended into a seemingly endless pattern of fights and reconciliations. On many of these occasions, the battles ended with Alan moving out, only to return a few days, weeks, or even months later. Whenever we were arguing, I became convinced that we should live apart so that Deb and Carrie would not grow up in an unhappy environment. Yet both girls missed their father acutely during his absences, and I was chronically torn. During one period when

Alan was not living with us, two-and-a-half-year-old Carrie told me emphatically that she wanted her daddy to come home and live with us again. Her eyes brimmed with tears and her pleas were heartbreaking. I was going around and around in circles emotionally.

We kept on with the counseling sessions with Dr. Hirt for a time, but nothing much was changing. Eventually, in August 1971, we stopped going altogether. I guess I just learned to expect less from Alan, and my marriage in general, and immersed myself in my work. I felt it was imperative for me to stop wasting so much energy on futile efforts, and put greater focus on more tangible goals, and my career as it progressed at Kelly Douglas.

I joined several business organizations—the North American Society for Strategic Corporate Planning, the B.C. chapter of the American Marketing Association, and the Association of Professional Economists of B.C., where I was a board member and vice president. I also became one of the first women members of the Vancouver Board of Trade.

By the time I had stopped seeing Dr. Hirt, Dr. MacGillivray was issuing me prescriptions for Librium, and I continued to take them daily. I also had a drink or two when I got home some nights, trying to unwind after a busy day. For the most part, my drinking was moderate, but on the occasional weekend I would get carried away. I felt quite guilty about these sporadic binges and confided in Dr. MacGillivray about them. This is reflected in an entry he made in his records regarding a visit I made to him on April 8, 1971, where he wrote: "Drinking alcohol to excess occasionally. ..."[1] His recommendation on that same visit? "Rx Librium." In November 1972, Dr. MacGillivray wrote in his records: "Drinking problem—prolonged visit. Advised to stop all alcohol."[2] And I did in fact heed this advice for weeks and months at a time.

The Compendium of Pharmaceuticals and Specialties clearly warned that patients treated with Librium "should be warned against the ingestion of alcohol."[3] And the widely acclaimed book Under the Influence, by Dr. James R. Milam and Katherine Ketcham, published in 1981, describes the danger of combining the two substances: "Anyone who drinks and takes tranquilizers or sedatives at the same time is toying with a chemical time bomb which could explode into multiple addictions, multiple withdrawal syndromes, convulsions, coma, and death. One drink plus one pill does not equal the effect of two drinks or two pills. Instead, the potency of the drugs is multiplied three times, four times, or even more."[4]

During the always ominous Christmas season, in 1972 Alan and I held a small party at our home. As the hostess, I was careful to limit my alcohol intake, and certainly had far less to drink than many others in attendance. Yet, by the end of the evening, I had become quite intoxicated and wound up falling on my driveway, hitting my head hard on the pavement. As a result, I had a nasty bump and considerable bruising, both to my head and to my ego. When I visited Dr. MacGillivray the following day and told him about the incident, he reassured me about the nature of my injury, but chastised me for drinking.

Despite Dr. MacGillivray's concern about my drinking habits, however, he regularly increased my prescriptions for Librium. In fact, during the same Christmas season, a time of year filled with heart-wrenching reminders of Derek's death, and within two weeks of the day that I fell on my driveway, he doubled the number of pills in my refillable prescription. The day after that, he issued me a prescription for Elavil, an antidepressant[5]—an interesting development, in hindsight, given that Librium is essentially a depressant drug.

Not surprisingly, Alan and I were back in the office of Dr. Hirt shortly after that, but soon recognized we were at a stalemate. Dr. MacGillivray then referred us for counseling to another psychiatrist, Dr. Alan Adler, although we were both rather reluctant at that point. Alan didn't seem to think he should be there at all, and I was becoming resentful that the focus seemed to be shifting onto me, my problems, my behavior. After all, I felt it was Alan's actions that had caused so much pain and turmoil in our marriage in the first place, and that he had never made any serious effort to change.

Our sessions with Dr. Adler turned out to be unproductive, and I began to feel rather detached from the whole situation, as though I were on the outside looking in. In retrospect, however, I realize that our sessions with Dr. Adler mark a subtle turning point in my story. As Dr. Adler later reported, "[Mr. Gadsby] wants to help his wife and I think one of the rationalizations for [his] helping her is to go under the guise of conjoint therapy. Only if Mrs. Gadsby feels that the family has a problem can she emotionally accept the fact that she is going through therapy ...

she is rather circumstantial and never seems to get to the point. ... I am not sure whether this is obsessional rumination but perhaps it is the beginning of organicity possibly secondary to excessive alcoholism."[6]

I obtained a copy of Dr. Adler's report many years later, when I was off all the pills; it was significant for a couple of reasons. First, Librium, like all other drugs in the benzodiazepine family, was recommended primarily for *short-term* and/or *intermittent* use. The reasons for avoiding prolonged exposure to benzos are extensive, well documented, and were fully available to any informed family physician or psychiatrist. Many articles were published in medical journals at the time (the early seventies) that discussed the potential for patients treated with benzos over extended periods of time to suffer significant concentration, cognitive problems and confusion, among other things. Yet when I saw Dr. Adler in March 1973, the prescription drugs I was consuming were apparently never considered as a contributing factor in my "obsessional rumination."

Second, what Dr. Adler referred to in his report as "excessive alcoholism" was based on my own admissions of drinking. In fact, these incidents were not chronic but occasional, and for the most part involved the consumption of no more than two or three drinks. But, given the fact that I rarely drank at all before Derek's death, I basically bought into the popular notion that I was unusually susceptible to alcohol, and that I might be developing a drinking problem.

But the tide had turned: the problem was me. Alan was only trying to help. And, although indirectly, I was labeled as emotionally unbalanced in some way for the first, and not the last time. In addition, while Dr. Adler and others were quick to blame alcohol for my problems, it apparently never occurred to them that the subtle changes they noticed in my behavior and thinking were also related to my growing drug dependency. In his 1992 book *Power and Dependence: Social Audit on the Safety of Medicines*, Dr. Charles Medawar, a medical researcher with a professional background in consumer protection and former member of the World Health Organization's Expert Advisory of Drug Policies and Management, states: "The history of sedative-hypnotic drugs to date has been marked by belated recognition of drug-induced psychiatric disorders— chronically mistaken as evidence of illness or a character disorder, rather than something to do with the drug."[7]

Dr. MacGillivray doubled not only the quantity for my Librium pre-scription, to 100 pills from 50, but the dosage, from 5 milligrams to 10. Yet as my intake of Librium increased, so did the severity of my conflicts with Alan. By the summer of 1973, it was not uncommon for our con-frontations to become somewhat physical. I would grab onto him in the heat of an argument, and he would push me away—that sort of thing. In August, my finger was injured quite badly during one of our nastier fights and I had it examined at the hospital.

Once I got angry, I found it absolutely impossible to let things go; I would insist on going over and over the same emotional issues with Alan. One night after his response to my tirade was not as I would have liked— he basically threw up his hands and went to bed—I later poured water in his face as he lay sleeping.

This sort of behavior was completely out of character for me. In ana-lyzing the situation today, I realize I had become a totally different per-son, far removed from the controlled and rational woman I used to be. Alan and I had been through incredible hardship and adversity before that time, but I had never reacted like this. This was new.

Although it was unknown to me at the time, the *CPS* also listed para-doxical reactions such as excitement, stimulation, elevation of mood, and rage among Librium's possible adverse effects.[8] Also, all benzodi-azepine drugs, Librium included, are highly addictive, and tolerance to their effects increases over time. In effect, my body needed more and more in order to avoid withdrawal symptoms between dosages. I know now that I was experiencing a constant cycle of "mini withdrawals" between pills, a phenomenon that manifests itself as a severe state of "rebound" anxiety, wildly fluctuating emotions, and mood swings. I did not in any way connect my growing volatility with my prescribed medications. After all, as I understood it they were being prescribed to help keep me calm. Whenever I felt particularly edgy or irritable, I took another pill.

The irony is that many people who become chemically dependent, myself included, view this rebound anxiety, edginess, and volatility as evidence of an ongoing need for the medication, not a symptom of its overuse. If the prescribing physician doesn't increase the dosage, the patient often does. Cross-addictions are also common, as people tend to drink to alleviate the escalating (drug-induced) anxiety. It is not uncommon for the doctor to blame the patient—whose judgment and insight are profoundly impaired by that time—for the improper use of his or her medication, or to blame the patient's problems on alcohol, as Dr. MacGillivray did with me.

Paradoxically, despite my growing chemical dependency and the escalating turmoil in my private life, my career was booming. My motivation and will to succeed had always been very, very strong, and the tougher things got, the harder I worked. I functioned far better in the controlled, predictable environment of the office than I did at home, where emotional factors were likely to trigger my mood swings and angry diatribes. Although I didn't consciously recognize it at the time, the more out-of-control my personal life became, the more effort and energy I put into my work and community service. I was on overdrive. As my self-esteem eroded, I tried to compensate by striving even harder in the world outside myself. After all, these were the only areas in my life that seemed consistent, and within which I received reward and recognition for my determined efforts. In fact, my three-year stint as chairman of the Conquer Cancer Campaign and my involvement with Highlands United Church and many other business-related organizations (both in my role with Kelly Douglas and otherwise) had given me a reasonably high profile, including lots of media exposure. It wasn't long before I was approached about the possibility of running for alderman in North Vancouver District.

While attending a dinner for the Association of Professional Economists, in the summer of 1973, I met Dr. John Reinstra, who was then president of the North Vancouver Chamber of Commerce, and I hired him to work with me on a major economic feasibility study for our company relocation. John knew me from my community work on the North Shore, and thought I would be a natural to run for alderman, given my business background and the fact that I was a "free enterpriser" as opposed to the only other woman on council at the time, who was left-leaning. He encouraged me to consider running in the upcoming election, and eventually arranged a meeting for me with then mayor Ron Andrews and a prominent businessman who was willing to help back my campaign.

I was quite keyed up by the prospect of running for alderman, and considered it an honor to be encouraged by these prominent members of the community. My enthusiasm, however, seemed lost on Alan. When I asked him what he thought of the idea, he was indifferent, and didn't seem to appreciate that my decision would have any impact on my available time with the family. I suppose, in my heart of hearts, despite the tumultuous state of our marriage, I would have liked him to convince me to spend more time with him, instead of taking on more work, but that was not to happen. Although I had come to expect very little input from him over the years, his lack of enthusiasm still hurt me. He really didn't seem to care what I did.

In the fall of 1973, I ran for alderman in the District of North Vancouver, with considerable backing from the North Shore business community and other volunteer groups I had been involved with. Before long I was producing brochures and other promotional literature, having election signs made and distributed, and seeking public opportunities to express my views on local issues. I welcomed this new role, and dove into my first political campaign with great enthusiasm.

I asked very little of Alan during my political campaign, but one weekend in early November he agreed to help me put up some campaign signs around our neighborhood. When he didn't get around to it in a timely fashion, I became annoyed, and set out with the signs and a heavy mallet to tackle the chore myself. Unfortunately, this endeavor landed me in the emergency department of Lions Gate Hospital that day, as I missed the mark with the mallet at one point and smashed my hand. This was just one of many injuries I received over several years, owing to my reduced psychomotor skills and general lack of coordination while on the pills.

My first political campaign was an overwhelming success, and I was elected to serve a two-year term as alderman in December 1973. On election night, Deb, who was then twelve, and Carrie, only three, were so excited that they marched around the house, saying "We won! We won!" It was quite unusual for a candidate to get into office on the first try, and I, too, was very pleased with my win. My new role with the District Council soon became the focus of my community activities. Between my full-time career during the day, activities with my children, preparation for council meetings, and the meetings themselves, which I attended many evenings, I was busy all the time.

In September 1974, my unpredictable behavior spilled over into my professional life for the first time, during a trip I took to attend the annual Union of B.C. Municipalities Conference in Vernon with mayor Ron Andrews and several other aldermen. I flew to Kelowna, and made the hour-long trip to Vernon by car to take part in the three-day event. The first day of the conference was hectic, and that evening there was a reception for all the delegates. Although I was somewhat tired after the long day, I attended the reception, talked with other municipal representatives, and had a couple of glasses of wine.

As the evening progressed, I felt increasingly tired and a little homesick, and excused myself so I could phone home before Deb and Carrie were in bed for the night. But when I reached them, I was far from reassured. Deb and Alan had had a nasty argument, and I was not happy with what I was hearing. After talking to her, then him, I began to get quite angry with Alan. It seemed to me that he just wasn't being very understanding or sensitive toward Deb; I felt he was handling the situation poorly.

Like any mother who has a demanding career, I struggled with guilt. I could not be everywhere for everybody, and there were many outside obligations that took me away from my children for days at a time. I always missed them when I had to be away, but tried to keep in frequent contact with them by telephone. Auntie had left us shortly after Deb started grade one, and I had hired a woman named Roberta Martin to replace her. Roberta was very good with both the girls. Still, my conflicting roles did cause me distress from time to time.

That evening in Vernon, after hearing of the fiasco brewing at home, I felt a real sense of guilt that I was not there for my daughter when she seemed to need some reassurance. Deb was a teenager at the time and just entering those sensitive, transitional years that transform a child into a young adult. I knew all too well that Alan could be somewhat emotionally insensitive, and I was upset that Deb seemed to be having the same problem with him that I had always had. After all that our family had been through, and all the counseling, it seemed that nothing had changed.

After hanging up the phone, I stewed about the situation, getting more and more annoyed. Before long, I had decided it was necessary for me to fly back to Vancouver right away. I called the airport to find out if there was a flight I could catch that night. There was, and I immediately headed back down to the reception, where I found Ron Andrews and told him that I had to fly back to Vancouver due to a family crisis. I think Ron was a little displeased at this development, but I'm sure he could sense that there was no stopping me. I was determined to get home to my children *immediately*. Nothing else mattered.

I called a taxi from my room and paced impatiently while I waited. It seemed to take forever to arrive. When it did, I'm sure the driver sensed that I was edgy and upset. I was in quite a state by that point and told him I had to get to Kelowna Airport *right away*, but he seemed quite unconcerned. I was irked by his casual attitude and annoyed even further by the fact that he seemed to be eyeing me inappropriately.

When we got out on the highway, I was quite uncomfortable with the whole situation and very anxious to get to Kelowna. It was a long drive and I was in no mood to be patient. After several miles, we turned off the highway onto a side road. I *knew* we were going the wrong way and demanded that we turn around and get back on route. The driver was shifty and evasive when I spoke up, and kept right on driving. I became increasingly frightened and shouted at him. I was a public official and had a plane to catch! There were people waiting for me at the airport! Finally, with a surly look over his shoulder, he slowed the car, turned around, and drove back out onto the highway. My heart pounded wildly for the rest of the trip and I considered jumping out of the car when we got closer to town, but it was only moments before we would be arriving at the airport and I didn't want to miss my plane. I hurried from the car when we got there, intending to report the incident immediately.

Of course I arrived at the airport even more upset than I had been when I left Vernon. I burst into the terminal and rushed to the ticket counter, nearly tearful with anxiety. I tried to tell airport officials what had happened, but nobody seemed to want to listen. I realize now, of course, that I appeared to be irrational. Although I did have valid reason to be upset, I was handling everything poorly. I was in a rage, blurting out my story to anyone within earshot. I *had* to get home; I wanted the driver found and questioned. I wanted everyone to *jump*.

When the plane came in, I stormed to the counter to demand my boarding pass. They were sorry, they said; they could not issue me a boarding pass. I was so upset I heard only fragments of what they said to me. "… in keeping with policy … visible signs of alcohol …" I couldn't believe it. Security guards hovered nearby, muttering among themselves. I had drunk only a couple of glasses of wine! Why were they doing this to me?

By the time the announcement was made that passengers to Vancouver were to start boarding the plane, I was livid. I snatched up my suitcase and marched toward the boarding entrance, shouting at airport officials indignantly. Security personnel swooped in and blocked my way. As the door to the tarmac closed in front of me, I lost my temper completely and hurled my suitcase against the door. The glass shattered in front of me; sharp fragments flew everywhere.

The next thing I knew I was at the police station. My memory from that point forward is foggy, as I had slipped into a state of near-shock at being arrested. I do remember being allowed to make a phone call to Ron Andrews in Vernon; he offered to come down to Kelowna to help me. Then I was locked in a cell. Then they let me out. Then I was at the Capri Hotel.

Entering my hotel room, the first thing I did, hands shaking, was open my suitcase and root frantically through it for my vial of pills. As I popped the lid of the vial, it flew from my hands, scattering pills to all corners of the room. I cried out, fell to my hands and knees, and crawled about, desperate to find all the pills. My hands were shaking so badly I could hardly return them to the vial. Later that evening I couldn't remember whether I had taken one or more pills. But I had to call Alan. Why was I coming home? he asked. "Everything is okay."

The next day I found myself in court, answering for my outrageous behavior the night before. I was tired and bewildered, and highly embarrassed, wondering why everything had gone so wrong. Why had I behaved so irrationally? What was I thinking? Had the taxi driver thought I was drunk as well, and is that why he tried to take advantage of me? Why had I overreacted and lost control? I didn't know.

I was officially charged with "mischief to public property," ordered to pay for the shattered door, and fined. I wrote a check on the spot and apologized, and just a couple of hours later I sat having lunch with Ron Andrews and Kelowna's chief of police. They were both very friendly and understanding, and conversation was kept on the light side. They viewed the incident as simply unfortunate, just "one of those things." A few too many drinks, nothing serious. But I was mortified. I felt foolish, totally confused, and drained.

After lunch, when Ron and I were on our way to the airport, the situation suddenly went from bad to worse. The words blatted from the radio: ... *North Vancouver Alderman Joan Gadsby ... too drunk to board plane ... damaged property ...* The nightmare was not over. How would I explain this? Would people at home know? I flew home with my stomach in knots. When I walked out into the Vancouver Airport after the flight, the first thing I saw was the latest edition of the *Vancouver Sun*; the headline, partway down the page, jumped out at me: "Drunken Alderman Fined for Mischief." Yes, people at home would know. I was front-page news.

CHAPTER SIX

More Pills—More Trouble

M Y KELOWNA INCIDENT was to have quite an impact on my life for a time. I was highly concerned about my job after seeing the damaging headlines in the *Sun*, and called Victor MacLean at home the evening of my arrival back in Vancouver. I stammered out the explanation for my distress at the airport, but I couldn't deny what I had done. I certainly tried to dispel the notion that I had been drunk at the time of my outburst, however, making it clear that I only had a couple of drinks. Much to my relief, Victor was very understanding about the whole thing and my job was not in jeopardy—although I'm sure I was the source of some juicy gossip among my co-workers for a while.

The North Shore newspapers were quick to jump on the story as well, and had a little fun at my expense with headlines such as: "Great Gadsby Airs Grievance." Despite the humorous slant, though, the news coverage focused on my reported drunkenness.

The whole episode left me feeling extremely confused. I couldn't explain or understand my erratic behavior; it was so out of character. I knew only that the embarrassment, guilt, and remorse I was experiencing were overwhelming.

The professionals I was turning to for help all seemed to assume that excessive consumption of alcohol was the source of my problem. And if it wasn't my drinking, it was my "behavioural and emotional problems." In a letter written later by Dr. Hirt regarding the Kelowna incident, he stated "Mrs. Gadsby is showing slow improvement in her ability to

understand and control her behaviour problems … she has not completed therapy yet, but I feel [she] is moving in the direction of maturity
and personal growth."[1] This was an interesting analysis, given that prior
to my being prescribed sedative hypnotic drugs no one had ever suggested
that I was immature, or lacked a clear focus on personal growth—quite
the opposite, in fact.

Years later, during the process of researching the effects of benzodiazepines and alcohol and reconstructing my life, I came to understand
what was really the matter with me on that occasion in Kelowna, and on
many, many other occasions after that. I discussed my history at some
length with Dr. Alan Clews, the former chairman of the British Columbia
Medical Association (BCMA) Alcohol and Drug Committee, who later
wrote me a letter in which he offered this analogy: "When thinking about
the effects of benzodiazepines on the mind, I find it helpful to see them
as another form of alcohol but with a different way of elimination from
the body. For example your past use of 15 mg of Valium would be the
equivalent of drinking a pack of beer a day but with the difference that
a pack of beer would be eliminated in twenty-four hours, whereas Valium
takes much longer. The result of this slow elimination is that after a week
on Valium the effect would have climbed to the equivalent of several
packs of beer a day. If alcohol is used in addition to benzodiazepines the
effect is multiplied."[2] (Valium was later substituted for the Librium I was
taking at the time of my outburst in Kelowna, but the two substances are
essentially the same.)

At Deb's high school, there was a lot of talk about my "Kelowna incident." Although she, too, found the gossip humiliating and hard to explain,
Deb just tried to ignore it all and shrug it off, as I did. She was more concerned about continuing to do well in her studies and sports activities.

In March 1975, I made a week-long trip back to Ontario to see my
mother. She had fallen and broken her hip, an injury attributed to osteoporosis. Her subsequent hip surgery had appeared to be a success, but
shortly after the operation she suffered a stroke. I arrived at the hospital
to find her in terrible shape. Her eyes were open but glazed. She could
not communicate and didn't appear to recognize anyone. It was terrible
to see her that way, and it triggered the familiar feelings of helplessness
and loss that I had experienced both with my father and then with Derek.

At one point my sister, Pat, wept openly while we were sitting with Mom in her hospital room, and I asked her not to. I was worried that Mom could sense our sorrow and fear somehow, despite her condition, and I wanted to show only love and warmth in her presence. I just couldn't accept that she was not really with us.

Eventually the doctors told us it was highly unlikely that her condition would ever improve; the damage done by the stroke was irreversible. A few days after that, I had to fly back to Vancouver. The whole experience had been quite disturbing. Although she was still alive, I knew that I had lost my mother; her unending love and support would not be there for me any longer.

I had been back in Vancouver only a few days when I drove up to Harrison Hot Springs to attend a Union of B.C. Municipalities presentation. After dinner one evening, my brother phoned me at the hotel in Harrison to give me the sad news. Our mother had died. After hanging up the phone, I sat on the bed in my room and stared at the wall. I felt hollow inside, but somehow detached from the situation: it just didn't seem real to me, and I had difficulty crying. Dr. Heather Ashton, in a research paper published in the *British Medical Journal* in 1984, refers to benzos having the effect of "blunting the emotions" and producing "emotional anesthesia," which may explain my lack of immediate response to losing my mother.[3]

The next morning I packed up my things and drove home, but after much consideration I chose not to go back east again to attend the funeral. The thought of being anywhere near caskets, graveyards, and the official ceremonies of mourning was unimaginable to me at that point.

Around the same time as my mother's death, in the spring of 1975, Dr. MacGillivray stopped prescribing me Librium and started me on Valium, five milligrams, three times a day. Within weeks, an argument that Alan and I were having escalated into what the police called a "violent, hysterical rage." One of the neighbors must have phoned them, and I was again arrested. This time I spent the entire night in jail, crying and alone. The next morning I was released and took a taxi home.

It's painful for me to acknowledge, but this type of behavior, although extreme on that particular occasion, was not unusual for me at that time. In fact, I was having many such episodes. Once I flew into a rage and actually chased Alan around the outside of our house with a .44 magnum pistol, firing it into the air! Alan had been a target shooter in high school, and he had always maintained an interest in guns and gun collecting. He had bought the pistol not long before this incident, and foolishly kept it and his other guns (some loaded) in the house. I have no idea why the neighbors didn't phone the police on this occasion, but one thing is certain: Alan afterward saw to it that his guns were no longer easily accessible. Thank God. Since I've been off the pills I've read stories in which family members and others have been injured, or even killed, as a direct result of addicts' paradoxical reactions to the "tranquilizing" drugs they were taking at the time.

I was also experiencing bouts of extreme paranoia and emotional hysteria. One night I rushed through the house turning out all the lights and closing the curtains before running downstairs to the farthest room and scrambling under the bed, filled with an awful fear of what, I don't know. I was often overcome by inexplicable dread, and I was having terrible recurrent flashbacks to the night Derek died. The words I cried out when I was told he'd died kept echoing in my head. "No, no, no ..." louder and louder, escalating to a shrieked *"No! No! No!"* I was both irresistibly drawn to, and horribly haunted by his image. If I turned to Alan for help I would only feel worse. It had been nearly a decade since Derek's death and Alan did not welcome opening that wound over and over again. I would scream at him, demanding to know why he couldn't help me. It was as though it all happened yesterday, and I couldn't work through it.

It was many years later that I learned about the pills' creation of "emotional anesthesia" in users. My emotions had been blunted by the pills ever since I was put on them in 1967, some seven years earlier.

Desperately unhappy, sick, and tired, I nevertheless continued to put on my professional face every day and carry on working. I spent an extraordinary amount of time and effort checking and rechecking statistics and reports to ensure their accuracy, because I wasn't sure I could trust myself to catch errors if I checked just once. I didn't realize at the time that my ability to concentrate had been and was being affected by the drugs I was taking.

By July of that year, there were major changes taking place at the office. It didn't look as if Victor MacLean would be staying on as president.

I had always liked and respected Victor, and was not happy with this development. I stayed on with the company for a while after the restructuring, but soon found that there were some genuine differences between my values and those of Victor's successor. I felt that morale within the company had been adversely affected by the change in leadership, and decided to take a year's sabbatical while I considered my career options. It had been a confusing, stressful year, and I welcomed the opportunity to get away from the pressure of my career, spend more time with Deb and Carrie, and try to make some sense of my life. I had been living in a personal hell, and for the first time in my life I really felt I needed to take time out.

I kept up my professional affiliations and obligations, however, and was still a member of various boards and committees in the business community. I also began to campaign again, as there was an election coming in the fall. I definitely wanted to retain my seat on council and thought that the coming term would be an opportune time for me to immerse myself in that role, since I was not going to be working full-time for a while.

Despite having more free time than usual over the summer, I did not feel rested or in better shape by autumn. In fact, I was feeling even worse. I continued to have intense, exaggerated reactions to things, many of them minor. I seemed to spend most of my time feeling frustrated, disillusioned, and angry. Desperately seeking peace of mind and spiritual renewal, I booked an extensive trip to Europe for the early fall—alone. I thought that a complete change of pace and some time away would do me good. With Alan and Roberta around, I knew Deb and Carrie would be looked after, and I would call them often. Off I went on my thirteen-country, three-week guided tour. By no stretch of the imagination, however, was I about to leave my troubles behind.

Traveling only seemed to make me feel lonely and disheartened. Why was all hope and joy slipping away from me? I used to love life. I had always worked hard, reached for my dreams and tried to give of myself. Why was my life now so filled with chaos? I could find no answers to these questions. And I missed my children and my home.

I made one friend, a fellow tourist. She and I chummed around as we visited the many sites and countries on the tour's itinerary, but for the most part I kept to myself. I was searching and troubled; I found it nearly impossible to unwind or relax. One night in London, after attending a function at the Palladium, I had a particularly bad time. Alone in my hotel room, I went over and over the same tired issues in my mind. I kept phoning home, lonely, confused, and crying. I called my sister in Toronto many times, weeping and repeating myself. I was reaching for help, but I felt desolate and disconnected. Nothing anyone could say was of any comfort to me. In Rome, too, I had to face up to unexpected emotions. I had wanted so very much to take my mother on a trip to the Vatican before she died, and my visit there, alone, brought on almost unbearable melancholy.

I returned to Canada in no better shape than when I left. I had resolved nothing, and soon fell back into the same old negative patterns. In the early evening of October 19, 1975, Alan and I were starting toward one of our usual arguments. This time we were fighting over in-laws. Alan's father had been quite insulting toward me on a number of occasions and, because of this, I was *insisting* that Alan break all ties with him. I couldn't see how unreasonable my demand was. I was furious with Alan for being so passive about the situation, and demanded that he show support for *me* for once.

My tirade soon moved to the subject of Derek's death, as it often did. Again I cried and raged and carried on, and again Alan withdrew from me. I began drinking sometime during the evening and the situation escalated rapidly. Around 10:30 that evening, the police were called to the house:

"... Mrs. Gadsby ... appeared to be very intoxicated and very insulting. ... Her words to the police were 'If you don't take that bastard away I will axe him up tonight.' Mr. Gadsby was very cooperative and ... appeared to be stone sober. Police asked why [Mrs. Gadsby] wanted her husband removed. She became even more infuriated, saying ... 'Just do as you're told, you sons of bitches.'"[4]

Apparently, I wanted Alan to leave the house and could not understand why the police, who had been summoned to help, did not assist me toward this end. The report went on: "Mrs. Gadsby came outside ... in a state nothing short of a 'mad woman.' She had previously attempted to assault her husband ... they had an altercation and he was trying to subdue her and she was striking at him. At this point she again stated to the Police Constable that she was going into the garage, get an axe and axe both of them up. ... Mrs. Gadsby came up behind Constable Turner, grabbed at him and knocked him slightly off balance. Constable Turner described her as being in a 'mad rage.' [She] took hold of Turner's right thumb with her teeth and began to bite and tear at him in a ferocious, animal-like manner. ... Mrs. Gadsby struck Constable Turner numerous times in the face and chest. ... They got her in the car ... then Mrs. Gadsby began to slam her head and feet against the window of the police car and kicked at all the windows. ... Police felt ... they would have to handcuff her so they opened the door to remove her from the car. ... As Constable Green[5] opened the door, Mrs. Gadsby attacked him with her fists and was screaming ... [and] made repeated threats to kill them both. ... They again put Mrs. Gadsby in the back of the police car where she attempted to crash head long into the rear window numerous times and again tried to kick the windows out of the police car. At this point [she was taken] to Lions Gate Hospital ... she was still crashing headlong into the screen area of the vehicle and also tried to kick the screen up. [When] police arrived at the hospital Mrs. Gadsby was nearly unconscious. [Nevertheless] ... going into the hospital it took three policemen to hold her down from the car to the hospital on a bed. After being given two needles, they still had to forcibly hold her for about fifteen minutes and at this point she was strapped to the bed by the hospital staff ... her speech was extremely slurred and she seemed unable to keep on a set topic."[6]

No doubt about it, my life had descended to a whole new level of chaos. I was charged by the police with three offenses as a result of my actions on that terrible night, two counts of assaulting a police officer and one count of obstruction. The papers had a field day with the story and, of course, my children and everyone around me suffered. Once again I was the topic of the day, an elected official and highly visible business-woman in the Vancouver community caught acting like a crazed animal.

However, while everyone close to me endured tremendous stress, hurt, and humiliation as a result of my actions, I seemed to have absolutely no insight as to the enormity of the situation, or the reasons behind my bizarre behavior. While I realized that something had gone terribly wrong, I was strangely separated and detached from reality, unable to feel the full effect of what I had done.

Unfortunately, it wasn't just through the news reports that my associates and political colleagues learned of the events of October 19. I had actually called a number of them, including the mayor and a fellow alderman, at the height of my frenzy that night. In fact, both of them had come to the house, at my insistence, and witnessed the whole incredible scene. Yet this, too, did not seem to sink in. I carried on with my political role as usual, fielding questions and trying to roll with the punches. I went about the business of obtaining a lawyer to deal with my assault charges. I simply did not comprehend the huge impact that my outrageous behavior would have on every aspect of my life, my family, and my career.

In his book *The Real Pushers*, Dr. Joel Lexchin (a key figure in Canadian health-care reform whom I met years later) quoted a California psychiatrist, H.L. Lennard, who said, "Drugs designed to change experience or behaviour ... affect the complex psychological and social processes connecting the individual to his physical and human environment. ... To the extent that [they] dull the senses, sedate, numb and immobilize, they de-differentiate human experience and behaviour."[7]

Looking back to that time in 1975, I can now understand all too well what Lexchin meant. By 1975, I was hopelessly "disconnected" from my environment, seemingly unable to associate my actions with their repercussions.

My legal representative immediately went about trying to obtain a psychiatric report from Dr. Hirt in hopes of having the matter withdrawn from the courts. Dr. Hirt's initial response did not include any mention of the paradoxical agitation and rage associated with benzodiazepine dependence. Instead, he implied only that I had occasionally used prescribed drugs and/or alcohol to *alleviate* my emotional difficulties, part of a personality structure that he described as having "a large hysterical quotient." "Mrs. Gadsby," he offered, "has been advised not to use alcohol under circumstances of stress or strain, but her emotional condition has not allowed her to gain sufficient insight to accept this recommendation."[8]

That bears repeating: My *emotional condition* did not allow me to gain sufficient insight. Dr. Hirt did not seem to think that my emotions were anything but normal when he first began treating Alan and me for our marriage difficulties. In fact, it was *Alan's* emotional condition that he took exception to at that time. When I first consulted a lawyer back in 1970 regarding my wish for a divorce from Alan, Dr. Hirt sent a letter to my legal counsel that stated, in part, "Mr. and Mrs. Gadsby have attempted to maintain their marriage in spite of gross problems of communication and an inability on Mr. Gadsby's part to share or to understand the needs of his wife … [he] was passive dependent, subtly hostile and always emotionally independent from her … unable to understand or partake in her continued grief at the loss of their child. … He played a psychological game in which he offered his wife affection and then not only did he not display reciprocation but flaunted another relationship before her … a divorce is needed to prevent further mental cruelties."[9]

So, in 1970, Dr. Hirt did not attribute our problems to any emotional instability on my part. But after initiating continuous and prolonged treatment with drugs originally prescribed to alleviate my stress and ensure my ongoing ability to cope, he now found that my emotional condition had deteriorated. In his 1975 letter, Dr. Hirt also failed to mention that the probable result of my system having been saturated for so long with psychoactive medications, which blunt and impair both emotions and cognitive functioning, was exactly that lack of "sufficient insight" that he described. The drugs I was being prescribed are widely known to triple or quadruple the effects of alcohol. Nothing about that appeared in Dr. Hirt's letter either; only the implication that I had a psychiatric problem and was prone to hysteria.

Less than two weeks later, I read a small article in the *Vancouver Sun* reporting the growing number of deaths associated with the use of Valium, especially in combination with other drugs, including alcohol. *Deaths!* I was very confused by this report. Both Dr. Hirt and Dr. MacGillivray were aware that I drank alcohol sometimes—in fact, they apparently believed I had a problem with it—so why was I being prescribed so much Valium?

The following day I wrote a note to Dr. MacGillivray, and attached it to a photocopy of the newspaper clipping. When I next saw him, I asked immediately about the warning inferred by the article, but he pooh-poohed the danger and advised me to continue with the Valium. He implied that I would be in far greater danger if I stopped taking my pills; they were being prescribed for a good reason. While I was far from convinced he was right, and confused about whom to believe, I certainly felt that I needed my pills. I knew that if I didn't take them regularly, I felt extremely edgy and irritable. I was frightened enough, however, to swear off drinking any alcohol at that point.

It was my lawyer who was not satisfied that the drugs I had consumed the night I was arrested had been given adequate consideration, and he pressed the subject further. In his second letter requesting information from Dr. Hirt, he asked directly about "the effect of the combined consumption of Valium and alcohol" and "whether Valium could in [this] case cause a reaction opposite to that normally expected."[10]

Finally, but only after having it specifically suggested to him, Dr. Hirt touched on the real issue. Yes, he answered, "alcohol potentiates Valium and Valium potentiates alcohol, which simply means that the effect of both is qualitatively doubled and tripled." Also, "too much Valium causes the patient to become ... disinhibited." Dr. Hirt went even further, stating that "there are scientific reports that show that doses of Valium in some women, strangely, cause an upsurge of the emotion of anger with a preponderance towards violence." Yes, he confirmed, "Valium in Mrs. Gadsby's case ... could certainly have caused a reaction opposite to that which one would wish, namely, uncontrolled anger as opposed to realized tranquility."[11]

Incredibly, Dr. Hirt immediately reversed himself. In the next paragraph of his letter, he stated that Valium was not to blame, that "the single factor to trigger this behaviour" was my own suppression and repression of strong reactions of anger with my husband. In effect, he blamed me for my inability to (appropriately) "voice such feelings at the instant at which they were perceived," or, in other words, he claimed that my outbursts were caused by the emotions I had repressed. But I was being prescribed drugs specifically intended to suppress and repress strong emotions! Where was the logic?

Finally, Dr. Hirt expressed his opinion that I was "in some ways extraordinary ... bright" but had "an internal psychic demon born of anger and frustration living within (me)." If I could simply learn to use my anger, he went on, rather than lose my temper, my life "would be quite remarkable and productive, unmarred by these strange incidents of explosive behaviour."[12]

In hindsight, I cannot now accept the lack of comprehension and insight shown by the medical professionals who were trying to help me. My doctors ought to have observed that not once prior to being treated with psychotropic drugs had I ever had a problem clearly and directly expressing myself, or lost control of myself explosively or with violence. The medical community's capacity for denial of the deleterious and paradoxical effects of mind-altering prescription drugs was monumental then, as it is now. And unfortunately, back in the fall of 1975, I was still chemically saturated and not fully able to recognize or analyze what was happening to me.

The escalating insanity in my life was, of course, marked by a growing estrangement from my children, whom I dearly loved. Although I made sure Deb and Carrie had the best of everything—a comfortable home, nice clothes, music lessons, sports involvement, and nanny/housekeeper when I was at work—I was certainly not functioning normally on any level, which, regrettably, I didn't realize during my years on the pills. I tried hard and sincerely believed I was responding to their needs and that I was a good mother. In retrospect, I can see that I overreacted to just about everything they did, and berated them if I felt they had done something wrong. Then I would feel guilty and confused, and try to make it up to them in other ways. My inconsistencies and unpredictable changes in mood and demeanor sadly drove them further and further away. And although I was completely unaware of it at the time, I had grown less able to fully understand, empathize, or even acknowledge the existence of their individual concerns and problems.

At times, in my irrational state, I would feel both girls were ungrateful for how hard I worked to take care of them, and, in my despair, on several occasions I would threaten to sell our home. Slowly and insidiously, I was losing the single most important reality in my life—my deep connection with my children.

Deb was more of a mother to Carrie than I was during those years, and was always protective of her. Deb had learned at an early age to take care of herself and, as a teenager, was determined, independent, and very bright, excelling at nearly everything she did. She earned top grades in school and was very athletic, participating in swimming, skiing, field hockey, and fencing, among other activities. When I look back, I realize how strong and mature she really was, and have to give her full credit for everything that she was able to accomplish during this awful time in all our lives.

Carrie, on the other hand, was always somewhat shy and melancholy, and very close to her father. She was highly sensitized to my erratic behavior and would often retreat to her bedroom or to be with her cat, "Gigsy," for comfort and solace, curling up with him for hours. She was always very creative, drawing and making art objects. She read a lot and loved playing her violin and taking music lessons at school. I purchased a University Scholarship Trust Fund for her, which was proudly displayed in her bedroom so that she'd know she would be going to university if she studied hard and did well.

Fortunately, in spite of our troubled and tumultuous home life, both girls picked up on my value system of hard work, honesty, and concern for others—ironic, perhaps, considering our dysfunctional existence when I was on the pills. And I was certainly full of pride in all of their achievements.

Needless to say, I lost my seat on district council in the election that fall following all the bad publicity in the media. The assault and obstruction charges against me were eventually dropped, on the condition that I see a psychiatrist regularly, but, by the end of 1975, I was no longer working, no longer had a political role in the community, and was at the height of my chemical dependency. I had asked Alan to move out for the umpteenth time, and I could sense that he was gearing up to attempt taking custody of the girls. My life had reached a new, all-time low.

CHAPTER SEVEN

A Dangerous Mix

O VER THE COURSE OF my year-long sabbatical I decided not to return to Kelly Douglas. I began looking for a new job during the summer of 1976. Since I had to continue to earn a good salary to take care of my children and myself, I was very determined to get back to work. I was restless and frustrated, but I hadn't had any episodes of violence since my arrest in October 1975.

Within weeks, I landed a challenging position as director of planning and development for the B.C. Liquor Distribution Branch, and started working there in the fall of 1976. There was a certain irony about the appointment, given my alleged problems with alcohol. However, I was not drinking at all at that point, and nobody I worked with seemed to be aware of or concerned about the publicized incidents of prior years. I eventually became one of two women directors at the Liquor Distribution Branch, with a staff of twelve in my department, predominantly men.

My personal life was in a sorry state, but I was suddenly immersed in my work again, and for a time I greatly enjoyed it. Initially, I lost weight and got very little sleep, but I welcomed the change and felt that getting back to involvement in a busy schedule was just what I needed. Free time had been of little benefit to me. I worked long hours at my new job, getting oriented and traveling around the province with the general manager, director of store operations, and my staff, visiting potential store sites regularly to evaluate demographics and market demand, and to attend store openings in new shopping centers, among other activities.

I was often asked to make brief speeches at store-opening ceremonies. I struggled somewhat with the ethical considerations of my job—alcohol had certainly never been a friend to me—and whenever I spoke publicly I encouraged my listeners to drink responsibly. I was acutely conscious of my role and my social accountability in that regard. I was sometimes asked to take part in wine tastings as a part of my job, but regularly refused these invitations. Nevertheless, I found myself in some conflicts at times. Drinking in the late 1970s was accepted, almost expected, in some situations. In fact, some of my colleagues drank quite a lot, and their excesses were not frowned upon.

I managed and directed the Branch's overall properties program throughout the province, administering close to two hundred stores, warehouses and offices. I was responsible for managing multi-million dollar budgets and leases, and recommended, directed, and coordinated major capital repair and upgrading projects for many Crown-owned properties. I evaluated alternative forms and methods of retail marketing and distribution, and conducted major consumer and marketing research projects. I also sat on the Executive Committee for the Branch, and played a key role in developing its overall strategy, policies, and procedures. It was a long and intensive learning curve, but I felt that in at least one aspect of my life, I was back in the driver's seat, doing something I was good at.

After hanging on by a thread for so long, my marriage to Alan had finally collapsed by the spring of 1977, and he moved out for the last time. Neither of us made any further efforts to reconcile. But our battles were not over. Although I was trying to keep things as simple as possible, Alan disputed nearly every detail of the legal separation that my lawyer prepared, and stalled the finalization process for months. I was earning very good money at the time and, although he, too, made a decent living, he objected to the amount of child support he was being asked to pay, and waffled back and forth with talk of fighting for custody of Deb and Carrie. Eventually I got so fed up that I personally walked into his workplace one day, papers in hand, and coerced him into signing. In the arrangement we agreed that I would buy him out for his share of our family home, and assume full financial responsibility for our mutual debts. In turn, he agreed to pay a set amount of monthly child support.

For the most part, I was relieved to be out of the marriage and felt that an enormous burden had been lifted from my shoulders. I relished the freedom with which I could now make decisions, and set about building up my assets, establishing RRSPs, and weighing various other investment options. I made careful plans for upcoming university expenses for both Deb and Carrie. It felt good to be planning for the future without having to consult with anyone else, and I was certainly glad that I had remained motivated and focused on my career through the rough spots over the years, because the financial demands on me at that point were substantial.

At Easter I took Deb and Carrie to Palm Springs, California, for a ten-day holiday. We enjoyed days of unending sun and warmth, the palm trees, swimming in the pool, "fruity date shakes," and seeing all the exciting sights. The girls also went horseback riding, and at night we would seek out new and interesting places for dinner.

In 1972, I had purchased a brand new Chevrolet Impala convertible in "midnight bronze" (chocolate brown) with a white top, which I had enjoyed immensely, and soon Deb had learned to drive it too. She seemed to truly enjoy the wind in her hair, and the carefree attitude that went with such a vehicle. She also liked my yellow Buick Le Sabre convertible, which she affectionately called "the yellow boat." Often the girls and I would take off for dinner or a scenic drive out to Horseshoe Bay, or up to Whistler on the panoramic "Sea to Sky" highway.

There was a lot of pressure on me, but I was working very hard, determined to succeed and keep my life on track. Somewhere along the line, however, I lost my resolve regarding alcohol, and started having the odd drink socially, albeit very, very carefully. At that same time Dr. MacGillivray took me off the Valium and began prescribing Librium again (I don't know why). I continued to take my pills every day.

I worked through the summer of 1977 without much of a vacation, and by the fall I felt like I wanted to do something really special. It had been a tough few years all round, with the loss of my mother and the end of my marriage, and I also felt a strong desire to show my appreciation to my sister, Pat, in some way. So I made arrangements for both of us to take a two-week Mediterranean cruise to Israel. Pat had always been there when I needed her and, although I don't think she realized it, she was actually one of the closest people to me. She was like my second mother, given our thirteen-year age difference, and through all the trying times, strange phone calls, and turbulence, Pat had been unconditionally supportive, never judgmental or reproachful. With both of our parents gone, I had come to recognize just how important she was to me, and how much I loved her.

In October, Pat and I met in Palermo, Sicily, where we boarded the cruise ship and embarked on a spectacular tour that began with a stop at Malta, visited the Greek islands, and then went on to Israel. Things did not start out very well for Pat, who suffered from seasickness for the first few days, but she eventually regained her equilibrium and was able to enjoy the rest of our trip.

A little passenger ferry carried us ashore to explore the various islands and take in the sights. We hired drivers, when available, to tour us around the bigger islands, and hiked and bicycled around the countryside on some of the smaller ones. We visited Athens, Crete, Rhodes, Kos, and Mykonos, and took in the rich history and culture of the whole area. I took dozens of photographs of the many historic sites—the Acropolis, the Parthenon, Old Jerusalem—as well as of the spectacular Mediterranean sunsets and the Sea of Galilee. Many evenings were spent on board the ship, where we gorged on the delicious food and danced to live music in the night club until late in the evening. Although the champagne flowed freely, I rarely touched any alcohol, only having a drink on a couple of occasions.

I was glad that I was able to take Pat with me on such a memorable holiday. In a way it made up for the fact that I had not been able to do the same for our mother before she died. And yet, despite the exotic surroundings, I again felt removed from it all, somehow not really present. Although I did enjoy myself, at a certain level it felt unreal, as if I were just going through the motions. I missed Deb and Carrie very much and called home to talk with them every day or two.

I was still far from a spiritual or a philosophical resolution of my grief and loss at Derek's death, and our tour of Israel had a profound religious resonance for me. We visited Bethlehem and other holy sites, and the experience of actually being in places I had read about in the Bible affected me powerfully. In my search for some deeper connection with God,

I was also seeking release from this grief that seemed to go on and on without any change, and could be unpredictably unleashed in flashbacks of shocking intensity.

After returning home from the cruise, it wasn't long before I began to feel very frustrated and disheartened again, and I didn't know why. I should have felt rested and renewed, but instead I was still very wound up, easily distracted, and unable to concentrate for sustained periods of time. I was also having a terrible time getting to sleep at night, and I attributed my trouble with concentration to being overtired.

At work I often felt so distracted that I could not integrate the complex information in front of me. I had a large, private office, with a spectacular view of the North Shore mountains, but often I would gather up my papers and go down the hall to work in our boardroom, where it was a little quieter and more isolated. But even sitting alone and undisturbed in the boardroom, I found that my train of thought wandered constantly, and I had to check back in my work to see what I had done just the day before. I could not remember what I had been doing or where I had left off. This had never happened to me in the past, and my frustration seemed endless.

Luckily, I was at a point in my career when I had several staff members that could help me with some of the details, and I could delegate a certain amount of my work, again chalking my distractibility up to fatigue and stress.

In October 1978, Dr. MacGillivray stopped issuing my Librium prescription and started me on Serax, another tranquilizer. I didn't know why at the time, but I would later realize that it was probably because I had built up a tolerance to Librium. He assured me that the tranquilizers were necessary to *minimize* my ongoing symptoms, and keep me calm and focused. I do not recall that he ever suggested that my long-term exposure to benzodiazepines might have been *increasing* my anxiety, though I now believe that was the case.

Within two weeks of the switch to Serax, I was back in his office. I was feeling even more agitated, and having an increasingly difficult time unwinding at night. I just couldn't stop my mind from running in a kind of frantic overdrive, often without resolving anything at all. I constantly felt overwhelmed and wound up, and I didn't understand why. He recommended that I continue with the Serax, and start taking Dalmane (a sleeping pill) regularly again before bed.

I was now medicated regularly day and night. In looking back, I can say without any hesitation that my mental functioning, temperament, memory, and general awareness became progressively worse during this period. Unfortunately, my ability to recognize this further deterioration was also obliterated. Later on, when I was off the pills, I came across a review of information derived from a psychiatric study conducted in London in 1991 on memory and mood impairment caused by benzodiazepines. In two studies comparing the cognitive functions of chronic users with various control groups, chronic users were found to be significantly impaired, but psychological questionnaires also revealed that these "subjects were unaware of experiencing such problems."

This paper, published in the British journal *Psychopharmacology*, also stated that "in view of the fact that the amnesic effects of [benzos] were reported in the 1960s in the anesthesiology literature, it is puzzling why so little is known in the 1990s about the cognitive effects of [benzos] on people who have taken these drugs daily ... over a period of months or years."[1] Of course the fact that I was on not one but two drugs at the same time only exacerbated the situation. The *CPS* back then cautioned that patients treated with Dalmane "should be warned against the simultaneous ingestion of ... other central nervous system (CNS) drugs" because of their potentiating effects.[2]

In his article "Benzodiazepines: An Overview," published in the *Ontario Medical Review* in 1982, Dr. Mark Berner (later chair of the Canadian Medical Association's expert advisory panel, which developed draft guidelines for the safe use of benzodiazepines in 1996), said that "not infrequently, patients have received one benzodiazepine in the day-time for anxiety and a second agent as a hypnotic (for sleeping) ... this practice is irrational."[3]

The most immediate effect of my increased intake of tranquilizers and sleeping pills was a further loss of general awareness. Countless situations just didn't add up. With my impaired level of emotional and sensory awareness, I just didn't see things coming and was chronically missing subtle signs of trouble. I was no longer my former, savvy self. I realize now that I was essentially operating without *intuition* for all those years.

One of the first examples of this occurred when I went on an overnight business trip to Victoria. At the time, I was a board member and vice-president of the B.C. Government Managers Association, and in this role I attended numerous meetings and conferences, many of them in Victoria. On this particular trip, soon after starting on the two prescribed drugs, I did some socializing in the hotel lounge with some colleagues before retiring for the evening. After I got upstairs and into bed, I became vaguely aware that someone was in my hotel room with me. At first I thought I was dreaming. I was groggy and disoriented, but eventually came around enough to recognize the man—I had been talking with him earlier in the evening—but I was at a complete loss as to why he was in *my* hotel room. As I struggled to make some sense of the situation, he made his way toward me and began to climb into my bed!

I jumped up and shouted at him, nearly losing my balance, demanding that he get out of my room. Luckily he did get up and leave, but I was very shaken and embarrassed by the incident. I wondered for weeks why it had happened. My memory of that whole evening was fuzzy and disjointed and I thought I must be missing something. Had I sent out some mixed signals? I still don't know.

Of course, this sixth sense—especially important to a woman—was not the only one I started to lose touch with as a result of my chemical dependency. I really didn't feel much of anything emotionally for years and years. My inability to feel and identify emotions was even more pronounced when it came to the emotions of others. I lived my life on autopilot, working extremely hard, but oblivious, I realize now, to so much around and within me.

Once I started taking the two potentiating drugs at the same time, I was easily enraged and very impulsive; I could flip from one emotional extreme to another. One night when Deb and Carrie were staying with their father, I began to feel lonely, and decided I wanted them home. I drove over to Alan's apartment and barged in with no warning at all, demanding that they pack up and come with me on the spot. I ordered the girls into my car, over Alan's protests; then I raced home with them, driving like a madwoman fueled by a memory of Alan calling the police as I was on my way out. It must have been very frightening for Deb and Carrie to be accosted by me in that frenzied, paranoid condition.

When we arrived at the house, I wheeled the car into the garage, quickly closed the door, and frantically hurried the girls into the house, ordering them to remain completely silent. Then I ran around turning out all the lights and closing the curtains. The phone was ringing incessantly, and the police eventually came to the door, but I didn't answer. Deb and Carrie were upset and traumatized, but I had absolutely no thought of how my actions affected anyone else. Not much later that evening, I gashed my arm quite seriously while stumbling around in the darkness trying to find something in the garage, and somehow got myself to the hospital, where I spent the rest of the night in emergency.

Another time when Deb and Carrie were with Alan, I acted on the same impulse and drove over to get them again, but I didn't quite make it to my destination. Although Alan's apartment was only minutes from my house, I got hopelessly lost and couldn't find my way there. In fact, I parked my car in his neighborhood and promptly lost it as well. I remember wandering for hours in the darkness, frightened and disoriented, without a clue where I was. I found myself on a large sports field near dawn, circling its perimeter aimlessly, and it was there that a taxi driver spotted me and picked me up. I had him take me home, where I collapsed in bed and slept for a while. When I woke up, I tried to put some of the pieces together. I made my way back to the vicinity of Alan's apartment in the light of day and, after some searching, was finally able to find my car. I never told anyone about what had happened, nor did I ask anyone for any help that day, because I was so embarrassed about it all.

Things got worse and worse, and I was regularly experiencing almost unbearable anguish and agitation. At times, in desperation, I had a drink or two to try to alleviate this—a not uncommon practice among people prescribed drugs—many of whom never drank alcohol before. Of course, this only added to the dangerous mix, and I became even more unpredictable. My home life was outrageous. I was regularly acting out in an unruly and abusive manner, and Alan was becoming extremely concerned about the girls living with me. Before long he initiated legal action to gain full custody of the girls.

Alan saw the most important issue of concern as my "alcohol-related problems" whereby I seemingly "lost control periodically" to the point where he feared for the children's "physical safety and emotional well-being."[4] In response to this, in an attempt to objectively determine who would be best suited to have custody of Deb and Carrie, the court requested a report from Dr. Hirt on both Alan and me.

Interestingly, despite my terrible condition, Dr. Hirt was in full support of the girls remaining with me at that point. In his report, he described my situation as follows: "Mrs. Gadsby ... has never used alcohol to excess over any sustained period of time. She appears to be an individual who cannot metabolize [burn] alcohol without a severe toxic reaction, that is, any amount of strong alcoholic beverage over three ounces, in amount, will cause her to become temporarily disoriented, to lose her sense of social judgment, often depressed in mood, and physically ill. She has ... been advised that unlike most people she does not metabolize alcohol in a safe way ... she is not alcoholic in the classic sense, nor even in a clinical sense, rather it is toxic for her ... The infrequent episodes in which Mrs. Gadsby has had brief periods of lack of control, are directly linked to this phenomenon of her inability to metabolize alcohol. It is not linked to her use of medication nor is it due to excessive use of alcohol. Without alcohol she is normal, bright, and very capable in both her work and in her relationship with her children."[5]

With these words, Dr. Hirt denied the enormous significance of the interaction between alcohol and tranquilizers, which he had seemed to acknowledge earlier. In their book *Under the Influence*, Dr. James R. Milam and Katherine Ketcham warn that "when a physician writes an alcoholic a prescription for a tranquilizer or sedative, he may, in effect, be signing the patient's death warrant."[6] But of course, I wasn't an alcoholic: I didn't need *any* alcohol to "become disoriented and lose my sense of social judgment," and had many psychotic episodes when I had not been drinking at all.

As I found out much later, the two different types of benzodiazepines I had been prescribed, and faithfully took every day, affected my central nervous system in much the same way as mixing one of them with alcohol would have. There is no debate about this; it is an established medical fact. Yet the medical establishment consistently attributed all of my problems to emotional instability and alcohol.

In his report to the Family Court counselor, Dr. Hirt went on to express surprise that Alan was seeking custody of the girls, and claimed that Alan did not seem to "show the depth of concern and behaviour which would suggest that he could become the senior parent for [them]." He also stated that he saw his move to take custody as "a manipulation rather than as one of serious concern."[7] By the end of the year, Alan had withdrawn his application for custody, having failed to convince anyone that our children were indeed living in a very precarious situation. At the time I was pleased about this, and naturally saw Dr. Hirt as my ally. However, looking back, I find it very troubling that Dr. Hirt dismissed Alan's justified concern for our children as unwarranted. He was fully aware of my deteriorating state and frequent rages.

The happy, loving woman I had once been was lost somewhere, estranged from herself. I was not someone my daughters could consistently count on. Regrettably, Deb had distanced herself from me a great deal by her senior year in high school, and lived a very independent life. She continued to excel in school, worked part-time, and wasn't home very much. At sixteen she began dating a young man named Martin, four years older than herself, whom she had met skiing at the top of Grouse Mountain. At the time, he was working with his father in a family painting business. My reaction to Deb's having a serious boyfriend was immediately negative. I harassed and berated Martin for months, making both him and Deb miserable; I even followed them in my car a few times. Needless to say, my suspicion and hostility were completely irrational, and fortunately their relationship survived. Deb married Martin (in 1981) and they had a remarkably supportive, loving relationship for eighteen years, until Deb's death from breast cancer in 1999. Their marriage was one of the best I have ever seen. I know now that I could not have asked for a finer son-in-law.

Of course, my harassment alienated Deb from me even further, and she was anxious to leave home. She didn't have a lot to do with her father by that point either, and finally, toward the end of high school, moved into an apartment with a girlfriend, not far from home. Regrettably, we didn't have much contact with each other as she went on with her life, graduating from high school with honors in 1979. Deb entered the University of British Columbia that fall, and I paid for her tuition and books, and she continued working part-time to pay for most of her living expenses. Soon afterward, Alan quit his job at CBC Television and moved to Victoria. I was relieved, but I'm sure Carrie felt all the more abandoned—although Alan initially visited her three times each week.

Without Deb in the house, Carrie had lost the only consistently stable influence in her day-to-day life. I am sorry to say that those years were truly a horror for her. I often broke and damaged things in the house during my rages, and at times Carrie tried to stop me. On more than one occasion I can remember her trembling with distress, and her fingernails digging into my wrists as she held me back. At times such as these, Carrie tells me that I often then berated her for overreacting. I simply did not comprehend that I was causing all of these problems myself. All I understood was that I was working like a robot, day in and day out, determined to provide for all of Carrie's needs, and she never seemed to appreciate me. At times, when I was enraged, I even threatened to put her cat to sleep, or to take away her belongings and privileges. My judgment was simply awry and I could not appreciate the seriousness of situations around me.

In a statement Carrie made pertaining to my lawsuit against Dr. MacGillivray in 1997, she described her childhood home as a place where fighting, yelling, and verbal abuse were normal. She went on to say that she had been *terrified* of me as a child. She tried to run away from me on many occasions, winding up at friends' homes, or at her father's. She dreaded the weekends, and especially the summer holidays, because "there was nowhere to escape." I yelled at her for the slightest infraction, and she recalls that if she did not do exactly as I wished, I would "freak out ... become threatening, bang things around and even throw things." During one such incident, which she recalled in court, I threw a plate at her and apparently said I was going to "decapitate" her.[8] Much of this I don't remember.

I loved Deb and Carrie very much, and yet my inexplicable actions continued to push them further and further away. In July 1979, I had my next run-in with police, jail, and the emergency ward. The police called it a "hysterical rage"; hospital personnel (accurately) called it an "overdose"; Dr. MacGillivray wrote in his records that I was "intoxicated." Three days later, I sat in his office in what he described in his notes as an "acute anxiety state,"[9] rambling on hysterically about my many problems. It's incredible that, after years of treatment with what was considered to be *anti-anxiety* medication, my anxiety had become "acute." Just eight days prior to that visit to Dr. MacGillivray, I had been prescribed thirty Dalmane pills and had overdosed on them. Yet there was no change in Dr. MacGillivray's approach to dealing with me. It was my fault; the drinking, he insisted. His recommendation that day? Rx Dalmane.

Although I felt very guilty and disheartened about the constant turmoil in my life, I continued to assume that I would be even worse off without my pills. If I was distraught and overreactive while on tranquilizing medication, imagine how I would be without it! I did my best to make improvements to my lifestyle, exercising regularly and eating well, and went about blaming myself for everything. I would get healthy; I would drink no alcohol at all; I would try harder. I operated like a machine, working feverishly, going to meetings and paying the bills. I was disconnected from everyone, with very few close friends. I tried my best to keep up appearances and control myself during the workday, but I didn't always succeed. My colleagues got occasional glimpses of some very bizarre behavior.

One evening I was invited to a dinner party at the home of the Liquor Distribution Branch's general manager in Lions Bay, about a half-hour drive from where I live. We all enjoyed the scenic views from his mountainside residence and a lovely meal. I made the mistake, however, of having a couple of glasses of wine along with everyone else. I thought I was sure to be all right, given the amount of food I was consuming that evening. As it turned out, I was not all right. The only way I can describe it is to say that my mind exploded. I began ranting, screeching, and crying, and rambled on obsessively about Derek's death and more, right in front of my business associates. I was erratic and delusional, and someone had to drive me home while another person followed with my car. I don't know what they thought at the time, or how they explained the situation to themselves, but somehow I managed to keep my job.

I had a few drinks at home one evening in October 1980 and, during the ensuing outburst, Carrie, who was only ten, fled from the house and ran next door, where she tearfully confided in our neighbor. It wasn't the first time she had tried to escape my tyranny, but this time things got very serious. The neighbor was duly alarmed by the terrified girl on her doorstep, called the police, and Carrie was apprehended by the Provincial Ministry of Social Services within hours.

I had never in my wildest dreams thought that something so horrible could happen. My daughter, whom I loved so much, taken away from me! But again, I couldn't seem to comprehend that *my* actions had caused this dreadful development.

After spending the night in a foster home in Vancouver, Carrie was placed with Vonda, a former nurse who then looked after her in my home while I worked. Vonda lived nearby, but I was prohibited from having any contact with Carrie for several days. She was even told that, if she saw me on the school premises, she was to avoid me and tell the teacher about it. The fear and confusion she must have felt are unimaginable.

I was frantic to rectify the situation; naturally, good old Dr. Hirt came to my rescue once again. *Again*, he stressed that alcohol, even in small doses, was acutely toxic to me. But my alcohol use was "not habitual or chronic," he reassured the courts. For the most part, I was "an extremely capable mother, a very reliable working person, and healthy in my social interactions," he said. Carrie, he went on, "in fact loves her mother," but is "naturally more concerned about herself." In light of past occurrences, Carrie, in his opinion, was so "overly sensitized and fearful of the misuse of alcohol that she may misconstrue even minor social drinking as a major event." Carrie was in a confused state, he offered, and should undergo a psychiatric evaluation. *My* medical and psychological prognosis, he insisted, was "very positive and had improved markedly and remarkably—particularly in the past year."[10]

No doubt about it, Dr. Hirt was in my corner. He had established himself as my therapist, friend, and supporter.

During the next terrible two weeks, I was given limited access to Carrie, under supervision from Vonda. I brought Carrie some of her favorite stuffed animals from her large collection, drew her pictures of daffodils, and wrote how much I loved her. I made every effort to rebuild her confidence and trust in me again.

A social worker was brought in by the court to counsel both of us, and Carrie was sent to a child psychiatrist. With Dr. Hirt's continuing help, and the intervention of my lawyer, the situation with Carrie was finally resolved and she returned home under the condition that I agree to hire a live-in nanny.

It was about that time, when I felt sincerely grateful to him, that Dr. Hirt stood up in the midst of one of our weekly sessions, crossed to his office door, and locked it. He then crossed back to sit directly beside me on the couch. I was taken aback at this, to say the least, but I was also feeling vulnerable, lost, and very dependent on him at that point in my life. And certainly I was surprised, and intensely confused, as things progressed from there to a flagrantly sexual relationship. For a time I even thought I loved him. I can see now that he took outrageous advantage of his position of authority, and that his approach to me was little more than overt sexual abuse. Three years later, I was asked to testify in a lawsuit alleging exactly that against Dr. Hirt, filed by another of his former patients. It seems I had not been the only one.

I chose not to testify against Dr. Hirt, in part because I was so ashamed, but mostly because I did not want the story to hit the news. Believe it or not, at the height of my chemical dependency I had decided to run for alderman again, and had in fact won in the November 1982 election. I was back in public office.

When I went to Dr. MacGillivray for a checkup that fall, he wrote in his records, "getting uptight"—"anxiety state ... losing weight, not hungry."[11] One month later, in December 1982, I again overdosed. This time I took twenty-four Serax, washing them down with beer. Dr. Mark Berner's previously mentioned report describes this sort of behavior (known as "suicidal ideation") as follows: "patients [feel] driven as if by some outside force to commit suicide without the concomitant wish to die."[12] This rings ominously true to me today. On that dark December evening, I have no memory of wanting to die. And yet I swallowed the pills, and barely escaped with my life.

CHAPTER EIGHT

Turning Point

I CONTINUED TO WORK AT regaining my daughters' trust. In 1982 I took Carrie on a long-promised trip to Disneyland in Orlando, Florida, which had just opened. We spent several days there, having a good time together and making our way through all the exciting rides and exhibits. It seemed that for the moment our relationship was near normal again. While in Florida, we rented a spacious condominium in Clearwater Beach, where my brother, Bill, and his family were also vacationing. Carrie enjoyed playing with Bill's two girls, one of whom was her age. She acquired a nasty sunburn and had to take it easy for a few days; then, when she was feeling better, we joined a group tour on a massive sailboat, had a picnic lunch on one of the nearby islands, and went searching for gigantic seashells.

When we returned home, I plunged into wedding plans with Deb, who, after a three-year relationship with Martin, was about to marry him. I went with her to pick out her wedding dress, and she had chosen to wear a picture hat, which had to be especially made to match her dress. We then busied ourselves with the detailed arrangements for the service and reception. Carrie was her junior bridesmaid, and very excited about the upcoming event. We had made plans for a church wedding if it rained that day, but Deb's wedding day was beautiful and they were able to be married outside, at Whytecliffe Park in West Vancouver, overlooking the ocean. The natural beauty of the water, trees, and flowers was a splendid backdrop for a splendid wedding. The bridal party came to the outdoor service in my two large convertible cars. Afterwards, we had a catered dinner for more than 100 guests—family and friends—and we danced the night away.

Unfortunately her father, who gave her away, chose not to attend the dinner in protest over his father not being invited. This led to a further estrangement in Deb's relationship with her father for many years to come. Nevertheless, both Deb and Martin beamed with happiness in their union that day. He and Deb were very much in love, and genuine soul mates.

A few months later, Deb graduated from the University of British Columbia with top honors in psychology and was offered a graduate scholarship. Instead, she chose to work in vocational rehabilitation in the mental-health field, and quickly established a leadership reputation for her innovative ideas for helping others gain independent living. She continued to maintain a close relationship with Carrie, carefully and lovingly guiding her as Carrie approached the teenage years. Deb was more than just a big sister, probably in part because of my own struggles. As a mother, though, I was very proud of my girls, and loved them both deeply.

I, too, had finally met someone I was attracted to. I dated Mark[1] for a couple of years in the early 1980s, and he was good for me in many ways. He was a pleasant, easygoing businessman with a great smile, the vice-president of an insurance company, and from a well-established Vancouver family. We had a lot in common, and did quite a bit of socializing together, a pleasure I had missed with Alan. Mark and I spent many weekends on the beach along the Sunshine Coast, where his family owned property. He also had a son Carrie's age.

I was not the easiest person to establish a healthy relationship with, and Mark, too, had some problems. He drank a bit too much, ironically at a time when I was again abstaining from alcohol, and he had a hard time understanding why I chose not to drink. In addition, he was newly separated from his wife when we met and, at times, was still quite involved with her. This, among other things, caused some tension in our relationship.

Our differences were not insurmountable, but between my prescription drugs and his drinking the odds were stacked against us. Some of our fights became quite heated, even violent on one occasion. I must say, however, that he was one of the very few people who ever noticed something was not right with me, besides those who witnessed my outbursts. He always said there was something wrong with my eyes, that they seemed distant and wandered unnaturally, though he never made the connection between my extreme moods and my pills. Mark and I broke up early in 1984, after going together for two years, but I still have many fond memories of our time together.

My personal relationships had become something of a mystery to me by then, and I didn't feel a strong connection with anyone except my daughters. Over the years, my facade had become the only identity I could still take pride in, and I put an enormous amount of energy into its upkeep. My public displays of outlandish behavior were isolated and random. My public image, in general, was one of a "doer"—someone working hard in both the public and the private sector to see that things actually got done. In fact, I consistently worked fourteen- or fifteen-hour days throughout those years—including the weekends, preparing for Monday night council meetings. My daughters were proud of my achievements in the community, and to those who did not know otherwise we looked the absolute epitome of a healthy, functional family. The private reality was, however, a nightmare. Deb was now happily married and in her own home, so that her involvement with me was more limited. Carrie, although she remained close to Deb, was obliged to soldier on with me at home. I did my best to be a good mother.

Financially, I had done well. A few years earlier I had bought a second home, as an investment, a mile from our home. It was an attractive California-style rancher, with a flat, sunny yard. It had a swimming pool, grapevines, beautiful roses, and a view of the city. At the time of the purchase, I thought Carrie and I would possibly live there. But Carrie didn't want to move. I guess she wanted something to remain constant and predictable in her life, and I didn't object.

As Carrie became a teenager, she blossomed into a strikingly beautiful young woman. She began dating, and naturally started to demand more freedom. I, however, was not prepared to grant it to her. It was as though I was in a time warp, unable to grasp that she was growing up. She was responsible and conscientious, never getting into any trouble, yet in my mind she was being extremely difficult. Her recollection is more accurate, however. I was the difficult one, to put it mildly. She wrote about it in an affidavit for the court years later, saying, in part: "As I was growing up, I realized that my mother's behaviour was being reported in the newspapers and that people were talking about her. In spite of this, she always tried to keep up appearances and did not seem to realize that anything was wrong. She was ridiculously strict with me about dating and often threatened, intimidated and frightened my boyfriends with her bizarre, unpredictable behaviour."[2]

A few years ago I attended a going-away party for Carrie when she was heading to Los Angeles to pursue her career in the film industry, and she reintroduced me to some of her old friends. A few of them had apparently been in our home on and off over the years, yet I had very little recollection of them. These memory lapses and forgotten years are a frequent topic of discussion among benzo survivors, and represent a tragic loss in our individual lives and in our lives with our families.

One night I became completely delusional and climbed up onto the deck railing in back of our house, thinking I could fly. Carrie frantically tried to coax me down from the ledge, crying and begging me to come to my senses. I was going to jump, and if I had would certainly have been badly injured, if not killed. Carrie has said she was constantly worried that I would kill myself, and that I talked about this often. She was so worried about it that, when I started acting up, she would gather up all razor blades, pills, knives, and anything else she thought I could harm myself with and hide them under her bed.

In December 1983, I landed in the emergency department at Lions Gate Hospital again after ingesting Dalmane, Serax, Elavil (an antidepressant), and alcohol to dangerous excess. Suicidal, they said. "Acute alcoholism and mental depression," wrote Dr. MacGillivray. Depressed? No doubt. For more than twelve years he had had me on tranquilizers that first cause and then worsen depression.

After that overdose, Dr. MacGillivray reported for the first time that he "took all pills away."

In her book *Coming Off Tranquilizers*, Shirley Trickett, a trained nurse with extensive experience assisting people to withdraw from benzodiazepines, listed these symptoms as potential withdrawal effects: "Increased anxiety, increased depression, insomnia, panic attacks, suicidal feelings, agoraphobia, outbursts of rage, flu-like symptoms, hyperactivity, hallucinations, confusion, headaches, dizziness, sweating, palpitations, slow pulse, tight chest, abdominal pain, nausea, nightmares, restlessness, increased sensitivity to light, noise, touch and smell; sore eyes, blurred vision, creeping sensation in the skin, loss of interest in sex, impotence, pain in jaw or face, sore tongue, metallic taste, pain in the shoulders and neck, sore heavy limbs, pins and needles, jelly legs, shaking and seizures."[3] The symptoms are greatly intensified by sudden withdrawal. In fact, death is even possible.

I never realized what I would go through when he abruptly cut me off the pills. As a result, I suffered tremendously. I went without sleep, had panic attacks, felt cold and then too hot, went through times of frantic activity, then collapsed into fits of crying. I was on the phone to Dr. MacGillivray within days of my cold-turkey withdrawal. He prescribed me both Dalmane and Serax again. He made no attempt to help me with a more gradual withdrawal from the drugs.

As always, however, his attitude to me was patronizing. When I went to him the following February in what he described, again, as a "chronic anxiety state," he wrote: "Discussed Xmas episode and booze and [she] *apologized* ... has been good ever since."[4]

I guess I wasn't "good" for long though, because I was in Lions Gate Hospital again in June the next year, with two black eyes after a nasty fall. Hospital personnel smelled alcohol on my breath, and wrote: "Patient has long history of alcohol abuse and psychiatric admissions. ... Difficult to assess ... very aggressive ... verbally abusive."[5] If I came in off the street and said that I had been strung out on various types of downers for years, which I got from a stringy-haired junkie pusher on the downtown east side, would they have dismissed the relevance of my prescription drug addiction?

Dr. MacGillivray seemed not to notice the relevance of my deteriorating health in other ways. At one point that spring I reported to him that friends had been telling me that I was too thin and looked sick. He apparently thought this was funny, and wrote, "Actually looks great! Happy with all her projects." Yet his own records indicate a significant weight loss over those months, and he recorded such comments as "chronic anxiety state ... running too fast ... eats on the run ... looks like she's lost weight"—within that same time frame.[6]

I left my job at the Liquor Distribution Branch in June 1984 after some shuffling of jobs and corporate restructuring. A new general manager was appointed, and, in addition, I was going to be accountable to a new director of management services. Unfortunately I found this fellow to be very prejudiced against women and he made my job quite miserable. By that time I had been considering a change anyway, and opted to get out. I was granted a six-month severance settlement, and took some much-needed time off before I started looking for something new and challenging.

It wasn't long before I lined up a job with Southland Canada, the company that owned Canada's largest convenience-store chain (7-Eleven Food Stores), as a full-time marketing consultant, accountable to the Canadian general manager. I started my new job in January 1985. I was involved with various aspects of the company's activities; however, my prime functions encompassed public affairs, government relations, economic feasibility studies, marketing, corporate planning, and business research. I was glad to make a fresh start and work with new people, and I traveled quite extensively with that job, at one point touring all the major Canadian cities, flying from place to place on a corporate jet sent up from Dallas. My life was again incredibly busy, and I chased around trying to keep up with it all. I think I was afraid to stop, because I knew as soon as I did my inner hell would catch up with me again.

Unfortunately, I continued to take my frustrations out on those closest to me, and in 1986, when Carrie was sixteen, she had endured quite enough, and left me to live with her father in a one-bedroom basement suite. She has said that it was "preferable to live in crowded, impecunious conditions than with my mother in a luxurious home with a floor to myself."[7] At the time, I sincerely could not understand why she had left, incredible as that may seem.

Once Carrie was gone, I was *really* in rough shape emotionally. I came home to an empty house every day and was tormented with intense feelings of loneliness and sadness. I often cried myself to sleep at night. I felt I was trying so hard, yet I had alienated everyone. One June evening in 1986 I walked to the top of my driveway and started screaming. Apparently I carried on for some time before a neighbor finally called the police, and I was charged with creating a disturbance. Once again, the case was eventually dealt with by court diversion, on the condition that I started seeing a psychiatrist again and attended the Alternatives program—for my supposed alcoholism—every three weeks.

I had stopped seeing Dr. Hirt some time earlier. My guilt and confusion over our sexual entanglement had left me bewildered and too unsure of myself to confront him about it, but I knew I had to get away from him. Much later I did tell Dr. MacGillivray about it, after other victims had begun to surface and go public, but he didn't have a lot to say. He seemed disgusted at my revelation, but I felt that this sentiment was aimed as much at me as at Dr. Hirt.

So off I went, skeptical and defensive, to another psychiatrist, Dr. Pankratz. According to his clinical notes, I reported "anxiety, depression, fear, and loneliness" as my primary concerns. I also told him about my episodic bouts with alcohol—occurring now about every two or three months—but that I had never been one to drink regularly. I confided to him about the intense, relentless level of anguish that I felt, and explained that I used alcohol for periodic relief from this terrible stress and tension.

Dr. Pankratz, like all the others, had very little to say about the drugs I was taking every day. He diagnosed me with a psychiatric illness and recorded in his notes early on that I showed "pressure of speech" and seemed to have some difficulty in focusing my attention.[8] These observations were apparently the basis for his leaning toward "the possibility of an underlying cyclothymic personality or even a mild bi-polar affective disorder." After another visit I was written up as "clinically hypomanic" and asked to consider Lithium to treat this "condition." He wanted to put me on *more* drugs! Another turning point. And yet another missed opportunity for someone educated in psychopharmacology to identify what I later realized was the real problem.

I found out much later that the *Diagnostic and Statistical Manual of Mental Disorders, Fourth Edition (DSM-IV)*, the primary diagnostic reference used by psychiatrists, emphasizes the imperative need for drug effects to be ruled out as a causal factor before diagnosing a patient with a psychiatric illness. To the best of my knowledge, this was never done in my case.

I didn't agree to the Lithium at first, and my decision to refuse Dr. Pankratz's treatment didn't sit well with him. His notes refer often to my unwillingness to be a patient, or to "accept" the cyclical pattern to my behavior (which would have satisfied his desire to diagnose me as manic depressive).

In July of that year I had my next accident. One sunny afternoon I had a couple of light beers while doing some paperwork out in the front yard. The phone rang, and as I jumped up to answer it I was disoriented, became dizzy and fell, landing hard on my right shoulder on the front-entrance walkway. The pain was intense. Although I had been calmly working in the yard only a short time earlier, my reaction to this sudden stress and pain was hyperbolic. Within a short time I found myself once more at the hospital.

The doctor attending me described me as "extremely uncooperative." He reported that I appeared to be "under the influence of alcohol" and that my condition was "certainly compromising any information [he] had." The doctor seemed somewhat perplexed by my state, saying that "as far as [he] could see there was no major neurological deficit although ... the examination was very, very difficult because [I] just wouldn't cooperate ... she doesn't even remember my name five seconds after telling her," he wrote.[9] Again it was assumed that I was drunk, yet I don't think I had consumed even two full glasses of beer that day.

At any rate, the X-rays of my shoulder revealed a very serious fracture-dislocation, and surgery was deemed necessary. However, they decided not to operate on me until the next day, in the doctors' words, "when she is sober." I lay in excruciating pain all night, without any pain medication or the aid of my usual sleeping pill. After surgery the next morning, I was required to stay in the hospital several more days. Deb picked me up when I was finally discharged, but it was over a week before I was able to return to the office, still wearing a sling, which restricted my movements in a particularly frustrating way.

In addition to working full-time, and fulfilling my duties as an alder-man in the evenings and on weekends, I was then serving as president and chair of various women's, health, and community associations. I also served on the advisory board for marketing and sales for many years at the Vancouver Community College, as well as on the board of the Association of Professional Economists of B.C. Ironically, I also served many years on the board of Lions Gate Hospital, where I had landed so

many times in a psychotic, drugged-out state. My service on the hospital
board was preceded by several years as vice-chairman of North Shore
Health—a community public health board.

I eventually met someone who would become very important to me,
a doctor I hit it off with right away. Dan[10] and I shared a passion for our
work, and a penchant for battling rigid bureaucracies. We started going
out for dinner together soon after we met, talking about business, political issues, our careers, and eventually our mutual attraction, despite the
fact that he was married. Although becoming involved with a married
man was something I thought I would never, ever do, our personal connection grew in a way that I had never experienced before, and things
became quite complicated early on in our relationship.

Two years later, Dan and I were talking very seriously of the future,
perhaps even a child together, and he was talking about getting a divorce.
He had lived in what he described as an "indifferent" marriage for many
years and wanted out, but he found the prospect of divorce difficult to
face nonetheless. It was a serious situation in which I felt many conflicting emotions, but, despite the significant obstacles before us, we felt that
we had a future together, and I loved him. However, one day, out of the
blue, he confided that he had a heart problem that was causing him
some significant concern. This news stirred a horrible fear in me, an
intense dread of losing yet another person close to me. I just couldn't
handle the thought that he would perhaps get sick and die prematurely,
and I really backed off. I became very uncertain about plans for a future
together.

Of course, he eventually began to have some doubts about me as well.
Anyone who was close to me for long enough during that period was
bound to witness some pretty strange actions, and in time he did. The
first incident happened during a quiet, romantic dinner in an elegant
West Vancouver restaurant, where, it is fair to say, I went berserk. Same
old thing—anger, rage, delusions. Something triggered it and I started
screaming randomly—although not necessarily at Dan—and he had to
hustle me out of there. He was shocked and bewildered by my outburst,
and dropped me off at home, seemingly disgusted with me. The next day
I was beside myself with regret. I felt humiliated and rejected, mortified
by what had happened, and actually phoned the restaurant to apologize.

There were other times, too, when Dan was taken aback by my sudden mood swings and strange behavior. He would lie to his wife about having to attend a meeting or work late, and come over at least twice a week, and I occasionally became outraged when he had to leave, knowing that he was going to a home and a family apart from me. Dan and I had even gone on trips together, and he had met many members of my family back east. It was as though I couldn't grasp the part of his life that was not right in front of me, or analyze it properly. I wonder now whether I would ever have become embroiled in such a difficult relationship if my level of perception had not been altered by the drugs I was taking at the time.

Dr. Peter Hotz, a psychologist I was still seeing in conjunction with Dr. Pankratz in 1986 (in order to satisfy the terms of my court diversion), described me as intelligent, competent, successful, and "possessing a fine full repertoire of behavioral skills." He decided that my underlying problem was related to "emotional avoidant features." He described me as "emotionally very vulnerable," and said that I appeared to "deny and rationalize away issues rather than deal with them." This behavior, he wrote, resulted in "self argument, circular thinking ..." Given his overall opinion of my intellect, he was puzzled by this, noting that I seemed to have absolutely "no emotional awareness of this process. ..."[11] This psychologist recommended that I undergo "sound reconstructive psychotherapy" and was of the opinion that my "alcoholism should be squarely faced"—recommending that I also attend Alcoholics Anonymous. Once again, no reference was made to the possibility that addiction to prescription drugs was a likely contributor to my state of "emotional vulnerability and circular thinking"; nor was there any suggestion that an addiction to prescription drugs should be "squarely faced."

I worked to the end of my two-year contract with 7-Eleven in 1986, and early in 1987 I was hired as the director of marketing for Canada by a British company, Cambridge Ltd., which marketed diet, nutrition, and health-food products. I was directly accountable to the Canadian president, responsible for advertising, promotions, public relations, marketing research, and product development. In essence, I was hired to put together a major strategic marketing program for the company's expansion into Canada. But I found myself struggling with the work, still having tremendous difficulties concentrating at times, and I quickly hired a very competent executive assistant to help me with a lot of the detailed work.

The company's parent company was in Norwich, England, and in 1987 I had to fly there to attend a conference. It was a long flight and I started feeling very strange after many hours in the air. By the time I arrived in England, I was spacey and uncoordinated, in a world of my own. As I got off the plane, I was badly disoriented and couldn't drive the rental car, as planned. The company's president and director of sales, who were traveling with me, were clearly puzzled. When we got to the hotel, I was very ill, and went straight to bed. I attended the conference the next day, but was feeling incredibly discouraged. It had happened again. Another fresh start had been scarred.

Dan came over for dinner the night I returned on a nine-hour flight from Britain, and we had a lovely salmon dinner. Afterwards we sat by the fire and talked for a couple of hours. There was really nothing extraordinary about the evening except that I felt particularly sad when he left. I felt very alone in the world, with my children gone, and my relationship with Dan seemed only to exacerbate my feelings of rejection and isolation. I was tired, depressed, and still somewhat embarrassed by what had happened on the trip. I kept going over and over things in my mind, and couldn't settle down, despite my fatigue. I was exhausted, yet agitated.

The night went on and on, and even my sleeping pill brought no end to the torture of my despairing thoughts. I wanted to scream and cry but tried to control myself, determined to maintain my composure this time. But the storm in my head was relentless and gaining momentum, and I felt as though I would explode. I took another Dalmane, then another, then a couple of Serax. After many hours of torment, I phoned Deb in tears, and apparently told her I was going to take *all* my pills. I remember feeling absolutely desperate for sleep, but again I *do not* remember any conscious desire to kill myself. Next, I have a vague recollection of struggling with Deb in the driveway and her driving me to the hospital. I had ingested approximately twenty Dalmane and twenty to twenty-five Serax. Had she not come over when she did, I would certainly have died. "OD —benzodiazepines" was recorded, for the first time, on the emergency admission at the hospital.

Later, Dr. MacGillivray denied in court that I overdosed on drugs that night. He said that I overdosed on *alcohol*. He even insinuated that I was *lying* about the pills I had taken on many occasions: "I would venture to say she probably didn't take many pills when she was in one of her drinking modes," he testified. "Most of the time she was out of the emergency within hours and, if she'd taken all the pills she said, she would never have gotten out of there in a matter of hours."[12] Four days after my March 1987 overdose, Dr. MacGillivray prescribed me more pills.[13]

I continued to see Dr. Pankratz, who was still pressuring me to go on Lithium, still convinced that I was "bi-polar," that is, manic depressive, and that my symptoms fitted neatly into that package. Yet the clear description of manic highs and crashing lows associated with that condition just did not fit my case. For one thing I had never, ever lost my impetus and interest in things, even when confronted with the most serious of setbacks. On the contrary, I was always eager and involved in a myriad of things; consistently proactive and motivated. Nevertheless, given the constant urging from Dr. Pankratz, I finally agreed to take the Lithium, on top of everything else.

I soon realized this was a terrible mistake. Just a few days into my Lithium regime, I was out for dinner with Dan at the famed Salmon House restaurant in West Vancouver, with its 180-degree panoramic view of greater Vancouver. Suddenly I was overcome with a terrible, frightening feeling. My eyes suddenly glazed over, everything went out of focus, and it felt as though my head had literally separated from my body. Feeling very alarmed, I asked Dan to take me home. I had not had any alcohol.

Once I was home, I phoned Dr. Pankratz and told him what I was experiencing. He seemed unconcerned about these deeply disturbing symptoms, and advised me to stay on the Lithium. He reassured me that this effect would lessen in time; it would "sort itself out" within a few weeks. I threw the Lithium away and never took it again. I assumed Dr. Pankratz had made a mistake about it, but I went on taking my other pills.

Once again, Dr. Breggin minces no words about the dangers of this sort of thing, saying in his book that "it should be emphasized that all minor tranquilizers combine with each other or with other central nervous system depressants—such as barbiturates, antidepressants, neuroleptics, lithium and alcohol—with a potentially fatal result. While they can be lethal when taken alone, they are especially dangerous in combination with these other drugs."[14]

In 1989, Cambridge Ltd. wanted me to move to Toronto, possibly to take over as president, but I didn't want to leave Vancouver, and so started looking for a new job. In March 1989, I was appointed to the position of marketing manager for B.C. InfoHealth, a provincial government agency. This was a major turning point for me in many ways. I had been on benzodiazepines for approximately twenty years by then, and my higher intellectual functioning had been altered in many ways I didn't yet realize. In a nutshell, I had very great difficulty learning new information by that point. I absolutely *could not* understand how to accomplish simple tasks on a computer, while everyone else seemed to be able to adapt quite quickly. To say that this was stressful and embarrassing for me would be a huge understatement. I had always been innovative and sharp, eager to try new ways of doing things. For the first time in my life I received a performance appraisal that was mediocre, and this was a heavy blow to my already damaged self-esteem and confidence.

Ironically, my role with B.C. InfoHealth was to put a strategic marketing plan together for the new computer systems being developed for key health-care facilities and hospitals. Yet I couldn't understand the basic premise of the technology I was trying to promote. I really, really tried, but it was useless. Absorbing new information was not my only problem, however. My difficulties with concentration and comprehension now reached into every area of my working life. I had to read *everything*, even letters, several times over, and underline key points in every document I read so that I could go back over them later. Of course writing had also become very, very difficult for me, and I had always been a fluent and effective writer—I had put myself through university, in part, with my writing skills. I knew there was something profoundly wrong, but I couldn't understand what it was.

My long battle was nearly over, however. A series of stressful events began to occur that were to be the catalyst to some major changes in my life. On Carrie's nineteenth birthday in June 1989, the car she was driving (one of mine) was broadsided by a speeding police cruiser. The officer at the wheel was rushing to the scene of another accident nearby at the time, colliding with Carrie at a speed well in excess of the legal limit. The car she was driving was thrown 180 degrees into a parked vehicle and demolished. Although she was not seriously injured, she was terrified to drive a car for months, and was having nightmares. Had timing or circumstances been even slightly different, she could very well have been killed. Of course, this thought rekindled nearly unbearable memories and fear on my part.

All reports and witnesses' accounts relating to the accident indicated that the constable driving was speeding without a siren. Yet it was Carrie who was charged with failing to yield the right-of-way, and the police officer was absolved of any wrongdoing. For months I battled over legal accountability and insurance, and I found myself at loggerheads with the police. Their refusal to accept responsibility for the accident infuriated me, and was further exacerbated by the unwillingness of the insurance adjusters to take the RCMP to task. They were clearly not willing to go against the police, and I was determined to fight for justice. I was experiencing firsthand the strong-arm manipulation that can be inherent in dealings with powerful bureaucracies. It was an eye-opening experience that troubled me deeply.

My relationship with Dan was also causing me a great deal of pain and anguish. In fact, I had finally come to the conclusion that the relationship, after five years, was futile, and I decided to end it. As described in the prologue to this book, I invited him over to tell him of my decision. We talked calmly about the situation over dinner that evening, and at first, the whole thing seemed to be going quite smoothly. We were both rather stoic about it actually, seemingly resigned to the inevitable split. But somewhere along the line, after dinner, things went terribly wrong. I began to scream, rant, and throw things, I became completely out of control and lunged at Dan's face and grabbed him by the tie. He fought me off and put his hands around my throat, understandably enraged. Gaining control of himself, he let go of me, turned away, and walked out of the house.

The door slammed, and I stood there trembling, in a state of shock and confusion. The sudden silence was unbearable. I turned up the volume on the stereo, and took a beer from the fridge. My heart was thundering. The next thing I knew I was fumbling with my pill container. The whole ugly scene kept replaying in my head. The room was closing in on me. I reached for my pills again and dumped out another one, and then another.

Near midnight, I found myself wandering from room to room, still torturing myself over the events of the evening. A favorite picture of Derek, smiling radiantly in his cowboy pajamas, set me sobbing uncontrollably, and for the thousandth time I began having vivid flashbacks to the night he died. Finally I snatched up the cordless telephone and started punching at the numbers. I called friends, and my family back east, Deb, and Carrie, desperate to talk to someone.

In order to let ambulance attendants into the house, police smashed in the glass panel next to my front door at about 3:30 in the morning. Carrie had called 911 after I phoned her several times crying and carrying on, and she arrived moments after the emergency crew to find flashing lights, the ambulance, police cars, and people rushing everywhere. All the furniture was pushed back, and I lay flat out on the floor while attendants worked on me. They were feeding a tube down my throat when Carrie came in. I wasn't breathing. Apparently, thanks to Carrie, who had directed the emergency crew to my house over the phone when they had trouble finding it, I was revived only moments before brain damage would have been inevitable.

When I awoke in the intensive care unit of Lions Gate Hospital the next day, there was a snarl of tubes and monitors attached to my body. Lights wavered above me and I struggled to focus my eyes. I had an intense headache, and no idea what had happened, or why I was there. Slowly I became aware of voices outside the room, distant and hollow. It was Deb and Carrie. They were arguing, and sounded very upset.

Pieces of the previous evening began making their way back into my consciousness. It was like a dream I couldn't quite recall, fragmented and distorted. The masked faces coming in and out of the room were a swirling sea of images, bleary and unfocused. They talked about me as if I wasn't there: " … pills and booze; I think she's the mayor or something." Laughter. Then came Dr. MacGillivray's face, frowning down over me. He shook his head disapprovingly, and his voice droned as if in slow motion, "What are you doing to yourself, Joanie? What are you *doooing*?"

I was released from the hospital the following day despite insistence from just about everyone that I stay for several more days. "Mentally and emotionally unfit," they said. They told me that I nearly died, that I had taken dozens of pills, but I didn't want to believe it. When Deb came in the morning to drive me home, she looked terribly tired and stressed. It was a cold, dreary day, and we didn't talk much as we drove up the hill toward my house.

But then she looked over at me and said, "We thought we were going to lose you this time, Mom."

There was something in her tone—a sadness, or resignation—that reached me in a way that nothing else ever had. With those simple words I saw what was happening through *her* eyes, perhaps for the first time. I found myself, for once, unable to reply. Her words would echo in my mind many times over the next few days and for the rest of my life.

The house looked like a bomb had hit it when I arrived home, and I spent most of the day cleaning up. Fear, guilt, shame, and confusion racked my mind in a ruthless cycle. Snippets of memory were coming through, and, among other things, I realized that I had called the chief executive officer of Lions Gate Hospital in my delirium. I didn't know him well personally, only through my role on the hospital board. He was a professional colleague. I could scarcely comprehend it. "I'm losing my mind," I thought, over and over.

Carrie came over later in the day. I could see the moment she walked in the door she was angry, and she wanted to be heard.

"I sat in that hospital half the night thinking you were going to die," she said, struggling to control herself. "How many more times are we going to go through this, Mom?

Again, I had no answer.

After Carrie left, as always, I attempted to distract myself with work. I spent ten hours the following day, a Sunday, poring through council paperwork, fighting to concentrate on the business at hand—property development, zoning, street beautification, creek diversions. But it was like an impossible jigsaw puzzle, and I was too troubled and exhausted to accomplish much. I went over and over the same things, unable to absorb the information in front of me. At work on Monday, I moved like a zombie, feeling completely disconnected, mentally and emotionally numb. I showed up to the council meeting that evening in much the same condition. The session was long and rancorous at times, and I felt far removed from my environment, completely confused and stunned by all that had happened. I was finally, truly at the end of my rope.

CHAPTER NINE

Withdrawal

W HEN I LEFT THE HOSPITAL after my nearly fatal overdose in February 1990, it was by the skin of my teeth. Because I was considered a danger to myself, forms had been prepared while I was hospitalized (pursuant to the B.C. Mental Health Act) that, in effect, were enough to commit me to the psychiatric ward indefinitely, against my will if necessary. However, Dr. Pankratz eventually decided not to file them, and I was allowed to leave the hospital on the condition that I saw him regularly upon my release.

I was back at the office the following week, despite having been in the intensive-care unit on Saturday. I was consumed with worry about fulfilling my responsibilities there, but work was impossible. I was still in shock regarding what had happened, bewildered by the seriousness of the overdose. I was supposed to be preparing a strategic marketing plan, and I kept bringing information together, but I had great difficulty putting the data into any kind of order. I wasn't capable of analyzing the material, or logically organizing what I had to do, much less committing anything to paper. Finally, after much frustration, I approached the president of the company (who knew nothing about what I had been through) and told him that I really wanted to work from my home, as there were just too many distractions at the office. He was somewhat hesitant, but he agreed to my request. Over the next few days at home, I tried and tried to work, but I couldn't concentrate there either. I began to get panicky. Giving up was not an option, but I didn't know what to do. After a week with nothing accomplished, I was distraught.

I was experiencing full-blown panic attacks now: horrible, mind-bending bouts of indescribable fear. I was also not getting *any* restful sleep at all. I finally phoned Dr. MacGillivray, and he called in a prescription for Restoril, another benzodiazepine sleeping medication to replace the Dalmane I had been taking. (I found out later that the *CPS* at the time cautioned strongly about prescribing Restoril to patients "when suicidal tendencies may be present.")[1] When my panic attacks recurred twice in the following month, he gave me samples of sublingual Ativan, a faster-acting form of benzodiazepine. In effect, he introduced two new drugs associated with suicidal ideation within a month of my most serious overdose.[2]

On March 1, 1990, still at home, I had an experience that I will always remember as a clear turning point in my life. I was sitting in my living room, listening to a new Zamfir tape; the peaceful, flowing music filled me with a sense of wonder and awe that I had not experienced in many, many years. My skin tingled, and tears came to my eyes. The music touched me and freed an emotion that was just beyond rational comprehension, and lasted just long enough for me to identify it. Put simply, I experienced the music's beauty. It was an overwhelming feeling. I felt joy, and at the same time a crippling sadness. I had long forgotten these simple pleasures; somehow I had been so strangely removed from so many things I used to enjoy that I had not even noticed.

I was so affected by my revelation that day that I sat down and made a new plan for my life—a new beginning. I would try to find this joy again, whatever it took. I would try to regain a clear perspective of what was important to me, to re-evaluate my priorities. I tried to think of absolutely everything I could do to fulfill my new plan, all the ways that I could put myself on the path toward regaining my wonder, my joy, my self.

One of the first things I did was resolve that I would *never* drink again. I contacted an old friend who attended Alcoholics Anonymous (AA) meetings regularly, and asked if I could go with her to one. She agreed, and I went to a meeting with the best of intentions, but the experience was strange. I listened to people talking about their compulsion to drink —the daily craving, the obsessive physical need, and I didn't recognize myself. I had certainly used alcohol irresponsibly at times, but I had never been driven to drink daily for any length of time, or to consume great quantities of alcohol. On several occasions I had even cut out alcohol altogether for a year or two at a time, with very little difficulty.

However, I decided to continue attending AA meetings. If nothing else, it put me in contact with people who were, like me, trying to make radical changes in their lives. I also resolved to go out for walks, sometimes along the West Vancouver seawall, where I literally stopped to smell the flowers for the first time in years. I was longing to recapture the moment of deep connection that I had made with the world, or perhaps with myself, when the music of the Zamfir tape had broken through my defenses. I gazed intently at the sky and the ocean, trying to break through again. But I felt that I was looking through a veil, removed and separate from almost everything and everyone. I genuinely wanted to live a better life, but all my attempts seemed futile. It was frustrating not to know what was wrong with me.

By early April I was seriously questioning my physical health. I was feeling debilitated beyond any reasonable explanation attributable to stress or pressure or depression or *any* such thing. Concentrating on my work was impossible, and I was now on sick leave. At last I had become convinced there was more to my problem than was being addressed, and I started to be concerned that my February overdose had caused me some damage. I asked Dr. MacGillivray to repeat the tests that had been done in the hospital, and those from my annual medical several months earlier. I also phoned the head of the intensive-care unit at Lions Gate Hospital, to ask if there was any reason to think I had suffered any brain damage that night. Had I stopped breathing for too long? He reassured me that I had not, and all the tests came back normal as well.

I continued to visit Dr. Pankratz. In his opinion, my suicide attempt in February was related to the crisis in my long-standing relationship with Dan, to Carrie's accident, and to the general stress of my "daily, driven, high-pressure life." He wrote: "She describes anxiety, irrational fears, anger, frustration, and even borderline paranoia. ..."[3]

On April 16, I attended an AA meeting in West Vancouver. I had just about decided that it was a waste of time, but I made myself go one last time. A well-dressed, middle-aged lady stood up and began talking. Her story began like all the others I had heard, and I was only half listening, when something twigged and I began to pay attention. She was talking about her delusional outbursts, rages, suicidal episodes, and terrible problems with concentration. Sure, she drank some, she said, but the main problem was *the pills*. Overdoses, police, hospitals, restraints, psychiatrists and doctors—*and their pills*. Her life had been reclaimed since she got off *prescribed medications*, tranquilizers and sleeping pills. She had been on them for years, just like me.

Her words stopped me cold. As I sat there, the idea flashed through me for the very first time that the medications I was getting from my doctor might be the *cause* of my troubles rather than the cure. Why *was* I on these pills? I had been on them for years and *they had never helped me*. I left that meeting with my stomach in knots, a lump in my throat, and my mind racing.

The next morning I confronted Dr. MacGillivray with my concerns. I told him I wanted to get off the pills, and I wanted him to help me. Why was I on them anyway? I asked. Why for so many years? Could they have *caused* some of my psychotic reactions? The pills were helpful. I needed *something*, he insisted. I would be in "real trouble" without them.

Dr. MacGillivray must have been rather threatened by my questions that day, because he did not enter my visit or the nature of my concerns in his daily records at all. He was later asked to explain this glaring omission in court, and claimed that his secretary must have forgotten to make the entry.[4] Yet all his other chronological records were in his own writing. Clearly it was he who decided not to record the details of our discussion that day. (The secretary, however, did bill the Medical Services Plan for my office visit.)[5] Dr. MacGillivray later denied in court that he had ever advised me to stay on the drugs at all. In fact, he stated, he "would certainly *encourage* [me] to come off the pills."[6]

That same day I phoned around in search of someone else to help me. I wanted information about the tranquilizers and sleeping pills, their effects, and how to get off them safely. By late in the afternoon, I had found Dr. Susan West, a Vancouver chemical-dependency specialist. Luckily, I was able to get an appointment with her right away, and she would prove to be the first medical person to be of any real assistance to me.

The next day, I drove to Dr. West's office, which was a long way across town. During our lengthy discussion, she gave me some very simple, startling information: After I provided an outline of my history, and explained that I had quit drinking alcohol on March 1, she told me that I was quite obviously chemically dependent on the pills. Benzodiazepines, she said, are insidious drugs associated with serious side effects, and known to cause some very bizarre and unpredictable behavioral problems. They were also highly addictive, she explained, and *very* difficult to withdraw from—worse than heroin. She did not mince words about the road ahead. I was not to attempt to do *anything* on my own, and I would need *a lot* of support. But I had to get off these drugs. Not only were they ruining my career and my relationship with Deb and Carrie, they were threatening my life.

Dr. West gave me some information to read that day, and asked me to come back several days later, which I did. Although she was of invaluable assistance to me, and opened the door to my new life, I was only able to see her for a month or so because, as I withdrew from the pills, among other problems I experienced, I found myself unable to safely drive my car that distance.

The next day, stunned and reeling from what I had learned, I brought my concerns to the attention of Dr. Pankratz, and told him I was determined to get off the pills, insisting that he help me. While he would not explicitly acknowledge that the benzodiazepines I was taking were a significant problem, he did at least show me how to incrementally cut the dosages—a quarter of a tablet at a time—over several weeks. He wasn't overly encouraging about my desire to stop taking the pills. I was unprepared for the extent of the torment I would suffer as I started to withdraw from the drugs I had been on for so many, many years.

I immediately cut my regular dosage of daytime tranquilizers by a quarter of a pill, and I started to experience difficulties. At first I found it increasingly difficult to swallow, and started losing weight. I felt more anxious and scattered than ever, all day, from morning until night. I was extremely cold all the time. In fact, one evening during that first couple of weeks, I left a heating pad wrapped around my feet for so long that they actually blistered and burned, yet I felt nothing. (My ankles are still scarred from that incident.) But I was religiously committed to my withdrawal plan, and targeted Mother's Day (May 13) as the day I would finally be free of the daytime tranquilizers—about three weeks away. I chose Mother's Day to show Deb and Carrie what I had done. Next, I would stop the sleeping pills.

Meanwhile (against all reasonable odds, I now realize) I was still trying to function professionally to some degree and keep up appearances. I was still on council, for one thing, attempting to carry on and fulfill my obligations there. But in preparing for council meetings, work that should have taken about an hour was taking about three hours to complete. Simply getting dressed and showing up to meetings once or twice a week required a monumental effort. It took every ounce of my will and determination to simply *get there*; participating effectively was nearly impossible. I couldn't concentrate on anything; couldn't read, couldn't think. My thoughts were going in every direction at once and I couldn't focus. At times I barely followed what was going on. Dr. Schmidt, one of my later neuropsychologists, described being on these pills as like having a pillow over music speakers on your stereo. When you remove the pills, you suddenly get a deafening blast; your brain explodes in a rebound reaction of "hyperarousal."

After a few excruciatingly stressful sessions, I finally confided in Marilyn Baker, then the mayor of North Vancouver District, about what I was going through. I didn't tell her everything, but enough to allow her to understand the change in my behavior and appearance. (By that time my weight loss had become quite noticeable.) Although she seemed quite surprised, she was also sympathetic and understanding, and I felt somewhat relieved that I had confided in her. I soon brought myself to tell one or two other close colleagues as well, and their reaction was also empathetic, even if they couldn't really understand what I was going through.

I was determined to keep going, despite some very strange experiences. One night while I was sitting across from a fellow councilor, his face began to look wildly distorted: very old, drawn, and fluid. I sat staring at him, horrified, trying not to show any outward reaction. I spent other meetings in a daze, stifling aggressive anxiety attacks. Eventually, more and more people started to notice that something was wrong with me. I was getting thinner and thinner, having lost fifteen or twenty pounds by then, and I spoke disjointedly, if at all. I was finding it hard even to put a sentence together. I was becoming more and more self-conscious and paranoid as the weeks rolled by, desperate to hang on to some shred of my life and my identity.

Nonetheless, I was fully committed to my goal, and was completely off the tranquilizers by Mother's Day in early May, when Deb and Carrie took me out for brunch. Although I was in no shape to go anywhere that day, I battled to get myself ready—my clothes hanging loosely on my thin frame. Deb and Carrie picked me up, as I was too fearful to drive, and I remember feeling dreadful at the restaurant, horrendously sick and shaky. I tried to eat the meal in front of me, but it was no use. "Swallow your food, Mom!" Deb insisted at one point, but I just couldn't do it. I chewed and chewed, but couldn't get it to go down.

By that time, I had confided in both my daughters about what I was experiencing, and they, too, were in the beginning stages of enlightenment regarding the extent of my chemical dependency. But it would be many months before we could really begin to comprehend the multitude of effects the drugs had had on nearly every aspect of our family life over the previous two decades. The intensity of my withdrawal was a real eye-opener for us all. During its early stages, what Deb and Carrie have said they noticed most (besides the obvious physical evidence) was my extreme vulnerability. They had never seen me in such a fearful, needy state, and they were bewildered by it. The Mother's Day card from Carrie that I mentioned earlier, in which she wrote "You are so different. Give me time" was given to me on that day. I had been drugged for her entire life.

I had not seen Dr. MacGillivray for a couple of months (since he advised against getting off the pills), but I eventually went to him to discuss my possible need for long-term disability insurance, since I was barely able to handle the part-time obligations of my role as alderman at that point. Returning to my full-time career was completely out of the question. I had no idea how long I could expect to be so debilitated and I was *very* concerned about my future. After an office visit on May 25, Dr. MacGillivray wrote: "she thinks she is having a chemical withdrawal reaction to substance abuse."[7] She *thinks* so?! After more than twenty years as my doctor, after having given me approximately 235 prescriptions for nearly 12,000 pills, was this notion really so preposterous to him? With what I know now about benzodiazepines, and what I realize he should have known as a trained physician, this comment is beyond comprehension.

Once off the daytime tranquilizers, I set as my goal getting off the Restoril at night as well, but, because I had a political conference to attend in Quebec City in June (a trip I was very apprehensive about), both Dr. West and Dr. Pankratz advised me to stay on the sleeping pills until I returned. When the time came for my trip, I flew to Toronto to squeeze in a visit with my family before the conference, and stayed with my sister for a couple of nights before going on to Quebec. She and my brothers expressed shock when they saw me looking so gaunt and pale. I dragged myself on a day trip to see a play in Niagara-on-the-Lake they had planned, and they drove me to the airport later the same evening to see me off to Quebec.

During the flight my anxiety was growing by the minute, and I had a terrifying feeling of unreality—body and mind separation—that I was becoming all too familiar with. I arrived in Quebec feeling very unsteady, and took a taxi to my hotel. I was fearful of everything and everyone by then. The world was whizzing past me and moving unnaturally, out of kilter. I was convinced that a man on the hotel elevator was after me, following me, and I hurried frantically toward my room. The long corridor was spooky and distorted, and I was in tears once I got inside, where I immediately wedged a chair back under the doorknob. Although I was exhausted, I slept very little that night, consumed as I was with fear and anxiety.

The next day I sought out a friend and colleague who sat on the board with me at Lions Gate Hospital at the time, Pat Boname (who later became mayor of West Vancouver), and confided in her about my situation. I told her in the best way I could about what was happening to me, that I was terrified, and that I needed to lean on her a bit. To her credit, she was very supportive. I don't know how I would have made it through the rest of that trip without her.

Unable to concentrate on anything for very long, I had given up on any notion that I was capable of taking part in the conference. I did go along on the day trips that were planned for the spouses of the politicians attending the convention—bus tours of the area, to look at developments, recreational facilities, and historic sites—but even these excursions were difficult for me. The sights and smells triggered many vivid flashbacks to my early life in Ontario, visions and snippets of my lost self. I was remembering my youth as though it belonged to someone else. The memories seemed like dreams, there one moment and gone the next. Where *was* that person? *Who was I?* I was extremely frightened at the time, not realizing that these feelings were normal during withdrawal. As well as triggering rebound anxiety, hypersensitivity to sensory stimuli, perceptual distortions, sleep disturbances, and impaired concentration, I found out later that benzodiazepine withdrawal, particularly in the acute stage, commonly causes feelings of derealization and depersonalization.[8]

Quebec City also brought back many memories of my French mother, and I suddenly started to mourn her loss while I was there as I never had before, missing her terribly. I sought out a Catholic mass at a church in Ste-Anne-de-Beaupré that she had spoken of many years earlier, and my visit there was extremely emotional. I was filled with grief, agonizing over her death as though I had just learned of it.

Flying back to Vancouver, I tried to distract myself by reading the *Globe and Mail*, but it was nearly impossible to concentrate. I mostly just scanned the headlines, and even they were hard to comprehend. After several minutes of this, however, one article jumped out at me; it was about the antidepressant drug Prozac, which I had heard about. Although I wasn't able to absorb much of what I read at the time, I understood that research conducted by Ralph Nader's Public Citizen Health Research Group in Washington, D.C., had exposed the incidence of adverse effects among its users.

Luckily, I had enough presence of mind to tear the article out of the paper that day, and one of the first telephone calls I made many weeks later, in the beginning stages of conducting my own research on mind-altering prescription drugs, was to that organization. (I was to find out that Public Citizen is a multifaceted consumer advocacy group involved not only in research, but in lobbying government, and providing lawyers for public-interest litigation to protect the health, safety, and rights of consumers concerned with issues such as health care and the environment.)[9]

Once I was back in Vancouver, I started a gradual reduction of my Restoril sleeping pill every night, pouring out one quarter of the powder in each capsule at first, and was completely off them by June 21. *I was drug-free for the first time in over twenty years.* And I had no idea of what was still to come.

It was probably a godsend that I didn't. In the weeks that followed, my withdrawal symptoms both intensified and diversified. If I fell asleep at all, I was tormented by nightmares. I was still filled with nearly unbearable anxiety, and sometimes got up in the middle of the night, turned the music up loud, and danced around and around the house, frantically trying to wear myself out. Ironically, it was about that time that I began reading Barbara Gordon's book, *I'm Dancing as Fast as I Can*, which completely astounded me.

I could hardly concentrate or focus at all, and I read the pages of that book over and over again, underlining key passages, crying with both fear and relief. It was all there! While Gordon's eerily similar story of her experiences with prescribed Valium—and the exacerbating medical/psychiatric response to her chemical dependency and withdrawal—frightened me, it was also one of the only shreds of evidence I had that I was not going insane. In describing her withdrawal from Valium, Barbara Gordon touched on virtually everything I was experiencing.

Over two and a half months of sheer hell, I had discontinued the use of all the daytime and nighttime drugs entirely. I now know that this process was far too quick, but the information I had at that point was sketchy at best, and I was determined to rid my body of the chemicals at the earliest possible date. The result was that I sincerely thought I was going to die each and every day. I started to experience an incessant ringing in my ears, and a tight band of pressure around my head that was accompanied by a horrible sensation in my brain, as though it was wiggling around inside my skull (others have described it like "worms"). I lost clumps of hair, and had chronic diarrhea for weeks. I started to record my experiences daily, using a tape recorder, and informed both Deb and Carrie that if I did not survive they were to listen to these tapes in order to understand what had happened to me.

My eyes became supersensitive to light, and almost impossible to focus, and my vision was very distorted at times. (I was actually prescribed eyeglasses at that time that I don't need today, although my eyes remain sensitive to light.) When I returned home one afternoon after a rare attempt to venture out for a bit, I got out of my car to lift the garage door and froze in fear when I looked at my house. It seemed to be moving as though it was alive, shrinking and expanding. I stood for a long time at the top of my driveway with my heart racing before I got the courage to move the car into the garage and go in the house. Another time when I was driving up the hill toward home, Grouse Mountain suddenly became huge and ominous, and seemed to be moving closer and closer to me.

In retrospect, I can see that I should not have been behind the wheel of a car at all. I had three accidents during the initial stages of acute withdrawal, all related to visual/spatial distortions and motor difficulties. I was muddled, shaky, mesmerized, and hopelessly uncoordinated. I was also extremely clumsy in other ways, dropping and spilling things frequently. My self-esteem and confidence were at rock bottom, and I worried night and day about the future; I had no idea when I would be able to return to my full-time career, and I feared losing everything I had ever worked for.

I experienced more disturbing flashbacks as the weeks went by, and at times they progressed into full-fledged hallucinations. One day when I was coming up Highland Boulevard toward home, I saw two young children walking on the side of the road, hand in hand. I was catapulted back in time, and those two children metamorphosed before my eyes— they *became* Deb and Derek. I started to cry, nearly crashing my car. Another time when I was out for a walk along Ambleside Beach in West Vancouver, I froze in horror when a little boy came running toward the restroom, wearing overalls similar to the ones Derek had worn in the hospital before he died. For a brief moment, I was twenty-six years old again, and that boy was my Derek. I broke down completely, overcome with grief. I ran through the park to my car in tears and drove straight to the cemetery, which I had not visited in several years.

But when I got there, *I couldn't find my son's grave.* Everything seemed different and unfamiliar, and I got completely lost. With the patient assistance of the groundskeeper, I eventually located it, and stayed there for a better part of an hour, crying uncontrollably. When I finally got back to my car I was barely able to walk.

I spent long spells looking at photographs of Derek during that period, trying to grasp the passage of time, at a complete loss as to where all the years had gone since his death. I felt as though it had happened yesterday. One day when I was looking at the collage in my bedroom, at a picture of Derek sitting in his sandbox, I felt that he spoke to me as though he was right there in the room. "I don't want to see you like this, Mommy," he said. That moment had a powerful spiritual impact on me, and I remember it as a flash of clarity in a time of total chaos. I began to make a list of "good things" that day, and literally anything that was joyful or remotely positive went on my list—love for my family, bright colors, the sea, trees, flowers, a sunny day, music. Anything. I read over my list whenever I started to feel I was losing touch with reality and I added to it each day. I was determined to rekindle my faith, to find hope again, and I prayed to God for guidance. I was going to get through this nightmare and live again. I would never give up.

After much discussion, Dr. MacGillivray finally filed the forms necessary for my medical disability coverage, listing an "acute stress–anxiety reaction" as the basis for my claim. "Can't sleep much, paces about, smokes too much, can't eat and weight loss," he wrote. He explained that I was "unable to concentrate on material at work" and "unable to continue in [my] present job because of constant stress."[10] Although these statements were true, there was not one word written about the fact that I was in the acute stages of withdrawal from the drugs he had prescribed me. Right from the start, all correspondence regarding my insurance claim was in my view tainted and biased, absolving my medical caregivers of any responsibility for my debilitated state. Dr. MacGillivray tried to make it appear that he was in my corner though, stating that I was "highly motivated to getting over this stress reaction," and that my "treatment" was going well.[11]

Contrary to Dr. MacGillivray's opinion, however, "treatment" was not going well at all. I tried to talk to him about my withdrawal symptoms, but he wouldn't listen. In July he wrote in his records that I was "upset and hostile about being on pills all these years" adding "is to blame doctors for this!?" This apparently puzzled him. I also continued to see Dr. Pankratz, as required, but there was little assistance coming from him either. He, too, continued to minimize my intense withdrawal symptoms, and molded everything I reported into a sea of psychobabble crafted to support his theory that I suffered from a bi-polar disorder. If I expressed any positive feeling, or was excited about anything (good or bad), then I was on a high—hypomanic or manic. If I was distraught, sick, or anxious during our sessions, I was depressed. One night I called his office in distress, very frightened by my complete inability to comprehend written materials while preparing for an upcoming council meeting, desperate for reassurance. The doctor replacing him that night was surly and condescending toward me. "You're obsessive compulsive," he snapped. "Take a pill." "Go to hell," I snarled back, slamming down the phone. I was starting to get the picture. The medical community was not my friend. If I did not agree with them, if I refused to take their drugs, they were not going to support me. With the exception of a select few who were telling me the truth at that point, I was on my own.

As time went on, I became more and more concerned about my inability to comprehend even the simplest things. I realized I couldn't even remember the Lord's Prayer, and spent about two hours going over and over it, having asked my gardener, of all people, to help me try to piece it together. Practical matters involving planning were impossible. For instance, I arranged for my front planter to be painted on the same day I had the foliage above it trimmed, and the clippings fell down and ruined the paint. I also had conversations that I promptly forgot, and found it impossible to make decisions. People were becoming very frustrated with me on all fronts.

However, despite my ongoing difficulties, I was also beginning to reawaken, ever so slowly, to the world around me. I sat on my sun deck every day and night by myself, and watched the horizon. New lights kept appearing, creeping higher and higher up the hillside in West Vancouver's British Properties, and the summer sunsets came to life before my eyes. I was actually *seeing* the swirling peachy colors for the first time in years, and I was mesmerized. And the trees in my backyard—which I had come to perceive as a solid green mass—slowly metamorphosed into an array of unique individual branches, swaying delicately in the breezes. I hadn't been able to see the detail in the stars or the clouds in the sky for as long as I could remember. I sat for hours that summer, fascinated by their beauty.

Other physical sensations began to come back as well, and I phoned my brother back east one day in childlike excitement to announce that I could feel the back of my teeth! And while driving with my arm out the window one sunny afternoon, the pressure of the wind against my hand brought tears to my eyes. These simple sensations were exhilarating to me, but, at the same time, I was overwhelmed by the realization that I hadn't known for all those years that I was missing anything. And some discoveries were not entirely welcome. For instance, I suddenly noticed the wrinkles on my face as though they had appeared there overnight. It was like waking up after a decade or two in a coma and being suddenly confronted with the signs of age.

Driving home with Dan after we had lunch one afternoon, I started to cry when I noticed the distinct ridges and texture on the mountains, where I had formerly seen only a big, dark, amorphous mound. I asked him to stop the car so that I could take it in fully, and tried to explain to him what I was experiencing. Over time, as he became more and more aware of what was happening to me, his understanding of my condition grew, and he did everything he could to help me. Although our relationship had changed, we had a longstanding love and respect for each other, and I relied on his emotional support for quite a time before we finally went our separate ways. I will always be grateful to him for helping me through that frightening time. He was one of the only people who fully understood how emotionally debilitated I was, and I sat cuddled up with him for hours some evenings, like a vulnerable child, with my head on his chest.

One thing Dan did not understand, however, was why I had ever attended AA meetings. Despite having witnessed some very untoward behavior on my part at times, he knew I did not have an alcohol problem. My medical caregivers had continually blamed alcohol for *all* my problems over the years, and I had continually protested. For once, I had someone to back me up.

Dan had started seeking out information on the effects of benzodiazepines (and withdrawal) on his own by then, and was appalled by what he found. In fact, he brought me many articles and reports on the subject early in my recovery that were, in part, the catalyst to my ongoing quest for answers. For instance, he was the first person to point out warnings in the *CPS* about various benzodiazepines causing paradoxical reactions, such as hyperexcited states, anxiety, hallucinations, insomnia, and rage. Most significant to me, though, was the caveat to doctors about these effects: "should these occur" the *CPS* warned, "the drug should be discontinued."

The *CPS* also warned that benzodiazepines were intended "for short-term and intermittent use" and that "the safety and efficacy of long-term use [had] not been established."[12] Furthermore, the use of more than one drug was clearly contraindicated. Under the listing for Dalmane in an edition of the *CPS* in 1979, the *CPS* noted that "careful consideration should be given if flurazepam (Dalmane) is combined with other drugs having known hypnotic or central nervous system depressant effects, because the pharmacological action of these agents potentiate the action of flurazepam."[13] (Dr. MacGillivray had me on two potentiating drugs for twelve years.) Regarding withdrawal, the *CPS* discussed the need to "reduce dosage gradually after prolonged excessive dosage to avoid possible epileptiform seizures." "Withdrawal symptoms," it warned, "are similar to those seen with barbiturates."[14]

Other information brought to my attention by Dan and others shortly after discontinuing these drugs came from numerous *Canadian Medical Association Journal* articles. A 1978 report claimed that "prescribing any benzodiazepine for acute, mild or moderately severe anxiety or insomnia is usually unnecessary, possibly dangerous and of questionable efficacy and consequence." A 1981 article from the same journal intended to "assist [doctors] in the rational and judicious use of drugs for the management of anxiety disorders" warned about "various unusual responses including nightmares, paradoxical delirium and confusion, depression, aggression and hostile behaviour" and that "awareness of the sometimes bizarre effects of these drugs is important."[15] The pieces of the puzzle were starting to come together. I was overwhelmed by the implications of what I was discovering. Through all those years, and all the suffering and embarrassment, why hadn't Dr. MacGillivray acted differently? And Dr. Hirt before him?

When fall rolled around, I was feeling a little better in some ways, but my problems with concentration were not improving. This was a terrible worry to me; my mind, my ability to analyze, and my ability to make decisions were the key to my livelihood. Toward the end of September, Dr. MacGillivray received a letter from the disability examiner handling my insurance claim, asking for clarification as to the "details of the complications prolonging [my] recovery," in the event that I remain "continuously disabled."[16] I was becoming increasingly concerned about Dr.

MacGillivray's reluctance to disclose *accurate* information for insurance purposes; in fact, I wrote him a note on October 15, 1990, which he kept with his records, saying "I don't feel Dr. Pankratz fully understands the symptoms I am still experiencing ... as a result of withdrawal from the sleeping pills and tranquilizers. ... I wish we could be totally honest about this."[17] It was never to happen.

In particular, my attempt to continue with my community service was always held against me. Dr. Pankratz, especially, raised questions about the grounds for continuing to authorize my insurance benefits, given my seeming ability to continue as alderman. The irony is that I was not functioning adequately in my political role at all. I was just hanging on tenaciously, unwilling to give up this part of my life. I never wanted to stop working, or to abandon the diverse career I had been building upon for years, and was trying very hard to at least continue with my community work. At that point I wasn't accepting the possibility that the effects of my chemical dependency were permanent. I always thought that, if I hung in there long enough, I would be okay, that I could make up for lost time.

The fact that my professional life was on hold was very distressing to me. It was my career in marketing that paid my bills; my position as alderman was community-service work. Actually, the hours and expenses incurred to attend meetings and community events, keep myself available to my constituents, and visit municipal sites cost me considerable money at times. One does not receive a salary or benefits as an elected official, but rather a stipend, or honorarium. I had gone into politics at the local level to contribute to the community, and to help maintain its unique character, certainly not for the money.

In October 1990, at the end of my term as alderman, things got even more confusing. It looked as though the position of mayor would be opening up, and I was approached by many of my supporters to run. I had been on council for a long time by that point, having topped the polls in five elections, and I was considered by many to be the logical choice for mayor. A campaign group came to me practically ready-made, and there was a lot of pressure on me to throw my hat in the ring. Although I was very apprehensive at first, I was swept along with the confidence the group had placed in me, and my ability to represent community interests. I kept thinking I would be back to my old self very soon, as I had been off the drugs for six months by then. I prayed that, by the time the new term started (if I won), I would be feeling better. I had worked so hard for so many years, and I felt I couldn't turn down the opportunity to run for mayor.

As if things were not difficult enough, we had only one month to put a campaign together by the time I agreed to go ahead. I confided in a few key members of my team early on regarding my health and the pill withdrawal, including Bruce Gilbert, a senior business executive and my campaign chairman, and they were invariably very understanding. Bruce drove me everywhere, and was a tremendous ally and supporter through that difficult time. For the first time ever in my political career, I had a whole team of people taking care of promotions, literature, signs—everything. I even had a communications person to help write my speeches. I became almost like a puppet, carried along by my ardent supporters.

On election day, I made a very credible showing, coming in a strong second, despite having mounted a short campaign and having had a budget that was about one-third the amount spent by my two main competitors. Perhaps mercifully, I was out of public office, and out of work. Although I was still not fully aware of the need to focus completely on my health, or for how long this need would persist, I was able to do so at that point, and came to realize later how lucky I was that I was not elected mayor at that time.

In November 1990, I was informed that an independent medical examination was required for disability-insurance purposes, and that an appointment had been booked for me with Dr. Edward Margetts at the Vancouver General Hospital for this purpose.[18] (It is interesting to note that Dr. Margetts taught psychiatry at the University of British Columbia during the time both Dr. Pankratz and Dr. MacGillivray attended classes there.) His involvement in my case proved to be nothing short of devastating. After my first appointment with him, he reported that I "did not seem willing to accept the explanation that the sensory-perceptive experience [I reported] would not be due to withdrawal from drugs stopped five months ago." He went on to write that "she has received adverse suggestion in this regard from a chemical dependency doctor" and "her enthusiasms for re-doing the medical and management structures indicate misinformation, misinterpretation, and poor judgment."[19]

Dr. Margetts also decided that "the panic attacks and stress which she emphasizes are largely the result of suggestive indoctrination." In essence, what Dr. Margetts was suggesting was that I was imagining my ongoing drug-withdrawal symptoms, that my criticism of the medical community was not rational, and that I was being brainwashed into experiencing panic attacks.

An article entitled "Benzodiazepine Dependence" written by doctors at the Department of Psychiatry at Charing Cross Hospital in London, England, in the early 1990s discussed the "persistence" of "prolonged benzodiazepine withdrawal syndrome" as considerable—explaining that "about one third of patients report significant symptoms ten months to three and a half years following withdrawal."[20] Terence T. Gorski, an addiction specialist in Illinois, has written that post-acute withdrawal is often mistaken for "denial and resistance, personality disorders, and mental disorders."[21] In an article written in 1993, Dr. Gorski lists the symptoms of protracted withdrawal as thought disorders (difficulty in thinking clearly); affective disorders (difficulty in managing feelings and emotions); memory disorders; sleep disorders; and psychomotor distur-bances (difficulty with physical coordination and accident-proneness).[22]

Yet in Dr. Margetts's opinion, I was not suffering from any with-drawal syndrome. I was instead "diagnosable as [having] bipolar mood disorder, long-standing but ... correlated with menopause." He went on to warn that I was "in a crusading mode at this time and may bother a lot of people via telephone and letter." His most heartstopping com-ment? "It may be difficult or impossible to *control her* without the help of psychopharmaca [emphasis added]."[23] More drugs! In a letter to Dr. MacGillivray, he elaborated further regarding my condition (and perhaps a method of "controlling" me), when he suggested that I "may well require hospitalization." He advised me to "pull back, to stop ... taking self-help suggestions and bad advice."[24] If I had taken his advice I would still be on psychoactive drugs today, if I was alive at all. I thank God every day that I never gave up.

CHAPTER TEN

Systemic Denial

FTER MY LOSS IN THE 1990 election, I had no job and no community role to occupy my time. It was something of a shock to me, but I soon recognized that I nevertheless had work to do: rebuilding my health, my life, and my relationship with Deb and Carrie. With the determination and drive I had always poured into my business and professional activities, and with the aid of my background in marketing research, I went looking for information on benzodiazepines. At the same time, I was seeking out people and resources that would maximize my chances for recovery in every way. However, I found my search for information and support was an uphill battle right from the start.

I fully expected the medical community at large to be helpful and supportive of my quest to get well. Dr. MacGillivray and Dr. Hirt were clearly not about to help, and Dr. Margetts's pro-drug report had been devastating, but their attitudes, I thought, were surely the exception. After all, they had played a direct role in creating my chemical dependency; they could not be expected to admit that they had been at fault. They had their individual professional reputations to think of. But I assumed that there were doctors, psychologists, and other experts in the field who would be knowledgeable, understanding, and encouraging. Unfortunately, I would soon learn that my expectations were naive.

My first contact was with Bob Smith, the CEO of Lions Gate Hospital, whom I greatly respected, and who quickly referred me to Dr. Stu Madill, the vice-president of medicine at the hospital. When I spoke to Stu, whom

I also knew from sitting on the board of the hospital, I explained that I had learned some very alarming facts about benzodiazepines, and that I was having trouble finding the help I needed to understand and recover from their damaging effects. Much to my surprise, Stu stated that he wasn't aware of a problem with benzodiazepines or withdrawal, and throughout our conversation, to my growing frustration, he continually minimized what I was going through. When I asked him if he was aware of anyone on the North Shore who could help me with the problems I was experiencing in withdrawal, he flatly, though not unpleasantly, said he did not. After I hung up, I was left with the uncomfortable feeling that he was feeling somehow threatened by my questions. It was not an auspicious beginning to my search.

I had been off the drugs for several months by this point, but I was still experiencing weird perceptual distortions. One thing I remember distinctly is that my own body looked utterly foreign to me. I was still underweight and my hair was thin and wispy, but often when I looked in the mirror, these changes were grossly exaggerated, and I saw myself as absurdly shrunken and old. My nights continued to be a grueling test of stamina, bringing restless hour after hour of the physical and psychological distress known to be associated with withdrawal. I often paced around the house, trying to shift my attention from disturbing thoughts and memories, listening to music, or recording what I was going through on tape. For Christmas, Deb and Carrie gave me a big foam mattress I could drag around from room to room so I could plunk down for a rest anywhere I wanted to, in front of the fireplace, by the patio windows, or outside on the deck. If I could drift off anywhere for even half an hour, it was a help.

I left Dr. MacGillivray early that year in thorough disgust, deciding to begin seeing a female physician instead. My thinking was that a woman might be better equipped to understand my problem, and would surely be more sympathetic to my plight. Dr. Joanne Trebell came highly recommended, and I quickly signed a consent form for Dr. MacGillivray to forward my clinical records to her. This, unfortunately, set me up to be viewed with some skepticism. The psychotic rages, the overdoses, and especially the psychiatric reports were all there in my file. The idea that my "crusade" against tranquilizers and sleeping pills was a manifestation of a bi-polar mood disorder was gaining momentum, and would come to taint nearly every aspect of my medical care. Although I liked Dr. Trebell and felt she was genuinely trying to help me, she didn't seem able to see past the label that Dr. Pankratz originally assigned me, and that Dr. MacGillivray now seemed eager to embrace. Henceforward, it seemed, everybody had something to say about my alleged "psychiatric disorder." Even the neurologist I was referred to for the numbness in my fingers (a common withdrawal symptom) was determined to bring this up continually in his reports—and he even attempted to once more prescribe Lithium. It is hard to be taken seriously when everyone thinks you are on a mission, misguided, or manic.

To this day, when I think about how easily this theory grew and metamorphosed into "fact," I am very concerned. If it happened to me, it can happen to anyone—and it does. This is enormously troubling to me. Again, the *DSM-IV* stresses that, before diagnosing a mood disorder, "the mood disturbance must ... not be due to the direct physiological effects of a substance (e.g., a drug of abuse, a medication).[1] Yet my doctors did not merely fail to apply this criterion; they actively denied its relevance, even after the issue came to light.

This failure and denial not only prevented me from receiving appropriate care and guidance, but threatened my financial survival as well. Dr. MacGillivray eventually wrote a letter in response to the earlier request from my insurance handler regarding the reasons for my prolonged disability, stating that I was "definitely psychiatrically disturbed." He went on to express "frustration" with me—but also that he felt a "moral responsibility not to abandon [me] ..."[2] (I certainly wish Dr. MacGillivray's sense of moral responsibility toward me had kicked in much sooner.) In the eyes of my insurer, therefore, I was diagnosed with an illness for which I was refusing treatment (i.e., drugs). This assessment—that I was uncooperative in my treatment—caused me ongoing problems, in that my disability benefits were continually threatened. And, by this time, my income had dropped to one third of what it had once been.

This chain of events is not unusual, apparently, and I have since connected with many other people with similar stories. Rodney Baker, a Vancouver-based crisis counselor who contacted me after reading a news story about my lawsuit in later years, told me that he had dealt with many people facing similar problems. Refusing to take drugs prescribed by a psychiatrist, it seems, is "proof" that you are suffering from a psychiatric disorder, and at the same time "proof" that you are not really ill but only misguided—or faking. It's a truly frightening and unconscionable practice that works to perpetuate the overprescribing of these drugs to vulnerable and uninformed patients.

Despite all this, I knew I had to keep trying to find help, and stayed on with Dr. Trebell, who referred me to many specialists, including a psychiatrist named Dr. Ruth Kennedy, who didn't seem to know *what* to do with me. In her clinical records regarding our first visits she wrote: "she reads books, collects literature about pills. ... She is critical and verbally abusive to doctors ... she repeatedly asked questions that are difficult to answer. Her use of intellectualization is impossible for me to deal with."[3] Dr. Kennedy also seemed very concerned that I was talking about initiating a lawsuit against Dr. MacGillivray, and it was obvious to me she did not want to become involved. Fortunately, my relationship with Dr. Kennedy in 1991 was relatively short-lived.

I visited the sleep clinic at the University of British Columbia early in 1991 with the hope that the complex testing performed there would shed some light on my relentless insomnia, and the hyperactivity in my brain that was responsible for it. I had read award-winning science writer Lydia Dotto's book, *Asleep in the Fast Lane*, and was particularly interested in research regarding the importance of certain stages of sleep—known to be interrupted or eliminated by some drugs, benzodiazepines included—and the effects of long-term deprivation of "normal" sleep. As well, a 1967 article I had come across by R. Greenberg, entitled "Dream Interruption Insomnia," seemed to describe the sort of insomnia I was suffering from. Greenberg wrote, "Treatment with Librium or Valium at bed time leads to initial improvement in sleep ... but over a period of time both these drugs suppress the amount of Stage 1 REM sleep."[4] And it was well known by that point that sufficient REM (rapid eye movement) sleep was critical to health, and that people withdrawing from benzodiazepines experience considerable insomnia.

I was looking at my insomnia problem from two angles: first, as a factor in my problems while I was still on the drugs; and, second, to learn more about how the brain recovers, or re-establishes normal functioning, after such long-term interference. "Sleep deprivation," Dotto writes, "... does cause severe ... problems with mood and the ability to perform many kinds of mental and physical tasks. Perceptual illusions, intrusions of fantasy into wakefulness, waking dreams and mild hallucinations are not uncommon. Some people also exhibit temporary psychotic-like behavior."[5]

Alas, my quest for enlightenment at the sleep clinic was also unsuccessful. In preparation for my visit there, I had filled out lengthy forms and questionnaires in which I fully disclosed my history. Yet all the information I had supplied about the drugs I had taken for two decades and the symptoms of my ongoing withdrawal from them, including the rebound sleeplessness, was deemed irrelevant and all but ignored. Once again, my previous psychiatric evaluations overshadowed everything.

"Past psychiatric history is positive," wrote Dr. Jonathan Fleming, director of the clinic, after my examination; "she has received a number of medications ... for the most part she was *managed* with benzodiazepines [emphasis added]." Further observations made by Dr. Fleming, obviously encouraged by preconceived psychiatric determinations, included these comments: "rapport was tenuous particularly changing when I challenged any of her views about her *illness* or said things about medications which she did not like. She was quite irritable ... there was a slight acceleration in her thought rate. There were no frank delusional ideas although her preoccupation about benzodiazepines is certainly an overvalued idea [emphasis added]." My sleep problem, he concluded, "appeared to be related to a psychiatric disorder."[6] Nothing else mattered. My thoughts, opinions, and, most significantly, any unpopular line of questioning were dismissed.

I have developed a great deal of compassion for others faced with this sort of indignity; I know that many of them are never able to fight their way to the other side of it, and often return to pills. I was very fortunate in that I started with above-average intelligence, a good education, money, influence, and a high level of motivation. Yet even for me it has been a grueling battle, which continues to this day.

During those early months of 1991, in addition to the time spent running from place to place, to appointment after appointment, in search of answers, I spent a lot of time with three friends—Madeline, Anita, and

Miriam—who were my anchors. Many days, one or more of them went for walks with me, often along the beach. The world was continuing to open up more and more, and I was rediscovering the sights and sounds of the natural world—trees, flowers, stars, moon, sunrises and sunsets in all their brilliance and beauty—which had been lost to me for so long. Every day and every excursion was a source of both wonder and bewilderment, but my senses were still misfiring in many ways. When I touched a tree in the park during one of our walks, I expressed surprise that it was so wet—it hadn't rained in days and the grass was bone dry. Yet, when Madeline touched the tree at my insistence, she said it wasn't wet at all, but sticky. My tactile discernment was decidedly off.

Not surprisingly. A 1985 article on the clinical management of benzodiazepine dependence in the *British Medical Journal* pointed out that, in withdrawal, "particularly frequently reported are instances of increased sensory perception … photophobia … hypersensitivity to touch and pain." The authors also mentioned that "gastrointestinal disturbances, headaches, muscle spasms, vertigo, and sleep disturbances are also frequent."[7]

Eating was still a major problem for me, and we made a point of trying out many different restaurants for lunch during our day-trips, trying to find a place where the food appealed to me. I had been living on not much more than milk and bananas for months at that point, eventually adding various breads and rolls, and different types of fruit to my diet. Heavy or greasy foods and meat were abhorrent to me, and I couldn't get anything down that was not easy to chew and swallow. I also experienced the above-mentioned "gastrointestinal disturbances," which were diagnosed at the time as irritable bowel syndrome. A 1991 article in the *Journal of Substance Abuse* by Dr. Heather Ashton, entitled, "Protracted Withdrawal Syndromes from Benzodiazepines," substantiated the fact that this symptom, too, could be attributed to the pills: "Gastrointestinal symptoms are extremely common during chronic benzodiazepine use and in withdrawal. Many chronic benzodiazepine users have been investigated by gastroenterologists and found to have 'irritable bowel syndrome.'"[8]

The paranoia and fear were also still with me after several months, but had become much less chronic. Although I felt reasonably well for stretches of time, I could still be unexpectedly overwhelmed at the most inconvenient moments. Once, I froze in terror when I reached the middle of Lions Gate Bridge in my car on my way to an appointment over town. My hands locked on the steering wheel and I felt I couldn't drive any further—I couldn't go forward, and I couldn't go back. The railings were narrowing in on me, and the rolling ocean waters below the bridge seemed to swell up closer and closer. My big yellow Buick convertible, not an inconspicuous car at any time, felt *huge* to me, as if it had suddenly grown to the size of a bus. Finally, I was able to inch, in terror, across the remainder of the bridge that day.

Such panic attacks are nearly inevitable among long-term benzo users in withdrawal, I was later to learn in my research. A 1980 study published in the *New Zealand Medical Journal*, stated that "on withdrawal [people] uniformly suffered from insomnia, panic attacks, agitation, depersonalization, and an increase in depression. Their suffering was obvious and they all described it as being the worst experience of their lives."[9]

And the incident on the bridge was certainly not the last time I had that kind of experience. On more than one occasion over several months I became similarly overcome with sudden fear when I was out in the car. I even pulled a U-turn on the freeway one day, suddenly intent on rushing back home, which had become my place of refuge from the world. When I became panic-stricken, or confused, or even distracted, I often became blind to my surroundings, with no appreciation of how my actions were affecting others. Another time I became so enthralled by the sight of beautiful wildflowers growing along the boulevard that I stopped my car in the middle of the road to get out and pick some. I then became dazed and embarrassed when I realized I had caused a traffic problem.

Another instance of sudden panic occurred one morning during a visit back east. I was staying at my sister's summer home on Lake Huron in Ontario and I had walked out to the water's edge on a point of land, when I suddenly noticed the Douglas Point nuclear power plant looming off to the east of me, a large, multistoried complex that looked, to me, like an enemy fortress. As I stood there, staring at it in confusion, a big barge-like vessel came around the bend and frightened me. For several minutes I was convinced there was a war on. My mind was playing tricks on me at every turn.

Throughout this time I continued to have a relentless, recurring pressure band around my head, and my eyes were so sensitive to the light and the sun that I had to wear sunglasses, even on dull days. Some days my eyes would still not focus properly. My coordination was still badly off and I would often drop things unexpectedly. And at times I would break into major sweats for no apparent reason. My skin felt like it had gone from sandpaper to silk.

Yet I clung to the hope that things would get better, and I thanked God every day that there were no more unintentional pill overdoses or suicidal thoughts in my life. In fact, I felt glad to be alive, to be given a second chance, even though I still lived with a flattened emotional response to most aspects of my life.

I developed a strong philosophical perspective and tried to live each day to its fullest. I had come to realize the validity of the saying that all the money in the world means nothing if you do not have your health. On my fridge door, I placed poems and inspirational messages, which I read every day. Two of them were especially helpful to me, and I pass them along with the hope that they may provide inspiration and support to others:

Promise for the Day
Avoid negative Sources, People, Places Things and Habits.
Believe in Yourself; consider things from every angle,
Don't give up and don't give in.
Enjoy life today—yesterday is gone and tomorrow may never come.
Family and Friends are hidden treasures—seek them and enjoy the
    riches.
Give more than you plan to give.
Hang onto your dreams. Ignore those who try to discourage you.
JUST DO IT!
Keep trying no matter how hard it seems—it will get easier.
Love yourself first and most.
Make it happen.
Never lie, cheat or steal. Always strike a fair deal.
Open your eyes and see things as they really are.
Practice makes perfect.

Quitters never win and winners never quit!
Read, Study and Learn about everything important in your life.
Stop Procrastinating! Take control of your own destiny.
Understand Yourself in order to better understand others.
Visualize it! Want it more than anything. Accelerate it.
You are unique of all God's creations—nothing can replace you.
Zero in on your target and GO FOR IT!
  Jeff Olsen—TPN

To laugh is to risk appearing the fool.
To weep is to risk appearing sentimental.
To reach for another is to risk involvement.
To expose your ideas, your dreams,
Before a crowd is to risk their loss.
To love is to risk not being loved in return.
To live is to risk dying.
To believe is to risk despair.
To try is to risk failure.
But risks must be taken, because the
greatest hazard in life is to risk nothing.
The people who risk nothing, do nothing,
have nothing, are nothing.
They may avoid suffering and sorrow,
but they cannot learn, feel, change,
grow, love, live.
Chained by their attitudes they are
slaves; they have forfeited their freedom
Only a person who risks is free.
  Author unknown

I shared these words with Deb and Carrie, and sent them back east to my sister and my brothers, because of their significance in my life.

My love for music was a constant companion during those long, lonely, frightening days and nights, and I would sing and dance around the house for hours on end. I couldn't get over the beautiful sounds and words in what were actually familiar songs from the past years, but which

I was now listening to with much more clarity. The words were no longer "muffled." It sounded like a full orchestra instead of a three-piece band. I was in awe.

Deb, who also loved music so much, spent hours taping my favorite songs, and other songs she wanted me to hear, and presented me one day with one of the most beautiful tapes I have ever heard. I lovingly and appreciatively played "Deb's Tape for Me" continuously in my car and at home.

I also started to see Carrie more often, and our moments together became so special. I had a lot to catch up on with both my daughters after so many years of estrangement. At times I would become tearful, overwhelmed with joy and happiness at being able to spend time with them. I was determined that nothing would stop me from rebuilding my health and my life. The pills had made such a mockery of everything I believed in.

I had my personal prayer that I repeated every day: "Thank you God for letting me live. Please show me the direction you wish my life to take, but don't make it so financially punitive. I love my daughters so much and myself." I was working very hard to rebuild my self-esteem and my confidence during those dreadful days and months. And I kept searching for my real identity, which had been lost for so long.

In the spring of 1991, I started to jog a little when I was out for my early morning walks on the sea wall in West Vancouver, and the exercise and fresh air helped me so much that I eventually made it a daily habit. I felt better after my run than at any other time of the day. It was very beneficial to get my heart beating and break a sweat—helping to rid my body of its toxicity. To this day I view my running (two and a half miles each day) as my lifeline, and consider it perhaps the single most important contribution to my recovery and return to health.

I was also by then receiving counseling at Alternatives, a local drug and alcohol counseling and resource center, and my experience there was giving me more hope. To my great relief, personnel at Alternatives were not the slightest bit surprised by what I was experiencing, and reassured me that it would eventually pass. They gave me literature to read on women and tranquilizers, and for the first time I became aware that many women of my generation had suffered, as I had, as a result of blindly trusting their doctors, and their prescriptions. I still had trouble reading, and went over and over the material, highlighting significant passages.

It was beginning to sink in that there were two very different schools of thought about what I was experiencing. For the most part, the mainstream medical community was like an ostrich with its head in the sand, ignoring or denying things it didn't want to see, the problems it created. Conversely, counseling health-care professionals working outside of the medical system, in the field of chemical dependency—those dealing directly with people in recovery—were highly knowledgeable and seemed to have lots of relevant information. These people knew. Yet they ran parallel to the medical mainstream, and I couldn't understand why the divergence existed.

I learned more about the very serious effects that benzodiazepines have on the central nervous system through a series of lectures I attended at Alternatives. I heard, again, about their side effects, including paradoxical reactions and violent behavior, and the fully expected horrors of withdrawing from them. Through the center, I met other men and women of all ages who were fighting the same battle. And finally, fortunately, I learned the name of a Vancouver doctor, Mary Stewart-Moore, who had a lot of experience dealing with chemical dependency and withdrawal. I saw her for the first time in March 1991.

The letters were flying back and forth with my insurers, and on August 24, 1991, Dr. Stewart-Moore wrote that I "was suffering from protracted withdrawal symptoms from Dalmane, Restoril, Valium, Librium, and Serax." She went on to elaborate that my mental and emotional symptoms were "fairly typical of … protracted withdrawal symptoms." Dr. Moore also explained that I was "essentially unable to handle any complex cognitive tasks because of the inability of [my] brain to process more than simple information and to remember tasks at hand." I had difficulty, she had observed, "even finishing a sentence or remembering what [I] set out to say." In her opinion, the prognosis for my being able to return to work was "guarded."[10] Finally, at long last, I had found a doctor who was willing to acknowledge that my problems stemmed from my past chemical dependency on the pills. But her prognosis for my returning to work was chilling. What would become of me if I couldn't return to my career? What about my financial future, and everything I had worked so hard for over so many years?

At the insistence of my insurance company, I was referred to Dr. Raymond Parkinson, another psychiatrist, for yet another evaluation. With great hesitation, I was obliged to go through the whole twisted tale yet again. I told Dr. Parkinson of Derek's illness and death, the subsequent prescriptions for tranquilizers and sleeping pills, the escalation of my problems through the years on the pills—the rages, the drinking, the overdoses, the hospitalizations—as well as the sexual abuse with Dr. Hirt. I also told him that I would not accept drug treatment at any point. To be sure, I was apprehensive about seeing another psychiatrist, *any* psychiatrist, but I tried to be honest, and to keep an open mind. With hesitancy and reservations, I also gave permission for Dr. Parkinson to obtain my various past medical and psychiatric records.

These records, of course, included those available from Dr. Hirt, whose response to Dr. Parkinson's request was both swift and reprehensible. He responded quickly, he explained in his letter, so that Dr. Parkinson "would not be unprepared" for dealing with me. In essence, Dr. Hirt contradicted nearly everything he had ever said to me and about me in the past; he seemed to want to ensure that I was viewed with bias and skepticism. First, he classified my earliest depression, following Derek's death, as "psychotic" in intensity, coupled with "paranoid ideation." (He had seemed to think my depression was entirely appropriate at the time it was occurring.) He then went on to discuss my "alcohol addiction" (which he had refuted in writing on many occasions) and my apparent "Jekyll–Hyde syndrome," elaborating that I occasionally went "berserk, out of control, vicious, amnesic, and delusional."

Dr. Hirt didn't, however, mention the role that prescription drugs played in contributing to these episodes. The clincher, and the obvious motive for his extreme and distorted summary of his dealings with me, was evident in his most offensive statement, wherein he claimed that I "would confabulate our sessions or simply remain amnesic about [my] office visits."[11] Interesting. I *made things up* about our sessions. My memory could not be relied upon. How convenient. (I later found out from a court watcher who attended Dr. Hirt's subsequent sexual-misconduct trial that "confabulate" was a favorite word with the doctor, one he used often in court in an attempt to discredit many of the women who filed complaints against him for sexual abuse.)

Dr. Parkinson, to his credit, appeared to have an open mind, and luckily he knew of me from my former days as an alderman, when our council meetings were televised, and from newspaper articles. Sensing that something was seriously wrong, he sent me for neuropsychological testing with Dr. Klonoff, a clinical psychologist and neuropsychologist and professor emeritus at the University of British Columbia, to try to shed some light on my ongoing difficulties with concentration and memory. I felt that Dr. Parkinson listened to what I had to say with genuine interest and caring, and did not refuse to acknowledge the possibility that the drugs had played a major role in my past behavior, or that I had suffered damage as a result of my long-term exposure to them.

In December 1992, I underwent extensive neuropsychological testing with Dr. Harry Klonoff. In his subsequent ten-page report to Dr. Parkinson, he stated, among other things, that "inefficiency was evident throughout the cognitive sphere, and that I revealed significant impairment of adaptive abilities dependent upon organic brain functions." There were "no indications of psychotic ideation or profound depression," he asserted. "Nor were there indications that Ms. Gadsby's emotional state would in any manner account for the presenting picture on the cognitive and neuropsychological tests." Given expectations based upon my past education and career performance, Dr. Klonoff claimed that there was "'objective evidence' of a decline in my intellect, decisiveness, and persuasive reasoning."[12] He also reported that signs of impairment on the cognitive and neuropsychological tests "could be accounted for" by the medications I had been on for twenty years, although he recommended further observation and testing. Dr. Klonoff felt I could benefit from a cognitive rehabilitation program, coupled with supportive counseling.

With his report, I felt that at last there might be some hope. This was the first time in a year and a half that my concerns about problems with concentration, decision-making, and memory were substantiated by objective tests.

Following up on Dr. Klonoff's recommendations, I sought out Dr. Ursula Wild, a highly regarded Vancouver neuropsychologist, who was to be a tremendous help to me. She, too, turned out to be a concerned, caring, and supportive health-care professional. Her experience and insight regarding brain-injured and drug-damaged individuals has been invaluable to me, and to this day I still see her regularly. In March 1993, I met with her for the first in a series of cognitive-rehabilitation assessment sessions.

After the initial testing period, Dr. Wild reported to my insurance company that my performance on tests involving planning and problem solving was "particularly surprising … given [my] background as a successful, goal-oriented, self-directed businesswoman." She also confirmed my "impaired performance" in processing written information, as well as with auditory and visual memory tasks. She concluded that a "considerable discrepancy [existed] between actual and expected level" of performance, and recommended not only cognitive retraining, but also "supportive counselling" and the teaching of "coping techniques" that would help me to "accept and adjust to the considerable limitations in [my] neuropsychological functioning."[13] Dr. Wild had no doubt whatsoever that my cognitive impairment was "due to long-term use of benzodiazepines."[14]

Alas, just as the real issue was beginning to fight its way to the surface, yet another psychiatrist was recruited by my insurance company to provide an independent expert opinion regarding my case. Dr. James Brown, whom I never met, reviewed material from just about everyone, including Dr. MacGillivray, Dr. Pankratz, and Dr. Margetts. Based on this information, he concluded, by paper diagnosis, that I should be given a "vigorous trial of treatment for mood disorder." Meaning drugs, of course, and plenty of them. He understood, however, that I had "declined any such treatment." Other interesting statements from Dr. Brown included comments such as "neither [Stelazine] nor benzodiazepines are known to cause dementia" (an interesting statement, given what I later learned) and "the withdrawal symptoms from benzodiazepine drugs usually last no more than a few weeks."[15] This damaging assessment from a psychiatrist who apparently knew little about or would not acknowledge the drug's effects, and who had in fact never interviewed me again threatened my continuing disability-insurance benefits, and my financial survival.

Thankfully, Dr. Moore, Dr. Parkinson, and Dr. Wild became, collectively, my supportive health-care professionals over the next five years.

My financial troubles were ongoing, but I felt that my journey toward improvement was nevertheless gaining some momentum. Time was my kindest ally, and, with its passage, the professionals I was seeing were regularly confirming my progress and the gradual return of my underlying personality, emotional state, and "normal" coping mechanisms. My mental, physical, and emotional health improved steadily the longer I was off the drugs.

While all this was going on, I was again approached by supporters to run in a by-election for district council, since one of the serving council members had been appointed a judge, thereby creating a vacancy. At first I was excited and tempted by the opportunity to get back to that part of my life and my identity, and I gave the by-election serious thought. Finally, after much encouragement, I agreed to run. The campaign slogan became "Let's Bring Back Balance and Experience," recognizing that in four previous elections I had topped the polls. I quickly realized, however, when I tried to put my campaign brochure together, that I had underestimated the difficulties I would still have to face. That process took an exhausting amount of time, since I was not yet up to speed, and I was concerned. Fortunately, my campaign chairman was a real doer and organizer, and handled a lot of the details that I couldn't.

The ball was rolling, and I won the election, largely as a result of an aggressive campaign, and my past reputation as an effective alderman. In retrospect, I realize that I probably should not have attempted so much at that point in my recovery, but I longed to regain some semblance of normal living and involvement in my community. I worked harder than I had in any of my previous terms in office—taking hours and hours to prepare for meetings, going over and over things, writing notes, and struggling. What I had normally done in one hour now took three hours. I would soon feel fatigued because of the extra mental effort I was required to put out.

Working as alderman again during that period made it very clear to me that my ongoing problems with concentration, memory, and information analysis were not over. Although I was getting better all the time in a physical sense (from my daily runs, a nutritious diet, and vitamins), and was benefiting emotionally from the help I was getting, my mind was simply not as quick as it had been. But I never accepted that

I would not improve eventually. I would never give up trying, no matter what it took.

I badly wanted to find out more about how I could help myself improve and recover, and I felt that the more knowledge I had, the better my chances were. Earlier on, feeling apprehensive and uncertain, I had phoned and visited a number of detox and treatment facilities, including the Betty Ford Center in Rancho Mirage, California; the Patty Duke Canyon Springs Hospital, also in California; and the Meridian Treatment Center in Lynden, Washington. In Ontario in 1992, I toured the Donwood Institute and treatment center in Toronto. My discussions with key medical and counseling personnel there were very productive, a gold mine for my ongoing research. These people were clearly *very* knowledgeable about the effects of drugs, particularly benzodiazepines, and referred me to Dr. Joel Lexchin, who had written a well-researched book entitled *The Real Pushers: A Critical Analysis of the Canadian Drug Industry*, published in 1984. I contacted Dr. Lexchin (who worked out of the Toronto Western Hospital) immediately, and was very pleased that he could meet with me that trip.

My meeting with Dr. Lexchin, a forthright critic of the drug industry and a key member of the Medical Reform Group of Ontario, was both revealing and troubling. His book, which I obtained upon returning home from Toronto, looked at the "mythology" of prescription-based medicine, beginning with pharmaceutical companies' advertising and marketing strategies, how profit-based interests influence and dominate the medical profession and its government regulators, and how doctors often rely on this biased stream of information with tragic results. Among many other things, Dr. Lexchin critically addressed the "widespread effect of drug dependency (especially among women) from the tranquilizer boom of the last two decades."[16] Nearly everything I read struck home. Dr. Lexchin was clearly very tuned in. Among other things, he wrote: "Benzodiazepines are frequently prescribed to lessen anxiety, fear or irritability, but in some minimally anxious subjects they have been shown to actually increase anxiety. It was found that violent, aggressive incidents occurred significantly more frequently when prisoners were on Valium than when they were not." Also, "a number of reports have emphasized the risk of suicidal thought induced by [benzodiazepines]."

Dr. Lexchin also discussed the federal Health Protection Branch's product monographs for these drugs, which warned—*many* years ago—that there was "no justification for the regular use of anxiolytic drugs in overt or covert manifestations of anxiety if they are considered to be within the normal range of human living. [They] … should not be routinely used for anxiety associated with normal tensions of unhappy personal or family situations, loneliness, interpersonal difficulties, normal grief or bereavement, expected reactions to everyday stresses, normal frustrations, trials and tribulations of human existence, or transient complaints of a nonorganic nature."[17]

Through Dr. Lexchin's book, I also became aware of the work of the late Dr. Ruth Cooperstock. Dr. Cooperstock, once a leading researcher with the Ontario Addiction Research Foundation, had studied the sociological roots of the trend to address valid psychological responses, especially those of women, with tranquilizing drugs such as benzodiazepines. She noted that this practice often placed women in even greater jeopardy by increasing their passivity, such that they were then less likely to leave a destructive situation. Her work also delved into withdrawal, as well as psychomotor, learning, and memory impairment following benzodiazepine use, which was of particular interest to me at that time. It appalled me to discover that Cooperstock's research had, for the most part, been published in the late 1970s and early 1980s. These problems had obviously been a topic of discussion for a long time. Why then, did I have so much trouble convincing doctors of my plight? How could they not know? Why were they putting people through such torment, even blatantly denying the existence of their suffering, when the effects and after-effects of these drugs were known so long ago? And why were there no regulatory measures in place to prevent this from continuing?

Dr. Lexchin also referred me to Dr. Mary Pat McAndrews, a Toronto research psychologist working, as she was, to effect change in the area of medical treatment and philosophy. Dr. McAndrews was then conducting extensive research into the area of cognitive impairment caused by benzodiazepines, examining people while they were on the drugs, during withdrawal, and after longer-term discontinuation. Her work focused particularly on the elderly, an appalling number of whom are prescribed these drugs, worsening any age-related dementia they may already be experiencing. I was able to arrange a meeting with Dr. McAndrews and some of her colleagues on that same trip to Toronto, and she provided me with much valuable information and insight. She gave me a bundle of research papers pertaining to the significant impairments of memory and cognition caused by benzodiazepines.

One of the papers Dr. McAndrews gave me was a review published in 1991 by the Department of Psychiatry at the De Crespigny Park Institute of Psychiatry in London, England, which stated that the amnesic effects of benzodiazepines had "attracted considerable research interest" some years earlier. A Medline search revealed more than 100 published studies between 1986 and 1990 that assessed benzodiazepine effects on human memory.[18] This aspect alone bothered me very much. I had struggled to perform in my career and in politics, all the while taking drugs that were known to impair memory. Many of the documents that Mary Pat McAndrews shared with me also discussed the phenomenon of patients' increased anxiety and depression while on the drugs, often intensified by the sheer frustration associated with failing memory and concentration. I could certainly relate to that. When I thought of how I had suffered in this regard, only to be prescribed more and more pills, it made me very angry to know that this impairment was actually a well-documented side effect.

The most disturbing aspect of the literature on cognitive impairment was contained in reports about *long-term* users. A paper published by the Department of Psychiatry at the University of Pennsylvania School of Medicine in 1986 discussed patients who had been on benzodiazepines for years and showed signs of "general intellectual impairment." "Furthermore," I read, "the impaired performance of these patients *failed to recover* after they gradually stopped taking their medication."[19]

And in 1993, at the Mayo Clinic in Rochester, Minnesota, extensive testing done on benzodiazepine-dependent patients, as well as on patients who had discontinued benzodiazepine use, revealed a cumulative memory and learning impairment; the researchers concluded that "the impairment does not necessarily diminish in time." One study showed that negative effects of long-term use persist even after detoxification when there are "no outward signs of withdrawal."[20] This was the first time I had seen these terrible possibilities starkly described on paper.

I contacted several lawyers to discuss my situation and my potential lawsuit against Dr. MacGillivray, which was becoming increasingly important due to my mounting financial losses. Most wanted a $50,000 retainer to start an action against him, and advised me I would be taking on the whole medical profession if I did (which proved to be true). I found myself leaving one lawyer's office feeling particularly angry at the ongoing threat to my livelihood, my future security, and my career that the long-term residual effects of the benzos represented. When I thought of how my relationships with Deb and Carrie had suffered over the years, and everything I had been through, it only added to my anger. There and then I decided to confront Dr. MacGillivray, to enlighten him regarding my ongoing struggle to overcome the damage done by the drugs he had prescribed so freely.

I had called him weeks earlier and made an appointment, but he had subsequently canceled it. And during a visit the previous summer I had brought to his attention Barbara Gordon's book *I'm Dancing as Fast as I Can*, but he had dismissed the book as "exaggerated." Now the real truth was becoming abundantly clear, and I thought he should know about it.

I marched into his office that day unannounced, and summarily informed his nurse that I wished to see Dr. MacGillivray immediately. I was obliged to sit in his waiting room for several minutes, but soon enough Dr. MacGillivray emerged and we retired to the privacy of one of his consulting rooms.

As I sat down I was hoping he would at last begin to rethink his stance on benzodiazepines, and perhaps acknowledge his lack of understanding regarding their damaging effects and how they should be prescribed, if at all. But mostly I wanted to update him on how I was still being affected now, after almost two years off all the pills. As I began to speak, however, I found myself struggling to contain my anger, and to state my case, and feelings; I was very upset and annoyed with him. "I've just come from a lawyer's office," I began. "I'm considering filing a complaint against you with the B.C. College of Physicians and Surgeons, and possibly a lawsuit."

He was certainly taken aback by this announcement on my part, and before he could get much further than "Joan …," I continued: "You should have known about the pills. I've been able to gather all sorts of information detailing the damage they do. It's there in the *CPS*, in lots of articles in the medical journals, everywhere! Why did you keep prescribing them for me?"

"Joan," he began again, "there is no doubt in my mind that you needed the medication. You were suffering from anxiety at the time."

"I have neurological damage that may never be repaired!" I shot back. "My career, my relationship with the girls, the humiliation I suffered, the embarrassment! My God, I can't change all the damage that's been done!"

"The medication has not done you any harm," he returned, his agitation clearly growing.

"I trusted you! How can you be so appallingly ignorant?"

That was too much for him and he abruptly stood. "Get out of my office," he demanded, red-faced and upset. "Now! And do not come back!"

With that, he stormed out of the consulting room. Feeling unsatisfied, frustrated, and disappointed, I left his office.

I ruminated about what had happened with Dr. Hirt as well. I also wanted to confront him. I wanted to tell him I was off the pills, and ask him how he could justify what had happened between us. The more I learned about the effects of the drugs, the more I realized he must have known how vulnerable I was. Why had he chosen my weakest moments to initiate sexual contact with me? I contacted his office to book an appointment with him, but, not surprisingly, he refused to see me.

I decided to file complaints with the B.C. College of Physicians and Surgeons against both Dr. MacGillivray and Dr. Hirt. Before I did, however, I decided to meet with the then deputy registrar for the college, Dr. Askey. I made an appointment on the pretext that I was simply researching the prescribing of benzodiazepines, without disclosing that I had ever been on them myself. I wanted to get a feel for the general political atmosphere around this issue, without mentioning my own experience, and I was soon glad I had used that approach. The information I gathered that day was unbiased and undefensive, and gave me a better feel for the mainstream medical approach to prescribing these drugs. At one point in our discussion, Dr. Askey said, "Joan, you and I are too intelligent to take these pills." I was flabbergasted. Is that to say, I couldn't help thinking, that it's perfectly all right to risk the health of anyone unfortunate enough (myself included, despite Dr. Askey's presumption) to be unaware of their damaging effects?

Shortly after that meeting, I officially filed my complaints with the college, the body officially authorized to investigate inappropriate prescribing habits and complaints against doctors. Their inquiry into Dr. MacGillivray's conduct amounted to a letter describing my charges, and asking for his response. Dr. MacGillivray's response speaks for itself: "To say that looking after Joan has been a tumultuous undertaking," he wrote in a return letter to the college, "is an understatement ... my associates will also attest to the fact that Joan has been a problem to deal with." Not surprisingly, Dr. MacGillivray used the psychiatric evaluations performed at the height of my chemical dependency against me, and cited my alleged "alcohol abuse and manic-depressive disorder" as my primary problems and, presumably, the reason for my being such a "problem." Perhaps most disturbing and hurtful were the outrageously presumptuous comments he made about my daughters' feelings about me, saying that they "both tolerate her as best they can, in so far as she is their mother."[21] He also wrote that "Joan's present crusade is to rid the population of the use of tranquilizers, sleeping pills, and anti-depressants. Unfortunately for her, she will likely require their use again in the not too distant future, as *her disease* catches up with her again." (I have now been off all the drugs for almost ten years, and no such disease has ever caught up with me.)

I soon rejected the notion that regulatory bodies governing physicians were there to protect the public's interest. My complaint against Dr. MacGillivray was considered by the College of Physicians and Surgeons for a mere sixty days before it was dismissed altogether. Their response cited "the extent of my recurring emotional problems" as justification for his prescribing "medications for symptom control." Again, as it had been time after time, the fact that the drugs I was on were known to *cause* these "symptoms" was downplayed. The college found "no serious fault" with the prescribing practice of Dr. MacGillivray (after 240 prescriptions for more than 12,000 pills) and even decided that the "level of drug intake over the years was unlikely to produce any physical dependency."[22] Even the College of Physicians and Surgeons, which should have known the seriousness of Dr. MacGillivray's overprescribing habits, were in denial about the problem, or were more concerned about protecting one of their own.

I was eventually called in by the College of Physicians and Surgeons to meet with one of their official investigators to discuss my complaint against Dr. Hirt. However, when I found out how convoluted and time-consuming the process of investigation was—and learned that the investigator knew me from my aldermanic role in North Vancouver—I decided to put this on hold, as it was likely to become a public matter. I also felt there was already enough on my plate. (I would have revived my complaint against Dr. Hirt in time, but he died a couple of years before I could do so.)

Despite these setbacks, there was one particularly happy development in my personal life in the summer of 1991. Now that my erratic behavior had stopped, Carrie decided to move back home. She discussed her observations of me during that time in an affidavit prepared for my lawsuit, when she wrote: "I now see her as a completely different person from the woman that behaved in such bizarre ways as I was growing up. I no longer feel as I did before that at any moment there might be an eruption ready to occur. I feel now that my mother's behaviour will be normal for the rest of her life. She seems very proud of us, her daughters, and she acts very lovingly towards me. I have great respect now for my mother … "[23]

It had been a lonely life for me since she had left home, and to have her home again was a precious gift. We began to develop a relationship that summer that we had never really had before. I remember touching her face in amazement as I began coming alive again, fascinated and overwhelmed by her lovely, soft skin, big brown eyes, and long eyelashes. She was a beautiful, bright young woman, now almost twenty-one years old, studying for her communications degree at Simon Fraser University, working part-time, and living a full, independent life. Where had the child gone? I had missed so very much, without even being aware of it.

We did our best to make up for lost time. She seemed pleased to be able to confide in me when she moved back home, even seeking my advice at times, and sharing her future career plans for the film industry. And her father began to show up at the house now and then as well, and he, too, was curious about the changes he saw in me. He was astounded by the extensive research I had gathered on the drugs' effects, and became very interested. It explained so much to him. The three of us even had dinner together occasionally, as we began to develop the healthy, supportive connection with one another that continues to this day.

Deb was more standoffish at first. She and Martin did occasionally invite me over for dinner at their home, but Deb was very busy with her own demanding career, and her marriage, and their free time on weekends was most often taken up with sailing through the Gulf Islands, or skiing in the winter. She was very supportive of my being off all the pills, and very proud of me, but surprised and concerned about their lingering deleterious side effects.

By the latter part of 1991, with my income reduced to approximately a third of what it had been when I was working, my financial losses were piling up. I soon had to sell my second investment property, which was an agonizing decision, and cash in some of my RRSPs to keep myself afloat. All that I had built—my security, my career, my whole life plan— was going down the tubes because I had been so badly, so unnecessarily, damaged by drugs.

For all these reasons, I filed a lawsuit against Dr. MacGillivray in June 1992. My statement of claim alleged that I had not been advised of the risks, side effects, and highly addictive nature of the drugs Dr. MacGillivray continuously prescribed for me from 1967 until 1990. It also alleged that Dr. MacGillivray failed to prevent my becoming addicted to these medications, or to assist me in the difficulties I experienced in withdrawing from them. As a consequence of Dr. MacGillivray's negligence in over prescribing medication, I claimed as loss and injuries: impaired senses, cognitive impairment, altered mood, and withdrawal symptoms. I also listed damages, including pain, suffering, and emotional distress; loss of amenities of life; loss of wages, both past and future; loss of earning capacity; cost of future care; and special damages.[24]

In addition to trying to recoup my considerable financial losses, I felt that proceeding with my lawsuit against Dr. MacGillivray would encourage discussion and public scrutiny regarding some physicians' irresponsible prescribing practices, and their apparent immunity from being held accountable. It was becoming more and more important to me to make a difference in this regard, to do everything I could to prevent others from having to experience the horrors that I had.

CHAPTER ELEVEN

Mounting Evidence

THE ROLLERCOASTER RIDE of my recovery was to go on through several more heart-stopping loops. In November 1993, just one crucial week before the District of North Vancouver election, the *North Shore News* published a "Report Card" on the incumbent councilors, giving me a "D" grade. It was an unexpected, cruel blow and I was devastated. What was supposed to have been an opinion-and-analysis piece on the performance of individual elected officials was instead a personal attack on me, for reasons never disclosed to me. The reporter attacked me as inconsistent for having espoused free-enterprise ideals even though I had received unemployment insurance in the past, and also accused me of incurring excessive expenses in my role as a councilor. (My expenses were in fact higher because I had taken a council-approved trip to Toronto earlier that year to attend the World Congress on Local Government.) The president of the North Vancouver Chamber of Commerce, where I sat on the board, also wrote to the editor expressing serious concerns about the paper's policy of grading incumbents, pointing out that no objective criteria were established for how grades were determined, and that the grades were not issue-oriented. I tried to recover my position by contacting the publisher and editor, and having a letter published in the paper just the day before the election. I had received more than a hundred phone calls from district residents who were outraged at the unfair treatment I had received.

Although it was not our habit to do so, Deb, Martin, Carrie, and I, after eating supper together at my home, went down to the district hall on election night. Our mood *en route* to the hall might best be described as hopeful. As the results began to come in, however, it was clear the newspaper article had had its effect; I had gone from topping the polls to a position very near the bottom. Deb and Carrie, who were always supportive of my efforts on council, were very disappointed and upset, and so was I. At first I couldn't or didn't want to believe it. It was a somber night.

During the next week, I received many more phone calls from supporters, who agreed with me that the newspaper article was "the worst kind of insult," "yellow journalism," and the only reason that I had not been elected. Since I had received little response to my concerns from the paper, I wrote to the CEO of the Southam Newspaper Group in Toronto, who were part-owners of the paper, and they replied that they would not intervene but suggested I take my concerns to the B.C. Press Council. After I wrote to the B.C. Press Council and appeared before them, my complaint was dismissed. However, "the Council expressed concern that some of the statements in the report card were of a personal nature and not entirely relevant."[1] It was not a very satisfactory outcome, but I had to move on with my life.

I knew that there were more than enough challenges still ahead of me on my road to recovery and rebuilding my life. More important, I was steadily gaining ground in several areas of tremendous significance to me. My relationships with Deb and Carrie continued to improve in a very meaningful way, and we were getting together for dinners more often as a family, Alan included. Furthermore, I was finally gaining the professional health-care support I knew I needed if I was to ever fully regain my health.

New challenges were not slow in coming. In 1994, Dr. MacGillivray's defense team notified me that they wanted to go to trial in November of that year in my lawsuit against him. At that point I was in the middle of a one-year cognitive retraining program with Dr. Wild, and I knew it was critically important to complete the rehabilitation program before going ahead with the trial. I had to determine my prognosis, and in turn the damages to be claimed in the lawsuit. Would the retraining make a difference? Would I improve enough to resume my career in the future? These questions were highly relevant to my legal claim. I also wanted to recover my cognitive functioning as fully as possible in order to handle the rigors of a trial—something of a double-edged sword, since the existence of this impairment was in part what I was seeking damages for.

It was a mad scramble, including the preparation of a thick affidavit of medical and health-care reports, but my lawyer and I were able to postpone the trial, thereby allowing me to complete my cognitive retraining, and gaining me time to gather the research materials and information to make the strongest possible case against Dr. MacGillivray.

The research I had done to date was only the tip of the iceberg. My quest for information on benzodiazepines began in my own backyard, but over the next months and years it would ultimately extend throughout British Columbia, and across Canada, the United States, the United Kingdom, Europe, Australia, New Zealand, and South Africa. I would uncover a vast body of research detailing all the deleterious effects of these insidious drugs.

One of my earliest efforts brought me to research conducted by the World Health Organization (WHO) Program on Substance Abuse, which indicated that the organization has been "fully aware of the abuse liability of benzodiazepines since the late 1960s," and that "although [they] had produced educational materials and supported training workshops on rational prescribing ...," its members "... did not have an optimistic view about the impact such activities were having on the day to day prescribing practices of many physicians in the world."[2] Charles Medawar, the former member of the WHO Expert Advisory of Drug Policies and Management, wrote that "the evidence suggests that the providers of medicine keep making the same mistakes, mainly because they have been allowed to deny how badly things have gone wrong."[3]

Closer to home, I came across the 1994 book *Strong Medicine*, by Dr. Michael Rachlis, an outspoken critic of Canada's health-care system, and Carol Kushner, a writer and health-policy analyst, which also discussed the "unhealthy alliance" between medicine and the drug industry.[4] In their examination of the multibillion-dollar prescription-drug marketplace in Canada, Rachlis and Kushner point out that the drug industry spends about 20 percent of its sales revenues on marketing, and only about half that much on research. The intention of the pharmaceutical marketers, they add, is to sell as many drug products as possible through doctors, and products that can be widely applied—for anxiety, for instance—have been a highly lucrative focus for sales.

I had maintained my connection with the Public Citizen Health Research Group in Washington, D.C., and they eventually sent me a book they had published in 1982 entitled *Stopping Valium*, by Eve Bargmann, MD, Sidney Wolfe, MD, and Joan Levin. This book was another excellent source of information, with well-developed sections on mental impairment, loss of coordination, impaired driving, extreme confusion, hallucinations, paradoxical rage, overdoses, and deaths, as well as the problems affecting newborn infants after exposure to benzodiazepines in vitro.[5]

If the doctors themselves were so firmly in the grip of the pharmaceutical companies' marketing machines, I wondered why the regulatory bodies, both government and medical, weren't doing more to control the use and abuse of these drugs. As my efforts continued, it in fact became clear to me that attempts made by government and medical ruling bodies to distribute objective information about drugs were minimal and ineffective. And yet this was clearly their responsibility. They had issued warnings regarding benzodiazepines over the years, but it seemed that the message, time after time, had been lost in a convoluted sea of denial, ignorance, politics, and profiteering.

There is undoubtedly a tendency for some doctors who have held certain opinions and beliefs for decades to be disinclined to accept new information, and to dismiss as "exaggerated" or unreliable any new ideas that would threaten the validity of their prior thinking or practices. Unfortunately, such physicians in many cases originally relied blindly on the information supplied by those who profit from selling the drugs (the manufacturers) to form opinions about their safety and appropriate use. In addition, there seems to be very little incentive for doctors to keep up with changes in medical thinking. While some physicians do this voluntarily, many do not, and the repercussions for failing to heed new prescribing guidelines are practically nonexistent. The human cost inherent in this situation is alarming, yet it continues, decade after decade.

Worst Pills, Best Pills, published in 1993, is another excellent book by the Public Citizen Health Research Group in Washington, D.C., which I obtained when I was in Washington in 1994 attending the Women of

Vision Leadership for the Nineties Conference at Georgetown University, and it also discussed the relationship between drug companies and doctors. It states that "too many physicians, too often believing that their accepted role is to end a patient's visit by writing a prescription, fall easy prey to the industry's drug-pushing strategies, especially because of the doctors' often-appalling lack of information. ...."[6]

Derek Dawes, head of Poison and Drug Control at St. Paul's Hospital in Vancouver, in 1994 gave me a copy of a 1993 research paper on drug-induced cognitive impairment written by Dr. James D. Bowen and Eric B. Lawson of the University of Washington's Division of Neurology in 1993, a report that supported many of my previous findings about benzodiazepines. I later met with Dr. Bowen in Seattle, and I was most impressed to discover that a chemical dependency team of doctors, psychologists, and other support personnel was working with him out of the Pacific Medical Center in Seattle. They appeared to be providing real support to people who had been adversely affected by prescription drugs. However, as I continued with my research, I realized that the positive approach I witnessed in Seattle was very rare.

My search for more answers next took me to the United Kingdom, where I learned that, as far back as 1967, two panels of experts advising the Committee of Enquiry into the Relationship of the Pharmaceutical Industry with the National Health Service expressed grave misgivings with regard to the interaction of profit and medicine, and characterized pharmaceutical advertising as flagrantly biased information, which was "uninformative [and] highly coloured." This panel recommended the formation of a "medicines commission," which they hoped would become "the accepted source of information on all matters concerning the use of medicines," thereby minimizing the dangers posed by a health-care system within which information on drugs available to doctors came "almost exclusively from the industry selling them."[7]

Unfortunately, many of the British panel's recommendations were never implemented, and, not surprisingly, nearly twenty-five years later (in 1990), the *British Journal of Addiction* published a paper warning that the prevalence of long-term benzodiazepine use represented an "epidemic in the making."[8] In a paper written by Dr. Malcolm Lader entitled "History of Benzodiazepine Dependence" published in the *Journal of*

Substance Abuse Treatment in 1991, he wrote: "The widespread usage of benzodiazepines has inevitably led to thousands of people becoming dependent, perhaps 500,000 in the U.K. and twice that number in the United States."[9] In fact, in London, England, the Victims of Tranquilizers (VOT) network was formed in 1993 with the initial intention of promoting understanding of "the suffering and molecular bio-chemical brain damage caused to thousands of British people by benzodiazepine tranquilizers prescribed by their doctors. ..." VOT addressed the "long-term physical, mental and sociological damage caused to thousands of innocent people who live in misery and suffering, often with their families and careers destroyed, because of years of profligate dispensation of dangerous benzodiazepine tranquilizers by doctors and drug companies. ..."

Its early initiative, it appeared, was to "persuade the government to both hold a public inquiry into the effect and use of these dangerous drugs by doctors, and to compensate victims in the same way as people injured by industrial accidents and diseases."[10] The organization documents complaints resulting from "the failure of the medical profession and institutions to recognize benzodiazepine addiction and the damage induced by those who prescribe the drugs," as well as "the failure of the National Health Service to provide appropriate treatment and after-care." Later, a 1995 VOT newsletter reported that the group had expanded, and was now a medical-legal support group as well as a strong lobby for claimants suing doctors and pharmaceutical companies.[11]

A very significant research paper "Adverse Behavioural Effects of Benzodiazepines" appeared in the *Journal of Family Practice* in 1997. Its authors—Dr. Sidney Zisook, M.D., and Richard A. De Vaul, M.D. of the Department of Psychiatry at the University of Texas Medical School—refer to their finding that "benzodiazepines are one of the most commonly prescribed classes of drugs in clinical medicine and that the risks of dependency (including ... increases in hostile-aggressive feelings and behavior and suicidal depression) are markedly attenuated by the physicians' awareness and acknowledgement of these adverse effects."[12] They expressed "increasing concern with overprescribing and indiscriminate use and the lack of clinical concern about these and other potentially serious adverse effects, including organic brain syndromes, sleep disturbances, paradoxical hostility, and rage.[13]

In Canada, important information regarding benzodiazepines has been available to doctors in virtually every medium imaginable for decades—research papers, medical reports, articles, books, films and videos, documentaries, you name it. *The Canadian Medical Association (CMA) Journal*, back in 1975, ran an editorial that reported the use of benzodiazepines as increasing in North America at the alarming rate of seven million prescriptions a year. The editorial expressed much concern that "the regulation of pleasure and pain in human life has gone beyond acceptable limits," and stated that "if the trend continues the entire population should eventually be tranquilized." The article further stated that "the use of these agents in the course of ... treatment for control of ... behaviour ... presents a definite moral conflict and the possibility of abuse of power by psychiatrists."[14]

In 1981, another article in the *CMA Journal* questioned the ethics of prescribing pills for emotional problems, and issued significant caveats regarding the potential addictive qualities of benzodiazepines, stating, for instance, that it was "often difficult for the physician to stop a pattern that he or she or another physician helped to initiate." The same article discussed the overall ineffectiveness of benzodiazepine treatment, and reported statistics regarding the higher frequency of visits associated with patients' previous tranquilizer use.[15]

In 1987, the opening statement on the College of Pharmacists of British Columbia's newsletter read: "This year, British Columbia's Drug Use Review Program is again focusing its attention on the overuse of benzodiazepines."[16] More recently (in 1991) the B.C. Drug and Poison Information Centre issued a report warning that benzodiazepine dependence may occur at therapeutic dosages when taken continuously for periods of time as little as two to four weeks, and that withdrawal is exceedingly difficult and potentially dangerous. This report, *Drug Usage Review*, clearly stated the very limited benefits and many risks involved with the prescribing of benzodiazepines.[17]

Yet many Canadian doctors, including my own, continued to prescribe Librium, Serax, and other benzodiazepines freely.

In 1992, the B.C. Medical Association (BCMA) issued a resolution that recommended physicians use great caution in the prescribing of benzodiazepines, especially for those with a personal or family history of alcohol or drug dependency, or for periods longer than two weeks.[18] In 1995, the Therapeutics Initiative, an evidence-based drug-therapy program at UBC that receives no funding from pharmaceutical companies, also issued a document to physicians cautioning that benzodiazepines should be prescribed only intermittently for short periods.[19] By this time, I had also met personally with the president of the BCMA, and the director of the UBC Therapeutics Initiative Program.

In October 1996, under the guidance of committee chair Dr. Mark Berner (who wrote articles regarding the adverse effects of benzodiazepines nearly fifteen years prior, notably: "Benzodiazepines: An Overview," an excellent paper published in the *Ontario Medical Review* in 1982), the CMA drafted new evidence-based guidelines on benzodiazepines arising from concern about their continued widespread use "despite uncertainty about their benefit/risk ratio." These recommendations stated that, "given the lack of evidence of benefit compared to placebo, and the significant association with adverse effects, anxiety may be best not treated with benzodiazepines." The recommendation regarding insomnia stated that "benzodiazepines, if used at all, should be considered only after sleep hygiene and non-pharmacological interventions are tried, and should be prescribed only for short term (up to 10–14 days) or occasional use."[20]

The new CMA draft guidelines also warn, in explicit detail, of the adverse effects I had suffered, such as cognitive impairment, memory impairment, impairment of attention and information processing, reduced reaction time and motor coordination, and impaired vision. They also mention that benzodiazepines greatly increase the risk of falls in elderly persons, and that doses equivalent to 5 to 10 milligrams of diazepam cause a level of impairment similar to 100 milligrams/decaliter of alcohol, or a blood alcohol level of 0.1, which is an indicator of being legally impaired. (I found this information particularly startling.) Withdrawal symptoms are listed as ranging from mild (sweating, tremors, palpitations, rebound insomnia) to severe (delirium, paranoia, seizures), and can encompass restlessness, agitation, anxiety, irritability; tremors, sweating, auditory (hearing voices) or visual disturbances (blurred vision, hallucinations); headaches, muscle aches, fatigue; disturbed sleep or concentration; numbness or tingling in fingers or toes; increased sensitivity to sound, bright lights, and/or touch; and an altered sense of smell.

Unfortunately, nearly three years later, these draft guidelines have still not been released, and I was advised on several occasions that they were still under "peer review." This process has undoubtedly stirred up fear among the medical profession of a possible legal backlash from patients who took these drugs for years on the advice of their trusted doctors, and who are still "hooked" on them. In essence, doctors have been asked to review and comment on the validity of material that calls attention to the dangers of drugs they have been prescribing for so long, making objectivity unlikely. Later I was told that the new guidelines were still in the "publication process."[21] Why so long? How many lives have to be affected or lost before action is taken?

While attending the National Health Forum in Richmond, B.C., in the fall of 1996, I met Dr. Dennis Kendal, the executive director of the College of Physicians and Surgeons in Saskatchewan, a very enlightened doctor who discussed the benzodiazepine issue with me in great detail. He was very knowledgeable and a genuine medical advocate for change. He seemed very interested in my activities, and even went so far as to write a letter to the CMA suggesting that they invite me, as a well-informed consumer advocate and researcher, to attend the follow-up sessions pertaining to the new prescribing guidelines. When I pursued this with a phone call to the CMA in Ottawa, however, I was informed that the list of invitees to the sessions had "already been prepared," and that it was "too late" to make any additions.

In 1995, in the midst of my research, a study conducted on benzodiazepine prescription patterns in my own North Shore community caused quite a stir when it was released and the story was given extensive coverage by the media. The findings of the study, entitled "Prescribing Benzodiazepines to North Shore Seniors: Time for Reappraisal," conducted by Dr. Nancy Hall, director of health promotion, and Dr. Kathy Bell, a geriatric physician, were released by North Shore Health. It revealed that 27 percent of seniors (30 percent of women, 20 percent of men) in our community were being prescribed benzodiazepines, at an average of 4.1 prescriptions per year, clearly indicating a lot of repeat prescriptions. The report listed these adverse effects:

Cognitive impairment:
- Impaired new learning
- Decreased short- and long-term memory
- Exacerbation of underlying dementia

Behavioral Problems:
- Paradoxical agitation
- Increased behavioral disinhibition

Psychomotor effects:
- Sedation, ataxia, and dizziness leading to falls
- Impaired visual-spatial ability
- Impaired operation of a motor vehicle, associated with increased accidents

Psychiatric symptoms:
- Appearance or worsening of depressive symptoms, often resolving after successful benzodiazepine withdrawal

Addiction and withdrawal:
- Addiction becomes more pronounced and withdrawal more difficult with long-term benzodiazepine use[22]

It was all there! And I could have eventually become one of those seniors, but fortunately by this time I had been off all these same drugs for over five years. The numbers were indisputably alarming, and I hoped that the publicity they stirred up would have some effect on doctors' attitudes, and at the consumer level. Seniors, whose health and energy are deteriorating, are a hard group to advocate for, and the side effects they experience from benzodiazepines can be subtle and are often incorrectly attributed to the aging process, or passed off as something else.

Concerns regarding benzodiazepine use by the elderly are certainly not new, however. Dr. Ray Ancill, head of Geriatric Psychiatry at the University of British Columbia, was quoted in a report published in *Your Better Health* magazine in 1991 entitled "Tranquility in a Bottle," saying that "many elderly Canadians stumble about in a kind of psychic fog" as a result of inappropriate use of benzodiazepines. This report also revealed statistics derived from a 1990 provincial health study that found that

"84,000 B.C. residents over the age of 65 are using benzodiazepines, and over 14,000 were getting amounts greater than that recommended by the Professional Advisory Committee of Pharmacare's Drug Usage Review Program." The report discussed the resulting complications of this overuse as including, among other things, "a kind of pseudo-dementia, that, in some cases, mimics Alzheimer's disease."[23] Yet Canadian doctors were *still* prescribing these drugs. Why?

My ongoing research revealed more and more of the same: *lots of studies, little action.* In 1987, an article in *The Annals of Internal Medicine*, the journal published by the American College of Physicians, discussed the "serious problem" of cognitive impairment and falls among elderly patients taking long-acting benzodiazepines.[24] The B.C. Provincial Health Officer's annual report for 1995 reported that approximately one-fifth of all men and women over the age of sixty-five had been dispensed tranquilizers and sleeping pills in the previous year, and warned of serious negative consequences such as confusion, decreased hand–eye coordination, and the loss of balance associated with falls and hip fractures. The report concluded that inappropriate prescribing not only indicated wasteful spending, but "may keep patients from recognizing and dealing with underlying problems" better treated with counseling.[25] The report recommended an awareness campaign to address this issue, but little happened. When I discussed this in two meetings with Dr. John Millar, the Chief Medical Health Officer for the province, who initiated the study, he implied that it was up to the Minister of Health to show leadership and allocate funds. Or, he indicated, *I* could do it through the media with some of my similarly affected colleagues—a further instance of "passing the buck."

What I was learning from my research was that benzodiazepine dependence in seniors has been scrutinized more extensively than for other demographic groups, and that attention focused on this group only because the data on prescriptions for the elderly are publicly available from Pharmacare and similar programs worldwide. Information about prescriptions to the general public, or those not covered through government medical insurance programs, is not as easy to obtain, as it is generally protected under privacy laws. Nonetheless, I suspect that there were similar trends of overprescribing in other groups as well.

Victims of inappropriate prescribing of benzos come from all walks of life and belong to all age groups. Women are affected more than men (roughly two-thirds of benzo prescriptions are issued to women, and one-third to men) not surprisingly, considering the early trends of gender-specific advertising campaigns. *It's Just Your Nerves*, a guidebook published by Health and Welfare Canada in 1981 (nearly two decades ago), addressed this troubling phenomenon directly, and contained numerous patient profiles and discussions of the tendency among physicians to use chemicals in addressing significant social issues affecting women, thereby worsening and complicating their problems, obliterating their coping mechanisms, and impairing their judgment.

An article published in *The Sociology of Health and Illness* back in 1979 concluded that the use of tranquilizers as a solution to social stress raised "clear moral and ethical issues that transcend the bounds of the medical profession and demand social, not medical answers."[26] In September 1987, an article titled "Women and Tranquilizers" that ran in *Modern Medicine of Canada* discussed research findings indicating that women visit primary-care physicians more frequently than men, and have a greater tendency to seek out medical assistance during times of life stress. Ironically, the (male) author observed, that "women deal with life crisis and stress in a more open, support-seeking and arguably healthier way than men,"[27] but he went on to add that these very attempts to seek support, and women's greater ability to freely express their feelings, were directly related to the higher level of benzodiazepine prescribing for women. This, the author suggested, ultimately caused them more problems than turning to the bottle would have done, as many men apparently do—the author also cited a U.S. Health Interview Survey that found that middle-aged men subjected to similar life stresses were far more likely to turn to alcohol than to visit a doctor.[28]

In the United States, statistics compiled by the Drug Abuse Warning Network regarding hospital emergency-department admissions show that benzodiazepines accounted for more suicide attempts each year than any other prescription drug. In one year studied, one in five drug-related suicides involved benzodiazepines, and 63 percent of all benzodiazepine emergencies were suicide attempts (intentional or drug-induced). Medical emergencies involving benzodiazepines peaked in 1975 and

1976, when 24,287 overdoses and 477 deaths were tied to these drugs.[29] In 1981, a study of 3,548 drug-overdose patients admitted to the emergency rooms of twenty-one Toronto hospitals revealed that 39 percent used benzodiazepines.[30]

The suicidal ideation created by these drugs was first referred to in 1966 in an article in *Psychopharmacologia* in Berlin, which noted "the development of suicidal thoughts,"[31] and in 1968 an article in the *Journal of the American Medical Association* referred to "the deepening of depression and an increase in suicidal thoughts and tendencies."[32] After that, references are frequent in medical literature. In 1972 an article in the *American Journal of Psychiatry* referred to an "ego alien suicidal ideation syndrome which was abrupt in onset and marked in severity and appeared in individuals who had been previously emotionally stable."[33] In 1982 an article in the *Ontario Medical Review* also referred to "ego alien suicidal ideation,"[34] and in 1983 a Raven Press New York publication referred to the drugs "blunting discretion and precipitating the taking of an overdose, combined with the amnesia and confusion created."[35]

In 1988, a bulletin of the Royal College of Psychiatrists in Britain refers to the amnesia caused and states that "the prescribing of benzos in cases of depression may have serious consequences and may precipitate suicide."[36] This was further corroborated in 1989 when an article in the *New Scientist* referred to benzos "provoking suicide."[37] On and on it went.

The effects of benzodiazepines in causing car accidents are also well documented in worldwide research. In 1982 an article was published in *Lancet* entitled "Driving under the Influence of Oxazepam (Serax): Guilt without Responsibility?" It notes that "benzodiazepines can blunt perception, confuse thought, and cause amnesia. The defendant described feeling 'fuddled and muddled' and driving less sharply than usual." This state of mind, if it was induced by the drug, would aggravate the difficulty of understanding that something was wrong, and of taking appropriate action, let alone suspecting a connection between the state of mind and taking the drug.

The case underlines the importance of warning patients about the possible effects of drugs on driving and other potentially dangerous activities and concludes that "a doctor who fails to warn his patient at least shares the responsibility for any accident that occurs as a result; in such a case the patient would seem to be entitled to recover damages from the doctor."[38]

In 1988, a research paper published in *Psychological Medicine* entitled "Cognitive Impairment in Long-Term Benzodiazepine Users" states that "the cognitive effects of long-term benzodiazepine may not only be debilitating but also may be dangerous.[39] Although benzodiazepines have not been directly implicated in road traffic accidents, Hindmarch (1986) estimated that up to 10% of drivers involved in car accidents had been taking psychoactive drugs, and that psychoactive drugs are responsible for the loss of 200,000 lives world wide on the roads each year."[40]

More recently, in 1996, a study conducted by the RCMP's Vancouver forensic laboratory indicated that sleeping pills had been detected in more than 40 percent of the blood samples taken from 1,441 dead or impaired Canadian drivers.[41] Another Canadian study found that elderly drivers who take tranquilizers are far more likely to get into serious accidents, the risk being between 25 percent and 45 percent higher than for other elderly drivers.[42] The effects of benzos in creating car accidents applies not only when people are taking the drugs, but also during the acute and protracted withdrawal stages, when a person is still affected by coordination, psychomotor, and cognitive problems. I had three car accidents in the first two years of withdrawal, and I realize now that, even then, I should never have driven a car, as I was endangering not only my life, but also those of others on the road.

In April 1996, Roger Korman, the general manager for IMS Canada (a division of Dun & Bradstreet Corporation and the largest health information company in the world), provided me with invaluable information and analyses about the prescribing habits of doctors at that time. Benzodiazepines continued to be prescribed in alarming proportions, even though antidepressants such as Prozac were showing a significant rise. Predominantly, benzos were being prescribed by general practitioners, with some physicians issuing as many as 620 prescriptions each quarter. Some of the top prescribing doctors issued ten refill prescriptions for each single new prescription, indicating significant long-term use of these drugs, in contraindication to all the recommendations and guidelines I was encountering in my research.

As time went on, and I collected more and more information and research, and interviewed literally hundreds of people nationally and internationally about the use of benzos, I came to realize that there were four key elements of the benzodiazepine problem: *unnecessary prescribing beyond a short term*; *serious and often dangerous side effects*, including addiction; the severity and duration of *withdrawal effects* (both acute and protracted); and the potential for *organic brain damage and potentially permanent cognitive impairment*. Literally hundreds of papers had been written covering these four topics. For me, protracted withdrawal and lingering cognitive impairment were of the utmost concern and a main focus of my time, energy, and efforts. I was still experiencing problems directly even though I had not used the drugs for five years, and it seemed these effects would continue for me.

In addition to those studies I've already mentioned, the following abstracts are only a sampling of the most significant findings I came across in my research in the area of cognitive impairment:

- **1987** Stefan Borg, "Sedative Hypnotic Dependence: Neuropsychological Changes and Clinical Course," Karolinska Institute, Sweden.
  Results: Neuropsychological impairment has been observed not only in connection with abuse or dependence, but also in long-term users showing no signs of abuse or dependence. Impairment seems to be present even after a period of abstinence.

- **1988** S. Levander, "Psychophysiology and Anxiety—Current Issues and Trends," *Pharmacological Treatment of Anxiety* 1:43–51, National Board of Health and Welfare, Drug Information Committee, Sweden.
  Results: Treatment with benzodiazepines may have negative therapeutic longtime effects, and may induce neuropsychological impairment, which in the worst case may be permanent.

- **1988** Susan Golombok, P. Moodley, M. Lader, "Cognitive Impairment in Long-Term Benzodiazepine Users," *Psychological Medicine* 18:365–74, United Kingdom.
  Results: Patients taking high doses of benzodiazepines for long periods of time perform poorly on tasks involving visual–spatial ability and

sustained attention. This is consistent with deficits in posterior cortical cognitive function. This implies that these patients are not functioning well in every day life and that they are not aware of their reduced ability. Further only after withdrawal do they realize that they have been functioning below par.

- **1989** H. Bergman, S. Borg, K. Engelbrektsson, B. Vikander, "Dependence on Sedative-Hypnotics: Neuropsychological Impairment, Field Dependence and Clinical Course in a 5-Year Follow-Up Study," *British Journal of Addiction* 84:547–53.
  Results: Despite some neuropsychological improvement, cerebral disorder diagnosed in a group of 30 patients who had been hospitalized 4–6 years earlier is often permanent through the years with neuropsychological status linked to long-term prognosis.

- **1991** H. Ashton, "Protracted Withdrawal Syndromes from Benzodiazepines," *Journal of Substance Abuse Treatment* 8:19–28.
  Results: Benzodiazepines may occasionally cause permanent or only slowly reversible brain damage.

- **1993** "Learning and Memory Impairment in Older, Detoxified, Benzodiazepine-Dependent Patients," *Mayo Clinic Proceedings* 68:731–37.
  Results: A neurological study in which twenty detoxified, benzodiazepine-dependent patients were matched with twenty detoxified, alcohol-dependent patients, along with twenty-two control subjects from a community sample showed that the benzodiazepine group had "significantly lower" scores on auditory-verbal learning tests. Most investigators believed that use of a combination of benzodiazepines had a "cumulative effect on memory" which "did not necessarily diminish with time."

- **1993** James D. Bowen and Eric B. Larson, "Drug-Induced Cognitive Impairment," *Drugs and Aging* 3(4):349–57.
  Results: Drug-induced cognitive impairment is a common cause of delirium and is frequently a confounding factor in dementia. Sedatives such as benzodiazepines have a particularly high risk of cognitive impairment.

- **1994** P.R. Tata, J. Rollings, M. Collins, A. Pickering and R. Jacobson, "Lack of Cognitive Recovery Following Withdrawal from Long-Term Benzodiazepine Use," *Psychological Medicine* 24:202–13.
  Results: Twenty-one patients with significant long-term therapeutic benzodiazepine use were given psychometric tests of cognitive function, pre- and post-withdrawal and at 6-month follow-up. The results demonstrated significant impairment in patients in verbal learning and memory, psychomotor, visuo-motor and visuo-conceptual abilities, compared with controls, at all three time points. Despite practice effects, no evidence of immediate recovery of cognitive function following benzodiazepine withdrawal was found. Modest recovery of certain deficits emerged at 6-month follow-up in the benzodiazepine group, but this remained significantly below the equivalent control performance.

- **1995** U. Tonne, A.J. Hiltunen, A.J. Vikander, B. Engelbrektsson, K. Bergman, H. Bergman, I. Leifman, S. Borg, "Neuropsychological Changes During Steady-State Drug Use, Withdrawal and Abstinence in Primary-Benzodiazepine Dependent Patients," *Acta Psychiatry* 91:299–304, Scandinavia.
  Results: Impairment on neuropsychological tests during steady-state drug use and withdrawal, and after discontinuation of benzodiazepines, was studied in primary benzodiazepine-dependent patients. This study confirmed earlier observations of neuropsychological deficits in long-term benzodiazepine-using patients and demonstrated that these changes are "partly" reversible by discontinuing drug intake.

- **1996** "Intellectual Impairment and Acquired Intellectual Deterioration in Sedative/Hypnotic Drug Dependent Patients," Department of Psychology and Psychiatric Clinic at Stockholm University, Sweden.
  Results: Every second patient dependent on sedative/hypnotic drugs showed signs of intellectual impairment. The general test profile indicated an acquired intellectual deterioration.

It was all there, known for many years.

While assembling this research, I continued with my extensive cognitive rehabilitation program on a weekly basis with Dr. Wild. Although I was determined to work hard at regaining my cognitive functioning, the many tests and exercises I was required to perform were at times confusing and exhausting. I worked with computer training programs, doing puzzles and visual, spatial, and logic exercises intended to retain and enhance my memory, recall, attention span, concentration, learning, problem solving, abstract thinking, and overall executive functioning. Dr. Wild would patiently explain the procedures over and over again, yet often I couldn't follow what she meant. Even when I felt as though I understood the instructions, my mind sometimes went blank when I tried to carry them out. The undeniable evidence of my cognitive limitations even now, after so much time had passed, was alarming. I could certainly bring a lot of information together, but it wasn't easy for me to sort it out into meaningful sections. I was determined to beat the odds, but I was very concerned. I wanted to resume my career and livelihood, and to re-establish my financial security, but I feared that might never be possible.

Only those closest to me were aware of my struggle. Around this time, political supporters approached me about running federally for both the Reform and the Liberal parties in the election of 1994. I was also encouraged to run as a member of the Legislative Assembly for all three of the main provincial parties in B.C.—there was even some discussion of the possibility that I might be a candidate for the provincial leadership, for either the Social Credit or the Liberal party. With regret, I had to acknowledge that, until I was fully recovered, I could not allow myself to consider these challenges. After all my hard work in business, the constant networking, and the years of community service, I truly felt my potential for growth had been stolen from me. I had always intended my involvement in business and politics to expand and diversify in the years to come, but I was becoming more and more fearful that I might never be able to resume the full scope of my career in either field.

At the same time I was honored to be nominated and selected by the Canadian University Women's Club as one of Canada's Most Notable Women in 1994, in recognition of my thirteen years of community service as a councilor. I was also one of two Canadian women invited to speak at the Women of Vision Leadership for the Nineties New World Conference in Washington, D.C., that year. The conference was attended by several hundred high-profile women from throughout North America who were committed to creating the society and world we would all like to see; my primary topic was "Business with a Social Conscience— Emerging Paradigms." I was also an active participant in workshops, including some on health, community, environmental, and human-rights issues. And, of course, I raised the issue of the overprescribing of benzos.

The timing of these accolades was ironic, given my ongoing difficulties, and it was very frustrating not to be able to take full advantage of the momentum I was gaining during that period, both professionally and politically. After attending the International Conference on Ethics in Long Beach California the following year, I was also awarded a Leadership Scholarship for Ethics in Business and Government from the Josephson Institute of Ethics in Marina Del Ray, California, one of the few Canadians who received this honor. Yet I had great difficulty writing a paper on ethics, because of my cognitive difficulties. My ability to make oral presentations had improved somewhat by that time, however, and that carried me through. I was also asked to consider taking on the presidency of Green Door Organics—a burgeoning natural and organic food organization—a position that came with a six-figure salary, benefits, and shares in the company. However, once again to my dismay, while I was able to chair meetings and gather relevant information, I still found myself having great difficulty synthesizing the data and putting together strategic marketing plans. I tried to cover up my deficiencies, using some coping strategies I was working on with Dr. Wild, but I wasn't confident that I could take on the role just yet.

Eventually the enterprise lost momentum and broke up as one of the partners left Vancouver. Once more I was faced with another ominous confirmation that the challenging and diversified marketing career I had loved so much, and which had been the source of my livelihood for twenty-eight years, was seriously compromised, as was my future financial security.

My interest and connection with the VOT group in Britain continued throughout this period, and I eventually spoke with the national coordinator of that organization, Dr. Reg Peart, a former nuclear scientist who continues to suffer some limitations today, more than a decade after discontinuing the various benzodiazepines he was prescribed for fourteen years. He saw his IQ drop to 80 for the first five years after discontinuing the drugs, and, like me, has suffered significant professional and financial hardships because he has not been able to resume his former career. Dr. Peart is in his sixties today, and remains dedicated to researching and advocating for the thousands of people damaged by these drugs. He has in fact provided me with hundreds of international research papers and references related to the effects of benzodiazepines that he has assembled over the past nine years, the most significant of which I have included in the bibliography and Appendices of this book.

When I told him of my pending lawsuit against my former family doctor, Reg brought to my attention a very similar lawsuit launched in New Zealand by a formerly successful businessman whose story is regrettably similar to my own. Bruce Barnett, who is now in his early seventies, once owned a luxury home and ran a multimillion-dollar television-rental business with stores nationwide, but lost everything once his doctor started him on a twenty-year descent into benzodiazepine addiction and drug-induced psychiatric illness. Bruce, whose slide into chemical dependency also began in 1966, was claiming more than $1 million from the Accident Rehabilitation and Compensation Insurance Corporation in New Zealand for lost income and expenses. Bruce is quoted in a newspaper article: "I did not know then that the tranquilizers, the benzodiazepines, re-route your mind as surely as pulling the wrong switch on the train track, or that they stop the mind from encoding properly, and affect rational thought. Nor did I know that they would dull my intellect and memory."[43]

As Bruce's mental and physical health deteriorated, he, too, was told he had a disease of the mind, was labeled manic-depressive, and was prescribed even more drugs, including antipsychotics. By 1975 he was starting to argue with his doctors that the pills were making him sick, but they insisted they were correcting a chemical imbalance, and that unless he took them he would likely end up institutionalized. He was further quoted in the same New Zealand newspaper article as saying: "This is a terrible problem ... you go to the doctor well or relatively well and they give you pills to take, then you are sick. Then they tell you that you were sick to start with." Bruce's legal claim included reference to the fact that the drugs had resulted in almost total loss of mental powers and a long-lasting and severe psychiatric illness.[44] I have spoken on the phone to him several times, and continue to follow his recovery and lawsuit with great interest.

Through VOT, I was also referred to Ove Carlsson in Sweden, a former executive in his fifties also going through a very similar experience—still not able to return to work after eight years off the drugs. As chairman of a growing patient-advocacy organization, he referred to 100 other members suffering from prolonged withdrawal syndromes.

Dr. Malcolm Lader, professor of Clinical Psychopharmacology, Institute of Psychiatry in London, England, a well-known researcher in the area of benzodiazepines, has written at least two papers referring to a "persistent withdrawal syndrome dominated by anxiety, either generalized or phobic or sometimes both, phobic behavioral disorder and panic attacks." In a 1991 paper published in the *British Journal of Addiction*, he refers to the protracted withdrawal syndrome as including persistent feelings of unsteadiness, neck tension, a "bursting" head, perceptual distortions, and muscle spasms.[45] In a 1994 paper published in the *Journal of Psychosomatic Research*, he refers to the fact that "many of the litigants involved in the large U.K. court case have suffered from prolonged disabilities of this type."[46]

A further research paper published in the *Journal of the American Board of Family Practitioners* in 1992 by J. Landry, David E. Smith, M.D., David R. McDuff, M.D. and Otis L. Baughman III, M.D., entitled "Benzodiazepine Dependence and Withdrawal Identification and Medical management," describes three disparate benzo use patterns with three distinct withdrawal syndromes.[47] In particular, reference is made to "a prolonged subacute, low-dose benzo withdrawal syndrome experienced by former long-term benzo users that can last for months and even years." In 1994 an article entitled "Management of Protracted Withdrawal," by Dr. Anne Geller MD, New York, and published in the *American Society of Addiction Medicine Journal*, describes persistent symptoms as including impaired concentration, derealization, and depersonalization, in addition to headaches, sleep disturbances, tension, irritability, and lack of energy.[48]

Although I felt that connecting with people like Dr. Reg Peart and Ove Carlsson validated my experience, I must say that hearing of their similar circumstances and struggles also brought on some very mixed feelings. Frankly, the fact that these individuals felt they had never fully recovered had frightening implications for me! I was very hopeful that my ongoing cognitive retraining with Dr. Wild would be of significant benefit to me, that I would continue to improve, but I was starting to realize that this was far from guaranteed. Nonetheless, I carried on with Dr. Wild's program with great determination and a positive attitude. I told myself I would get completely better.

I eventually learned of another group of more than 100 men and women, based in California, called the Tranquilizer Users Recovery Network (TURN). In TURN's excellent newsletter, section after section tackled the issues at the forefront of my mind regarding the consequences of prolonged tranquilizer use: "How long? How long? How long?" asked one headline. "Help, What's Happening to Me?" and "Will I Ever Recover?" were other examples.[49] If nothing else, I was relieved to know that I was not the only one asking these questions.

Late in 1994, I connected with Anna De Jonge, who had started a patients-rights advocacy group in New Zealand committed to helping people in their benzo claims against doctors. She and her members expressed concerns regarding the "closed-shop policy" that exists within the medical system, the inadequate accountability of doctors, and the need to encourage compliance with existing laws and codes of practice and legislation affecting proper health care and medical treatment. Anna has over thirty years of experience in the medical profession, and has helped patients advocate for their rights and the need for informed consent for more than eighteen years.

Another very important book, *Toxic Psychiatry* (1991) by Dr. Peter Breggin, who is described as "the conscience of American psychiatry," was given to me by a former long-time user of these same drugs. Dr. Breggin, a leading critic of psychotropic drugs and the psychopharmaceutical complex, has had a full-time psychiatric practice in Bethesda, Maryland, since 1968 and is a graduate of Harvard College, formerly a teaching fellow at Harvard Medical School, and a full-time consultant with the National Institute of Mental Health. He had a lot of credibility for me, and his exposé of the multibillion-dollar psychiatric drug industry was the most thorough, fearless discussion of the topic that I had come across to date. It was alarming. One section directly addressed the seriousness of long-term benzo consumption on mental function and the potential "brain shrinkage" or "brain atrophy" associated with the drugs. At least there were *some* medical doctors who were issuing a wake-up call to their peers regarding the harmful effects and the epidemic of dependence on legal drugs.

Dr. Garth McIver, a well-known chemical-dependency doctor who had recently returned to Vancouver, and a member of the North American Society for Addiction Medicine, brought several papers and books written about benzodiazepines to my attention in 1996. He too knew of the seriousness of benzo overprescribing, and acknowledged that we were "on the same page," and encouraged me to continue to pursue my advocacy efforts. One of the books, written in 1990, entitled *Benzodiazepines: Current Concepts, Biological, Clinical and Social Perspectives,* had a section on the forensic implications of benzodiazepine use. I saw the author of that section, a U.K. psychiatrist, H.A. McClelland, as a potentially strong voice of warning on the subject. Dr. McClelland delved deeply into the many disruptive side effects of benzos, including psychomotor and memory impairment, amnesia, dependence, paradoxical aggression, emotional disinhibition, and impairment in learning new verbal and visual information, as well as "evidence that cognitive defects are found even in therapeutic regimes continued long-term."[50]

What I found particularly interesting was his discussion of the responsibility of the doctor in prescribing these drugs, and the potential for lawsuits "when untoward effects arise from this treatment." "The doctor has a duty of care to the patient," he stated, "and if there is a breach of that duty, leading to harm to the patient, then this can lead to a claim for negligence against the doctor." He went on to define one of the main areas of physicians' legal vulnerability with respect to benzodiazepines as pertaining to informed consent: "Have the risks of benzodiazepines, including dependency and side effects, been properly discussed with the patient?" he asks. "Any legal action for negligence would have a high chance of success if side effects developed for which the patient was unprepared and, as a result of which, unforeseen consequences developed."[51]

Dr. McClelland refers to benzodiazepine use as "involuntary intoxication," and cites instances of crimes such as murder, assaults, theft, and shoplifting, as well as car accidents, that occur when people are under the influence of these drugs and unaware of their dangerous side effects. He also mentioned the early activities surrounding the Benzodiazepine Solicitors' Group in Britain (actively supported by the VOT), who were then investigating approximately 1,500 lawsuits against manufacturers of benzodiazepines, as well as prescribers of the drugs, and government health authorities. (The number of cases later expanded to more than 5,000, represented by 1,000 firms of solicitors, making it the biggest personal-injury group action ever brought before the British courts.) The bulk of these cases were being fought with the support of legal aid and, unfortunately, in 1993, a judge ruled that providing legal aid for this massive action was no longer financially viable. Public funding for the cases was suddenly frozen, and the internal audit relating to these products was suspended. As a result, related lawsuits against prescribing doctors and health authorities were also struck.[52] This was a travesty of justice, and I can only surmise that this too was a concerted attempt to silence victims and survivors of benzo overprescribing.

When I spoke on the phone to Dr. McClelland for the first time, asking for further information about this litigation group, he was very cooperative and informative, but I soon realized that he assumed I was a doctor. In his subsequent fax to me, addressed to "Dr. Gadsby," he was quick to disclose that he did not do any work for the solicitors' group, and was "pleased to say" that his forensic reports were for the defendants, one of the pharmaceutical companies being sued. He also decried the fact that, when legal aid was pulled from these cases by the government, £30 million (the equivalent of $75 million Canadian, not a penny of which was received by victims) had already been spent.[53] I later discovered that Dr. McClelland, who was obviously very knowledgeable about the dangers of benzodiazepines, had appeared as a witness for the pharmaceutical companies in the lawsuits against the drug manufacturers in Britain. Needless to say, I was extremely disappointed. He was not an advocate for medical accountability and systemic change, but rather a defense expert witness for the medical establishment.

Nevertheless, discovering the U.K. group and their members' 5,000 lawsuits had a big impact on me. I was not alone. Other victims/survivors were seeking compensation—thousands of them, their lives devastated the same way mine had been. They, too, were taking on the system, the politics, the injustice. The more I learned, the more motivated I became. As well as pursuing a potentially precedent-setting lawsuit, I was intent upon putting myself in a position to exert influence for systemic change in any way I could. I was becoming more and more determined to get the message out to the public about the dangers of benzodiazepines.

In 1994 I made contact with the executive director of the B.C. Alcohol and Drug Education Service, and was somewhat surprised to find that their focus was mainly on society's alcohol problems, and on such approaches as educating kids through the schools. Although these objectives were obviously important, I felt they were rather narrow. While just about everyone knows about the perils of alcohol abuse and addiction, as well as the problems associated with illegal drugs such as heroin, cocaine, and marijuana, very few people really understand the very serious ramifications of using mood-altering prescription drugs dished out indiscriminately by hundreds of thousands of doctors. There wasn't any patient-education effort being made in relation to iatrogenic chemical dependency, or any patient advocacy being done by the Alcohol and Drug Education Service. As a result of my inquiries there, I put my name forward to be on their board, and it wasn't long before I was appointed. Right away, I set to work trying to draw attention to this issue.

At a seminar put on by the Pacific Addiction Institute at the University of British Columbia in 1994, I met a woman about my age named Linda[54] who had been through every bit as much as I had with prescribed benzodiazepines. When she was just a young girl, Linda had experienced chronic gastrointestinal problems. But when her family doctor was unable to determine a cause, he concluded that her symptoms were "all in her head." Thereafter, doctor after doctor minimized or dismissed her ongoing discomfort, and she was eventually prescribed Valium to address her "emotional" problems. She was never warned of any risks associated with the drugs she was advised to take day and night for years. Whenever she questioned the situation, she was, in fact, encouraged to continue with them, and was repeatedly assured that she had problems for which the pills were a viable remedy.

By the time Linda was in her thirties, she was hopelessly addicted to benzodiazepines, having been prescribed such drugs as Ativan, Serax,

Librium, Dalmane, and Valium continuously for years, and e
she started to use alcohol with the pills, to alleviate the escalatin
caused by the drugs. Not surprisingly, she was eventually to land in the
emergency department of nearly every major hospital in the Vancouver
area after overdosing on combinations of drugs and alcohol. She was
often institutionalized for up to a month at a time, only to be sent home
with more pills.

Linda became more and more unstable and unpredictable over the
years, behaving erratically and irrationally at times, and her physical
health deteriorated to the point of near-death on many occasions. She
was dangerously thin, and suffered from pancreatic disease, liver dysfunction, and jaundice. Her bone marrow had also begun to disintegrate.
Linda was finally referred to an addiction specialist and learned that her
many emotional, physical, and behavioral problems could be directly
related to her long-term use of benzodiazepines. Over the twenty-five
years, she had always thought the drugs were a treatment for her "illness,"
having been diagnosed as both manic-depressive and schizophrenic at
various stages of her chemical dependency.

I also met with Dr. Ray Baker, the head of Addiction Medicine at the
University of British Columbia, and a chemical-dependency specialist of
some prominence who developed the program for medical students and
who regularly spoke at conferences throughout North America on addiction. I was interested in finding out more about his approach to the
overprescribing of tranquilizers and sleeping pills. I brought him a lot of
the research materials I had assembled, a number of which he had never
seen. I found him to be quite responsive and knowledgeable at our first
meeting, and for some time afterward. However, once I told him I had
been there myself, and that I was very concerned about the extent of my
cognitive impairment, and that I was proceeding with legal action against
Dr. MacGillivray, his attitude toward me changed dramatically. When
we met in person again, he was guarded and apprehensive. It was clear
that the implications of my actions for change were not lost on him.
In fact, after one of our discussions, Dr. Baker went so far as to e-mail
numerous doctors in Canada and the United States about the serious
medical/legal significance of my claims. I know many people have found
Dr. Baker to be very helpful in treating them for chemical dependency,

but they are not people who have been willing to "rock the boat" and express their anger toward the medical community.

I ran into a similar roadblock when I met with Dr. Doug Graham, head of the alcohol and drug program for the B.C. Medical Association in May 1994. It was quite evident that he knew a great deal about the dangers of benzodiazepines going back to the 1970s, but he seemed not particularly interested in helping me with the movement for systemic change. He eventually became uncooperative, and later stopped returning my calls altogether. He was obviously, first and foremost, a loyal supporter of the medical establishment, and certainly not an advocate for change.

Time after time, I had the same experience: The door was initially open, but once doctors working within the system found out about my pending lawsuit, things changed abruptly. Clearly, the issue I was discussing was entirely too controversial, and even those who were inclined to agree with me in principle were wary of saying anything that might alienate them from their colleagues. For those with a vested interest, I was threatening.

The more resistance I encountered, however, and the more political and medical denial I witnessed, the more I realized that consumers needed to know more about these drugs, and they weren't likely to get the information from their doctors. I decided that a television documentary exposing the sordid problem of benzos was sorely needed to create awareness. I began to make phone calls and inquiries, and after some digging I eventually linked up with Jack McGaw, an award-winning TV producer and the former host of CTV's national investigative news program W5. He had some familiarity with the issue and knew of other people affected; moreover, he had spent most of his life investigating controversial issues through the medium of television. He agreed to work with me on the project. My role, as co-executive producer, was to help raise funding for the project, help bring together a team, and supply the research (which I had already done). It would take three years to make this project a reality.

I was also re-elected to the board of Lions Gate Hospital in 1995, and immediately brought the topic of overprescribing to the table there as well. Dr. Nancy Hall's recently released report referring to the high incidence of benzodiazepine prescribing to seniors, particularly on the North

Shore, provided a good launching pad for a campaign to bring more attention to the issue. Not surprisingly, my efforts were again met with uneasiness and objections. I pointed out to my colleagues that many people are introduced to benzodiazepines during hospital stays, which is sometimes appropriate (before major surgery, for instance) but often unnecessary. Once they leave the hospital, they often get refills and soon become chemically dependent for months and years, research shows. This element of the problem alone warranted the board's attention, I added.

After quite a struggle, I put forward a motion to investigate the problem through the hospital's Therapeutics and Quality Control Committee, but, suffice it to say, the whole topic met with stonewalling. Certain parties were already quite upset about Nancy Hall's study and the conclusions drawn from it, which dared to point the finger at many local doctors' prescribing habits. The head of the pharmacy department at the hospital was asked to be part of a proposed committee to look at the problem, but he made it quite clear that he was not at all eager to be involved.

Several years later, however, this same person spearheaded an initiative known as "academic detailing" in British Columbia, a program that provides physicians with impartial prescribing advice from a clinical pharmacist (whose salary is paid by Pharmacare) during individual visits several times a year. This project went about achieving its results in a non-confrontational way, but its objective was to reduce the escalating financial costs of inappropriate prescribing, and in fact the program began in response to quickly rising spending within Pharmacare. Although the offshoot effect of this program helps to protect patients, it was initially geared to saving money, not lives. It did nothing to help people who were already hooked on the drugs, who needed help and proper medical supervision to end their addiction. Nonetheless, it was, and continues to be, a step in the right direction.

A similar situation exists in regard to the triplicate-prescription program in British Columbia, another potentially valuable initiative introduced to cut costs and encourage a more responsible pattern of prescribing. This system requires that one copy of each prescription for certain drugs, now including benzodiazepines, be kept by the physician, and another copy by the pharmacist; a third copy is forwarded by the pharmacist to Pharmacare for entry on "PharmaNet," a computer database accessible by pharmacists, thereby providing them with up-to-date information on patients' prescription records. While the system is intended to detect potential adverse interactions of drugs, it is rarely used to call the prescribing physician's judgment into question, and has a tendency to target "bad consumers," not "bad doctors." Pharmacists are far more likely to use the information on PharmaNet to intercept patients who may be "double-doctoring," rather than doctors who are overprescribing. It is worthwhile to note, however, that a 1995 study conducted by Dr. Molly Thompson of the B.C. Ministry of Health Research and Evaluation Branch concluded that physicians' "prescribing practices did not correspond with current guidelines." Nothing new in that! But what was particularly significant about her study was that "of those people dispensed potentially inappropriate prescriptions, 68% received them from a single physician,"[55] which indicated much less double-doctoring than the medical profession would have you believe.

As well as serving on the board of the Alcohol and Drug Education Service and the Lions Gate Hospital board in the mid-1990s, I also became a member of the North Shore Detox Services Committee. In my role with this committee, which was to continue for two years, I was able to bring to the table my personal story regarding my horrendous experience with tranquilizers and sleeping pills, my medically unsupervised drug withdrawal, and the appalling lack of services and resources available to me on the North Shore during that time. In 1996 a much-needed, long-overdue withdrawal-management program was eventually set up to provide supervision for people withdrawing from both prescription and non-prescription drugs, and/or alcohol, at home. Within the new program, a nurse coordinator, outreach counselor, and program physician made up a team to assess detox needs, assist patients during withdrawal, and refer these clients to appropriate community resources. I was very pleased to finally see this program in place, but unfortunately it is still not well publicized or utilized. The last time I inquired, approximately 100 people had received help in getting through some kind of drug withdrawal. Not many, but it was a start.

By the mid-1990s, my activities, research, and advocacy had ruffled more than a few feathers. But the more I spoke out, the more people came forward, many of them seeking help. It seemed that just about everyone had a relative, friend, or acquaintance with a story. I was inter-viewed for the CBC television program "Fifty Up," which aired across Canada in 1996, and focused on the cognitive effects of benzodiazepines and this aspect of my recovery. Ironically, the producer of that program, I found out, had done a two-part television program investigating over-prescription of Valium and its side effects, which aired back in 1983 on CBC TV. After the 1996 program was broadcast, I received many more phone calls and letters. Although I was not able to respond to all who called in from across the country expressing strong support and interest in my advocacy activities, I spoke with as many as I could.

By the end of 1996, my year-long cognitive retraining sessions with Dr. Wild had reached a conclusion. "No further significant improvement" could be expected.[56] It was time to move forward with my lawsuit.

CHAPTER TWELVE

Lawsuit in the News

MY COMPLAINT AGAINST Dr. MacGillivray was set to go to trial in late February 1997. The cognitive impairment I suffered as a result of long-term benzodiazepine use, originally confirmed by Dr. Klonoff (the neuropsychologist who did the first round of testing in December 1992), had been reconfirmed not only by Dr. Wild in 1993, but also by Dr. James Schmidt.

Dr. Schmidt, who had conducted four days of independent neuropsychological tests on me late in 1995, had prepared a twenty-two-page neuropsychological report of his findings, indicating that, among other things, I had suffered a "consistent pattern of disruption of cognitive functions" that had "an adverse effect on passive attention, problem solving and organization, and general learning and retention of material." This, in turn, had an impact upon "higher-order language functioning, affecting both comprehension and expression in both written and oral spheres."[1] My cognitive functioning had improved noticeably since the first round of testing (in 1992) and was above average, but still below expectations for someone with my education and background. The only psychiatrist to see me regularly once I was off the drugs as a condition of my disability, Dr. Parkinson, also provided an expert opinion, stating that despite the fact that I could "clearly not function at previous levels ... at no time" in the years since withdrawing from the drugs had I shown "any evidence of major affective [bipolar] disorder and that I did not require active psychiatric treatment."[2] These statements by Drs. Schmidt and Parkinson were of great significance to me both personally and legally. I knew that

Dr. MacGillivray's defense team would try to prove I suffered from psychiatric disorders to explain away my cognitive difficulties, and Dr. Parkinson's clear indication that I did not have any symptoms of these in the five years since discontinuing the pills was of crucial importance to my case.

I had interviewed about a dozen lawyers with experience in medical malpractice, and discovered that most of them wanted a substantial retainer to take on my case. This was not easy for me to come up with, given my declining financial situation, and it gave me a clue to just how thoroughly the odds are stacked against the average citizen in the kind of David-and-Goliath mismatch with the medical establishment that I was preparing for. Canadian doctors facing malpractice suits have their legal fees paid by the Canadian Medical Protection Association (CMPA) out of Ottawa, which has millions of dollars in reserves. (The CMPA coverage, incidentally, is paid for in part by doctors, but is also subsidized heavily by the federal government through taxpayers' money. In 1996, for instance, the B.C. government contributed $15.75 million toward doctors' medical and legal liability insurance.)[3]

Interestingly, in response to the need for a more level playing field, the Allied Lawyers Response Team (ALERT) was formed in the United Kingdom after legal-aid funding was pulled from the complainants in the class-action suit launched there against benzodiazepine manufacturers and doctors. ALERT is a group of lawyers who were "no longer going to wait until injured patients come to us," according to Graham Ross, one of the organization's participants. "We are going to research and develop litigation against drug manufacturers, government and authorities as soon as we learn of potential problems … in that way … we will help reduce the numbers of people avoidably damaged by products and drugs." Mr. Ross has also said that "medical treatment causes illness. You would expect that by now some system was in place to control this problem."[4] I agree; you would expect so. However, this is not the case, not in Britain, and certainly not in Canada.

Robert Strand[5] had agreed to take my lawsuit on a contingency basis, with his fees payable as a percentage of a successful judgment in the trial. Robert came well recommended as a tough trial lawyer and I felt he was a strong advocate. In a letter to me, he had told me he was "looking forward to breaking new ground in this particular area of law."[6]

I had been working with Robert for more than a year when I began to see that he was feeling somewhat overwhelmed by the immense amount of research and evidence I had amassed, and the many complex aspects of the case I wanted to discuss with him. And for reasons that I suspect were related to our contingency agreement, he did not always seem willing to take the time necessary to familiarize himself with the evidence. I knew that, in medical malpractice cases, clients who are unable to pay legal costs in advance are often relegated to lower-priority status by their lawyers.

I was prepared to work very closely with Robert to find expert witnesses, supply pertinent research, and help plan the overall strategy for my potentially precedent-setting case. I had been researching benzos for more than six years by this time and had met many potential expert witnesses. In addition to recouping my financial losses—which were in excess of one and a half million dollars—I had come to realize that my success would be very significant to countless others in the same position, and could have a huge impact upon the medical community and their duty to obtain "informed consent" from their patients before embarking on these kinds of harmful drug treatments.

As I continued to supply Robert with more and more specific evidence pertaining to the many aspects of my case (i.e., the inappropriateness of long-term use of benzodiazepines, the side effects and potential brain damage associated with this use, that they should not be given to people who display addiction tendencies or are known to use alcohol, that patients should be monitored closely for side effects, that the physician has a duty to assist and supervise the patient through withdrawal if chemical dependency has occurred, that two central nervous system drugs are not to be administered simultaneously), he became somewhat overwhelmed and impatient with my expectations of him.

In fact, the rapport between Robert and me eventually deteriorated. He was quite short-tempered at times, and I didn't like his tendency to make unilateral decisions, sometimes going against my specific instructions; after all, I was his client. For example, we had agreed to have a jury trial—after discussion, we had both thought it was very important for a positive outcome in my case—but then he later decided against it.

I kept hoping everything would fall into place, however, and we moved ahead to the point of legal discovery. Things hit a low point when he told me to "shut up" in front of Dr. MacGillivray during his pretrial discovery. This humiliation was difficult to accept, but Robert later apologized over lunch for his short temper.

Later on, at a pretrial conference in October 1996, when he and the defense lawyer were asked by the judge if a settlement conference was proposed, he did not respond, in spite of the fact that I had advised him previously that I would like to try to settle out of court. I stood up to be acknowledged by the judge, and to say "I would welcome this," but he abruptly told me, "Sit down and be quiet." After the pretrial conference was over, he said to me in a threatening manner as he was leaving the courtroom, "If you do that again ..." This took me completely by surprise, and I didn't know what to make of it. Things did not improve after that, despite my attempts to understand and reconcile our differences, and he subsequently withdrew from my case in November 1996.

This left me in the highly undesirable position of finding another lawyer who could take on the case, with the trial just four months off, in February 1997. The trial was expected to take about fifteen days, and a cancellation could mean up to a two-year delay, and I certainly did not want to see that happen. I had far too much at stake, and I wanted to get on with my life.

After considerable searching, I eventually found another lawyer to take my case on a contingency basis. The law firm Shirley Khan worked with advertised its medical background, its legal team with seventy years' personal-injury experience, and its success in medical-negligence cases resulting in major injury and loss, including brain damage. Shirley had ten years in personal-injury law, had been married to a brain surgeon, and came from a family of doctors. Her assistant (a woman) was a former doctor. I thought they would be a good team.

I worked feverishly for days to provide Shirley with the information she needed to represent me in the case, which was exhausting and confusing for me, given my cognitive limitations—writing summaries and other documents in point form, reconstructing events in my life, listing incidents of overdoses and paradoxical reactions and correlating these to pills I was on and Dr. MacGillivray's actions, summarizing known side effects and contraindications from the *CPS*, and providing names of some potential expert witnesses. She seemed confident and attuned to the overprescribing of these drugs and their significance, and I trusted that she would quickly get up to speed regarding the various aspects of my legal claim. There was, after all, a fairly well-established information base, and I was prepared to work very closely with her in putting together the case strategy. Her expertise and experience as a medical-malpractice lawyer was what was needed to pull it all together.

Both Alan and Carrie had agreed to be witnesses to what life with me was like both when I was on the pills and after I stopped them. Theirs would be significant testimony. As we approached the trial date, however, Deb informed me that she didn't wish to testify in court. This was, of course, disappointing, but I respected her decision. Deb disliked publicity; she had a busy career and generally just wanted to be free of all the "Sturm and Drang" that had characterized her earlier life. She supported my legal actions against Dr. MacGillivray, as she knew only too well how seriously all our lives had been affected by the pills.

I had a good feel for what had to proven at a medical malpractice trial for negligence—that is, that the patient was harmed because the physician failed to meet the required standards of skill and care. Specifically, a patient must prove four points in order to recover damages: (1) that the physician owed him/her a duty, (2) that the physician did not fulfill that duty, (3) that he/she suffered an injury, and (4) that there was a causal connection between the physician's breach of duty and the patient's injury.

Despite my positive first impression, as the trial date approached, I became increasingly concerned that my lawyer still had a lot of preparation to do. On the second day of court proceedings, it was revealed that she had not amended my statement of claim to reflect my asset losses— that is, my investment property sold as a direct result of my financial situation, the lost rental revenue, and RRSP withdrawals—despite the fact that financial documentation concerning these and other losses had been assembled well beforehand for a settlement brief. The judge would not allow any amendment after the fact. Other documents necessary to establish my financial losses, including substantial past and future income, and damages of approximately $2.4 million, including a lucrative job offer turned down because of my cognitive problems, were not presented as evidence.

Legal issues aside, the whole experience surrounding my lawsuit against Dr. MacGillivray quickly became rather surreal, and I watched with some incredulity as my whole life was opened up for public scrutiny. It didn't take me long to realize I was in for a very emotional and stressful experience. Almost immediately, court testimony graphically illustrated the decline of my life—once full of hopes and dreams and potential—into one of mediocrity, inconsistency, and chaos. It was very difficult for me to sit through much of it with my dignity intact. It was also disconcerting to see it played out so clearly. What seemed obvious in retrospect had been a complete mystery to me at the time, as it had to everyone close to me. My life could have been so different.

My lengthy turn on the witness stand over two and a half days, particularly my cross-examination, was a grueling test of stamina, and Jim Lepp, Dr. MacGillivray's chief lawyer, was a formidable foe. He was well prepared, as was his assistant, and very intent upon establishing that alcohol was the primary cause of my problems over the years. He used every comment ever written in Dr. MacGillivray's records regarding my admitted drinking habits to try to support this theory. Of course I had never denied that Dr. MacGillivray had occasionally chided me for my drinking; the point was that I never understood that drinking in combination with the medications he was prescribing could endanger my life, or cause disinhibiting, violent, paradoxical reactions.

Mr. Lepp also tried to suggest that I enjoyed the "euphoria" the drugs gave me, thinking I could "fly like a bird" (the night Carrie had to coax me down from my deck railing) and so on. When I pointed out that this same *euphoric* person more often crawled under beds in paranoia, he quickly switched gears and suggested that these "mood swings" were a manifestation of my mood disorder—I was being treated by a psychiatrist over the years, was I not? One minute I was an alcoholic drug abuser, simply seeking euphoria, the next I was the victim of a rampaging psychiatric disease—whatever suited the strategy, and whatever best clouded the real issue. At other times he went on and on about my "outbursts," and how I let my anger build until I just blew up, insinuating that I was just a hothead, unable to control myself. I pointed out to him that I had had no problem controlling my anger before or after my years on the drugs. I illustrated this by pointing out that I was pretty ticked off at him, for instance, but was not about to come over and hit him, or bite his finger, as I had the police officer's on that one occasion. He replied that he'd try not to get too close.

Of course the convoluted psychiatric paper trail created over my years on the drugs was used to maximum effect. It was amazing to see this brought to light chronologically, building and compounding upon itself until it had a sordid life of its own. Testimony from the doctors who created it was used extensively, to my great frustration, and the onus was on my lawyer and our expert witnesses to prove that all of the psychiatric mumbo-jumbo had been contrived to serve as a smokescreen for those whose livelihood relies upon denying the damaging effects of mind-altering prescription drugs. It wasn't an easy task, and, as the trial progressed, I began to believe that Shirley was missing numerous opportunities to make and substantiate this point.

To be sure, conceding the drugs' causal role in creating psychiatric symptoms (well documented by research over many years) would have been an act of self-incrimination on the doctors' part. And when lawyers fail to obtain testimony from medical professionals to support such a connection, judges and jurors simply don't have the information necessary to recognize it. As a result, the fact that complainants' psychiatric and behavioral problems came about *as a result* of their medical treatment, or during withdrawal from this "treatment," can be difficult to establish legally, and requires a skillful, highly competent lawyer.

Jim Lepp also tried to suggest that, once I brought the 1975 article regarding the deaths associated with mixing alcohol and Valium to Dr. MacGillivray's attention, I continued to take the pills with full awareness of the risk. Of course, no one had ever told me at the time that Librium, Serax, Dalmane, or Restoril were the same as Valium, and I explained this. I had never heard the term "benzodiazepines" back then, and did not understand that they all had essentially the same effects. And, of course, the real relevance is that Dr. MacGillivray all but dismissed my concerns regarding Valium at that time, reassuring me and convincing me I should continue taking the drugs. Jim Lepp brought up incident after incident of my being injured, arrested, or acting out—attributing my state of confusion and unsteadiness solely to alcohol, yet the significance of the combination of drugs in my system (for twelve years both sleeping pills and tranquilizers) was denied or ignored. The fact that the effects of the pills were never noted, recorded, or discussed during many hospital stays worked against me as well. Nearly every time I had gone off the deep end or injured myself, and wound up in the hospital, medical personnel inevitably made a note that I seemed to be under the influence of alcohol.

In addition, all of the emotional, mental, and physical distress I confided to Dr. MacGillivray and various psychiatrists during my chemically dependent years were used to support the theory that I suffered from "chronic anxiety" and, ironically, as justification for the ongoing drug treatment (which was actually causing the anxiety). Later, my lawyer pointed out that "chronic anxiety" seemed to be a regular entry in my medical chart by the late 1980s (after years of *anti*-anxiety treatment), but was not once mentioned in the earlier records, in the 1970s. It all came down to a chicken-and-egg argument, and I only hoped that the judge was listening very carefully.

When Alan took the stand, nervous but dignified, to give his testimony about our early life together, the birth of our children, and our early plans for the future, he painted a near-perfect picture. Among other things, he recollected that I had been a good companion and wife, and a "very, very protective mother." He called me a "go-getter," eager to achieve in all areas of my life. He talked about our move out west, my easy adaptation to change, and my love for our children. He remembered me then as solid and stable, consistent throughout major challenges. He denied ever having witnessed any untoward expression of anger or rage during his years with me *before* the pills.

He was also asked about Derek's illness and death, and it was very difficult for us both to have to relive that terrible experience in a public forum. Alan had to discuss the anguish we went through, the grieving, and the joint attempts at counseling after Derek's death. As I sat watching, I knew we were sharing a unique bond of resentment at the nature of the questioning. Was I diagnosed with anything during those sessions, Alan was asked. A mental disorder? Dr. MacGillivray's attorney tried to establish that I began behaving irrationally directly after Derek's death, that it was this tragedy, specifically, which marked the beginning of my mental and emotional deterioration, but Alan steadfastly denied it. Aside from the tremendous grief I was experiencing at the time, he stated, my mental state and behavior were entirely normal immediately after Derek's death. When asked about his thoughts on the eventual prescriptions for tranquilizers, Alan said that he "had no reason to think that [I] ought not to take them. The doctor was prescribing them. ..."

In the years following, however, Alan testified, I began to be "a little exaggerated" in my reactions to things. I was often "unreasonably angry." Alan recounted incidents during which the police were called, when officers had to calm the children. It was "horrific," he said, "and not something I had been used to ... she was acting in such an exaggerated way; she could not be calmed down." He testified that at times he felt it would have been more appropriate to call an ambulance, but I was so erratic that the police had to be summoned. Of course Alan's testimony eventually came around to describing the ferocious rages, the violence, the times I was taken to jail or the hospital. He described me as very dangerous at these times, the incident with the gun being only one illustration. "It's just such a refreshing thing to see her as she is now," he offered finally, describing our relationship in recent years as "very, very, good." She is "an entirely different person than in the seventies and eighties; I find her amazingly patient, calm and rational. ..."[7]

Unquestionably, Carrie's testimony was the most painful of all, drawing a bleak picture of an incredibly troubled childhood, filled with "uncertainty ... chaos and disorder." She told of various violent incidents, like the time she spilled some food and I threw a plate at her head, and testified that my behavior was "erratic and strange, totally bizarre, uncalled for." She told one story about coming home after she and I had a small argument and finding the locks had been changed on the house—"I was not even allowed to come in and get my clothes." At such times she had to go stay with her father, but she admitted that such times she *wanted* to go live with her dad because she "just couldn't take the day-to-day uncertainty." I threatened to have her cat put to sleep, to sell the house, that she would never see her friends again. She described me as abusive toward her friends, sometimes saying nasty things about their parents. "The stigma of my mom's behaviour definitely pervaded my life," she testified. "Her reputation preceded her, and it was a scary thing for anyone that I knew to have to meet her." Life at home with me for Carrie during those years had been a relentless and abusive ordeal, I'm sorry to say. There's no other accurate way to describe it.

As I listened to Carrie, I longed to turn back time and change everything, but instead I could only sit helplessly, wiping away tears and listening to her tell of a monstrous life I could hardly recall. As Carrie sat there in the witness stand, looking so beautiful in a black jacket with white blouse, she, too, began crying, and I was unable to stop myself from speculating about how living in such a crazy way through her formative years had shaped her personality and trust for the world. "I felt I had to watch over her," she testified, "so I often chose not to go out." She told of hiding all the pill bottles when things started getting out of hand, and my frequent talk of ending it all. "I always knew there was something wrong with her," she went on; "it was sort of an understanding in our house that she wasn't all there, so to speak, that something was affecting her. ..."[8] Carrie described how she distanced herself from me for a while, but how, by the grace of God, things began to change dramatically soon after that, as I stopped taking the pills.

After her testimony, Carrie and I went out of the courtroom together and I put my arms around her, hugged her, and told her how much I loved her, and I thanked her for sticking with me through the years.

Although I thought I had prepared myself for Dr. MacGillivray's testimony, there is nothing I could have done to avoid the overpowering feelings of anger and resentment it brought up. In light of what I knew by that time, and the years of hell my family and I had been through, absolutely nothing he said made any sense. Listening to him so offhandedly discuss my difficult years as his patient, and the murky rationale he used for treating me with the pills, was excruciatingly painful for me. There he sat, much heavier since I'd last seen him, calm and smug in his suit and tie, as though it was all just an annoying inconvenience to him. Immediately, his comments about initially prescribing the drugs attempted to paint a misleading picture: "I just wanted her to take it for two or three days until she got a few good nights' sleep so that she could get her problems ... into perspective."

He attributed every single run-in with police, every emergency admission, every overdose, every violent episode to alcohol, not pills. On the other hand, Dr. MacGillivray kept assuring the court that he had warned me of the potentiating effects of the two substances taken together. In effect, he seemed to leap back and forth, either denying the dangerous interaction of the two, or saying he warned me of it.

Dr. MacGillivray also denied any association of my chronic injuries, falls, and accidents over the years with the known side effects of benzodiazepines. These were not a result of the "unsteadiness" that he claimed he warned patients about when he prescribed benzodiazepines; they happened because of my drinking. There was seemingly no end to his contradictions. He spoke often of my perceived "alcoholism," yet on another occasion, when my lawyer questioned his practice of supplying potentiating, lethally interacting drugs to someone considered to have an alcohol problem, he said, "I think most of the time she wasn't drinking, I honestly believe that. ..."[9]

On my overdoses and his response to them, he said that he took the drugs away on some of these occasions, but that, after a few days, I would invariably come in "really needing something." When my lawyer suggested that I was obviously suffering acute withdrawal effects at such times, having stopped the drugs cold turkey, and that I needed to be advised about what to expect, he simply denied it. The whole thing was absurd, or would have been, if it had not had such an enormous impact on my life.

Although it was very hard to get a feel for how it all sounded to others, I felt, at least, that the nature of Dr. MacGillivray's testimony raised one crucial question: how was I supposed to know what was happening to me, with a clouded-up, drugged head, when the doctor treating me appeared not to identify it either? He was still denying the potentially deadly interaction of the pills and alcohol, even in retrospect. Eventually, my lawyer cornered him on a couple of key points: Why did he never associate my violent rages with the "paradoxical reactions" described throughout benzodiazepine listings in the CPS, which he said he referred to? And why would he keep endangering me by continuing with the pills, when it had been shown time and again that I was not abstaining from alcohol? But he seemed to miss the point.

"Surely you must have been frustrated with her?" he was asked.

"Very."

"I mean, you tell her not to and she says she won't drink and then she does it again."

"Mmm-hmm."

"So why is it, then, that it kept happening over and over, and it happened for eighteen years? Can you tell us?"

"Well, [in] medical school," he responded, "we were given lectures that it was our duty to look after some people in society … even though my three or four partners kept telling me that we had to *get rid of* this particular patient out of the practice because a lot of them, of these kinds of people, cause you a lot of problems. …"[10]

When asked about his switch to Restoril over Dalmane after that 1990 overdose, he said it was because the Restoril was shorter-acting, but earlier references indicate his ignorance regarding the long-lasting effects of *any* of the drugs he had prescribed. Why wasn't I on Restoril earlier, if he thought it was better? he was asked.

"She was doing very well with Dalmane and there was no reason to change," he explained.

"Even though she had many episodes over the years, she was doing well?"

"What episodes? Her alcoholism?" he retorted.

Testimony revealed that I was back on day- and night-time pills within days of that final overdose. Approximately two weeks later, I was back in Dr. MacGillivray's office reporting terrible panic attacks, and he gave me, for the first time, a *third* potentiating drug, Ativan. Shirley asked if there was "no harm with that combined with Serax."

"Well, she's going to take one or the other."

So, under his instructions I was to take Serax three times a day, Restoril at night, and Ativan when I had panic attacks. "You don't want them both," he offered. Was I then to plan ahead for my panic attacks and not take the Serax? And if you don't want them both, why did he prescribe all three? As I sat there listening to him, I honestly wondered if he might have been trying to "get rid of me" permanently. Had I died during one of my overdoses, it might well have been a relief to him.

When Shirley read passages from numerous reference sources regarding the potentiating effects of tranquilizers and sleeping pills, he didn't flinch. She questioned him with topics covered in medical journals that he admitted having regular access to, page after page of warnings and documentation on the effects of benzodiazepines: "nightmares, paradoxical

delirium and confusion, depression, aggression and hostile behaviour"
—on and on. When asked whether he ever saw any of these articles,
all of which likely crossed his desk, he admitted he "might have." He
couldn't recall.

After having scores of these passages read to him, when asked if he
"still believed" that I was treated appropriately, he was adamant. "I think
Mrs. Gadsby got very good treatment in those years and I don't think
probably it would have changed much, in retrospect." Did he still believe
there was a place for longtime use of benzodiazepines? Yes, he did. "It's
a very safe and efficacious drug."

He was asked what he would have done had I remained his patient,
if my episodes ("situational stresses," he called them) had carried on
time after time. Would he have kept me on the drugs? He answered that
he "probably would have."[11] It was just so frustrating. He *still* didn't get
it. I firmly believe, given all I have learned and now know about tranquilizers and sleeping pills, that if I had stayed on as Dr. MacGillivray's
patient after my last overdose and stayed on the pills, I would not be
alive today.

At the end of his testimony, the judge, obviously wanting answers to
questions not brought up by my lawyer, asked Dr. MacGillivray why he
would deny that I overdosed on drugs. "It probably was more to get attention that she said she took the pills, rather than actually taking the pills,"
he explained.

One witness brought in for the defense, Dr. Desmond Dwyer, a family
physician, cited the high percentage of the population using benzodiazepines as a *positive* point. In some cases, he claimed, he, too, prescribed
them over many years, thousands of them. "I would think that the vast
majority of family practitioners do," he offered, "and ... current indications from the medical literature and the teaching of family practitioners
is that long-term use of these in selected patients is wise and therapeutic.
... I find them a very safe and useful drug." His response to adverse
reports? "A substantial number of the studies were done in substance
abuse centres," he claimed, and "dealt with a population that was using
more than one drug ..." Of course I was using more than one drug—
three in the end! I wondered how many others in substance-abuse centers were like me, or were perhaps people with other substance-abuse

problems whose doctors did them a great disservice by prescribing benzodiazepines as well, then blamed *them* for their further deterioration and cross-addictions. Dr. Dwyer, in all seriousness, insisted on the witness stand that benzodiazepines "are not habituating."

Dr. Pankratz,[12] my psychiatrist from 1985 to 1990, had his turn on the witness stand, brought in by Dr. MacGillivray's defense team. He was asked about a report in which he wrote that I might have several problems, one being my use of alcohol and its "disinhibiting effects" and the other a psychiatric problem. There were no notes about the "disinhibiting effects" that drugs might be having on me. Dr. Pankratz testified about attending me in the hospital following one drug overdose, when his notes indicated he also questioned the possibility of a "major affective disorder ... bipolar type." "This patient is well known to me," he wrote—"[and has a] long history of alcohol abuse. ..." But I was there with a drug overdose! This fact was dismissed, overlooked, or denied over and over, year after year, by doctor after doctor.

Since I was a former public figure involved in a controversial lawsuit, my story was covered prominently in the media once court proceedings began. Reporters from the *Vancouver Province* showed up on the first day of the trial, and ran a lead story on the front page of that paper the following day, accompanied by a photo of me in front of the law courts. "I Was Addicted" screamed the headline. And for four more consecutive days the *Province* ran follow-up stories with captions like: "Kicking pills frightening ... I thought I was going to die. ..." The *Vancouver Sun*, the *North Shore News*, and other local newspapers also ran articles covering the court proceedings. Local radio stations also carried stories.

It was very upsetting at times, but nonetheless the various news stories drew a wide response. Despite the sensational slant of some of the coverage, numerous people appeared to be reading between the lines, and the response from the public was overwhelming. Through the entire trial, the Benzodiazepine Call to Action Group members and I were besieged with calls from people, many of them unknown to me, many of them similarly affected by these drugs, most of them wanting to know how they could get off the drugs, since there seemed to be so little help available. Others called to congratulate me for my courage in initiating the lawsuit and taking on the medical profession.

One person who responded to the media coverage during the trial and contacted me was a man about my age, also a professional, who I will call Glen. After reporting a panic attack at age twenty-three, Glen was prescribed benzodiazepines for what his doctor called a "biochemical imbalance," and Glen wound up taking them for *twenty-nine years*. I have never known anyone to have been on them longer, or who suffers more from their long-lasting effects. Tragically, during his long addiction, Glen also lost his wife to suicide. At the time of her death, she had been on Valium for years.

When Glen tried to cut back on the tranquilizers by himself at various times, withdrawal kicked in with enormous ferocity, and he suffered from acute anxiety, agoraphobia, and racing, confused thoughts. By the time he realized the extent of his chemical dependency, he was faced with a dreadful choice: keep taking the pills and working—or risk losing his job, along with his means of supporting his family. Glen's story parallels mine in many ways. For one thing, he also started to drink alcohol to alleviate his continually growing anxiety. He too was unaware of mini "withdrawals between pills creating anxiety." Despite enormous instability in his life during the years on the drugs, Glen eventually worked his way up the corporate ladder to a position as vice president of finance for a large company, and battled through his days on benzodiazepines. He frequently had to dash to the bathroom to conceal anxiety attacks, where he waited until he was able to pull himself together again. When he confided in his physician that the pills weren't working any more, and discussed his debilitating symptoms, the doctor's response was to *double* his dosage.

Glen finally lost his job at age forty-eight, for what his employer called "confused thinking." This turning point was the catalyst to getting off the drugs. Glen did it alone, without medical supervision, and he describes the following months as an "excruciating agony" of migraine headaches, chaotic thoughts, blurred vision, vertigo, agoraphobia, and nausea. He was barely able to leave his house. He had a friend drive him everywhere for four months, as he was incapable of operating his car due to visual/spatial distortions, psychomotor difficulties, coordination and concentration problems. Today, five years later, Glen is able to work (for himself) part-time, but bright lights and crowds still bother him, and he often loses track of his thoughts in the middle of conversations. And he too is trying to come to terms with a "very limited memory" that stretches from 1965 until 1990.

Eventually, Dr. Ursula Wild was called to testify regarding my residual cognitive difficulties—a critical part of my claim for damages—and about our work together in trying to overcome them. She confirmed the neuropsychological deficits described in Dr. Klonoff's 1992 report, particularly my problems in reading and auditory tasks, and my "heightened vulnerability to interference and distractibility, and the subsequent problems with learning and memory abilities." She noted as well "considerable difficulties with information processing and executive functions, leading to difficulties with problem solving and decision making, as well as impaired judgment." On my inability to integrate things, she described my tendency to get fixed on something and not be able to "unstick" myself. "She was bringing me all the trees but never saw the forest," Dr. Wild explained. She went on to say that "the neuropsychological deficits that [Joan] continues to experience are directly related to her long term use of ... [benzodiazepine] medications."[13]

It was distressing for me to hear Dr. Wild describe my cognitive problems so bluntly, even though I had discussed these matters with her many times. There was something about the frank objectivity of the courtroom that made reality uncomfortably stark. I still find it hard to accept what has happened to me, and, to this day, I tend to forget that my mind does not always work in the manner it used to, although I continue to utilize the compensating techniques Dr. Wild taught me, as well as others I have learned on my own.

Dr. Barry Beyerstein, a professor at Simon Fraser University and a prominent psychopharmacologist specializing in the field of "biological psychology" (particularly in the area of drugs that affect the brain and nervous system), was one of our most knowledgeable and important expert witnesses. During his testimony, Dr. Beyerstein explained to the court, in layperson's terms, the effects that benzodiazepines have on the brain and behavior, during which he referred to "clouding of consciousness ... despondency, dizziness, motor incoordination, all the effects of drunkenness basically, a dry gin." He went on to explain that, in increased dosages, the drug has effects on the mind that "go beyond the level of disruption of consciousness to delirium, and appearing staggering drunk."

Dr. Beyerstein was asked if a person taking benzodiazepines on a regular basis would be cognizant of his or her altered behavior. "Interestingly enough," he answered, "one of the things that is impaired is the ability to recognize the impairment. ... A person who has been taking the drug for a long time ... may not be aware that their performance ... is significantly worse than it was before they started using the drug." Dr. Beyerstein also offered that "the only time an individual recognizes he or she is addicted is when they no longer have the drug. ... These can be insidious things. ..."

Yet another important point that Dr. Beyerstein established was that withdrawal symptoms, in general, "are the opposite to the effect of the drug itself. It has a rebound effect." He explained that, "in extreme cases, this can be lethal because a long-depressed nervous system ... swings all the way into extreme agitation and convulsions, and without medical management" some people "actually die from it." He said that, although this was rare, symptoms of "extreme agitation, the rebound of extreme unpleasant anxiety symptoms, and great disruption of sleeping [and] terrible dreams" were not. There can also be "psychotic-like episodes where people are terribly confused and frightened and disoriented."[14] With regard to my ongoing cognitive problems, Dr. Beyerstein concluded from his review of the literature that there was a "high probability that complications arising from long term, high-dose prescribing of these tranquilizers were a contributing factor to the mental difficulties that Drs. Wild and Schmidt (had) documented." He also discussed the four- to six-year follow-up study done in Sweden that showed benzodiazepines to be capable of having long-term effects that far outlast the time the drug is in the brain ... due to structural damage to cells in the central nervous system which ... don't regrow.[15]

Dr. Beyerstein's evidence was crucial to my case. As I listened, I felt he had more than substantiated every material point in my case: that benzodiazepine use can mimic alcohol use, that the person prescribed the pills is often unaware of their subtle behavioral side effects, that severe withdrawal symptoms can ensue after long-term use, and that there was a high probability that my ongoing cognitive difficulties were directly linked to my long-term ingestion of the pills. In addition to this important testimony, Dr. Parkinson, my psychiatrist for longer than five years, also confirmed (through a deposition) the earlier assessment of Dr. Klonoff, that I suffered from cognitive dysfunction.[16] Unfortunately, a report dated December 13, 1996, by Dr. Mary Stewart-Moore, my chemical-dependency doctor for five years after I was off the pills, which stated that "I do believe that the long usage of benzodiazepines has caused long-term mental difficulties for Ms. Gadsby," was never entered as an exhibit. Nevertheless, with the appearances of Drs. Wild and Beyerstein, and with the forthright deposition by Dr. Parkinson, I hoped that our evidence at that point was comparatively clear and convincing.

The defense leaned heavily on my ability to answer articulately and knowledgeably on the witness stand, and remember things about my past, as evidence that I had not suffered any cognitive impairment. I tried to clarify that this sort of memory is quite different from, say, reading or hearing various bits of completely unfamiliar information and comprehending that information *without great effort*. Fighting to create awareness of the lingering cognitive damage caused by benzodiazepines has put me in the odd position, at times, of having to convince others that I still have subtle cognitive deficits, when I try to do exactly the opposite in my daily life. My training with Dr. Wild continues to reinforce strategies and techniques to overcome and minimize the outward signs of these deficits.

As testimony continued, however, my lawyer seemed to be missing numerous crucial opportunities. She often failed to elicit the desired testimony from key witnesses, not getting them to comment upon and confirm the validity of important research documents submitted as evidence. This even frustrated the judge at times: "Take your witness through his report," he prompted. "You're 'rambling,'" he commented at another point, "What are you saying?" He even prodded her at times: "Well, ask him if that's so." I became increasingly concerned and frustrated. My spirits were dropping by the day as I saw valid evidence brought forth, only to slide off into obscurity. In contrast, defense witnesses were invariably well briefed before court, often right up to the minute before they were called to testify.

In addition to the report prepared by Dr. Moore, one prepared by Dr. Parkinson didn't make it in as evidence either. Perhaps most troubling was her handling of another one of our most important witnesses, Dr. Jim Wright, a clinical pharmacologist and specialist in internal medicine, and director of the Therapeutics Initiative at the University of British Columbia, whose expertise in the area of the appropriate utilization of prescription drugs was key to our case. Just six days prior to the trial, Shirley apparently had failed to respond to a defense letter listing the key witnesses to be called (and not called), and had therefore lost the opportunity to call Dr. Wright as an expert witness. The defense argued strongly against his appearance, stating that Shirley had agreed not to call him. This very serious error had devastating consequences for my case. Although we were able to call him eventually, at my insistence, it was only as a rebuttal witness, which severely restricted the scope of his evidence.

Dr. Wright had prepared reports questioning the duration of Dr. MacGillivray's continuous prescribing and his rationale for switching me "from one benzo to another over the years."[17] Another report cited "potential and real harm in continuing benzodiazepine use over longer than a one month period," stated that benzos "are contraindicated in patients who are known to continue to use alcohol," and discussed withdrawal effects, including anxiety. Dr. Wright would also have confirmed that "all of these side-effects and risks including cognitive impairment were well known in the 1970s and 1980s," and that "after a suicide attempt with benzodiazepines the continued prescription of benzodiazepines is inappropriate."[18] His testimony was all lost. In the judge's words, these two crucial reports weren't "identified" by Dr. Wright in his testimony.

Drug-store records and receipts regarding my prescriptions were never entered as exhibits, although they would have proved that Dr. MacGillivray had prescribed benzodiazepines twenty-six additional times when he stated that he had no records of doing so.

My despair reached a peak when, just before the concluding arguments were to begin, the judge felt it necessary to *ask* Shirley to present the relevant case law. Her brief was less than a half inch thick, with few references, while the defence had two three-inch binders with thirty-nine references in their Book of Authorities. With crucial expert witnesses and treating physicians not being called to testify, I had become very alarmed. I could scarcely believe what was happening. On several occasions, Alan and I met with Shirley to go over my concerns, and I also documented these in writing to her throughout the trial and during recesses in the proceedings.

My life, my career, my future were on the line; my financial losses were piling up; the reasons for the lawsuit and recovery of my damages were being put in jeopardy. By contrast, the defense team had come out with "all guns firing." It was obvious that for them the case was extremely important: no expense was spared, no effort was too much. They had a lot at stake in my potentially precedent-setting case, and Jim Lepp was purportedly overheard by one benzo survivor to say they "had to win at any cost." If I were to win there would be a snowball effect, with many others waiting for my trial judgment before launching their own lawsuits against their doctors for overprescribing the same drugs.

Deb and Carrie's love and support for me during the trial meant more than I can say. And in the early mornings, every day before court started, I went for my two-and-a-half-mile run along the seawall in West Vancouver, which helped tremendously in coping with the stress.

In the evenings, I would phone Deb and brief her on what was happening in court. She and Carrie continued working full time throughout the trial and tried to maintain normal lives, in spite of the publicity surrounding the lawsuit. But I knew I had their love and support in what I was doing. And they knew they could always count on me and my love for them. I had always tried to teach them to stand up for what they believed in and I was "walking the talk" with my lawsuit. But as the trial reached its final days, I could not help feeling both discouraged and upset. The trial concluded on April 29, 1997. As I waited for the judgment, I reflected that Shirley Khan had probably never appreciated the enormous impact that winning the case and setting a legal precedent could have. Not only Dr. MacGillivray but all doctors who had overprescribed would feel the legal repercussions. Winning the case could make a huge difference, and not just for me, but for countless others in Canada and worldwide, directly affecting their lives and possibly preventing many other cases of irreparable harm.

On June 30, I received the disappointing but hardly unexpected news. My lawsuit had been dismissed. In his forty-seven-page judgment, Judge Clancy touched on many troubling issues, but none more troubling for me than this one: "The court was referred to many articles and reference materials on the use of benzodiazepines," he wrote. "Most were not adopted by experts and therefore have little proven value." (In other words, Shirley had not asked our experts to confirm the research findings.) On the specific question of causation, Judge Clancy found that we had "failed to show" that the use of benzodiazepines had caused my continuing cognitive deficits. He did not accept the opinions of "non-medical" witnesses, including neuropsychologists! In essence, the judge was saying that, because Drs. Wild, Schmidt, and Beyerstein were not doctors of medicine, but of psychology-related disciplines, their evidence did not carry the same weight. He dismissed Dr. Wild's testimony, in part because "she had not seen the reports of Dr. Hirt, Dr. Pankratz, Dr. Margetts, Dr. Brown, and Dr. Hewko" (all psychiatrists and prescribers of these kinds of drugs). In other words, because Dr. Wild's observations in treating me were not biased by psychiatric misconception, the significance of her findings of my cognitive impairment was dismissed! Given my "history," the judge wrote, "I find it far more likely that the interplay between her personality problems and her excessive use of alcohol have caused the psychological deficits from which she suffers today."[19]

In response to my claim of negligence in the matter of having been simultaneously treated with two potentiating drugs for twelve years, a practice that was clearly contraindicated in the literature and prescribing guidelines at the time, the judge said that "there was no evidence adduced to the effect that two central nervous drugs should not be used at the same time. No medical witness stated that it was inappropriate to prescribe daytime tranquilizers and night-time sleeping pills."[20]

This oversight compounded the other issues to a devastating degree. It affected the judge's view of Dr. Beyerstein's key testimony, particularly his statement that I had been a long-term consumer of benzodiazepines in high doses. During cross-examination, our expert witness, Dr. Wright, had testified that the daily dosages of each drug prescribed to me were within recommended guidelines. The relevance of the fact that I was on two drugs at the same time for twelve years—thus experiencing double and triple the effects—had not been established.

In weighing the evidence about benzodiazepines as a contributing cause of my documented cognitive impairment, the judge also considered the possibility of an underlying mood disorder or excessive consumption of alcohol. He referred directly to Dr. James Brown's firm diagnosis of a bipolar mood disorder. This was the psychiatrist whom I had never met. He also cited Dr. Margetts, the psychiatrist who thought I should perhaps be hospitalized when I disagreed with him during my acute withdrawal, and who suggested I would perhaps be hard to "control" without more drugs. He also considered Dr. Fleming's observations at the University of British Columbia's sleep disorder clinic; this was the doctor who, after reading my prior history, attributed my sleep disturbance during withdrawal to a "psychiatric disorder." Unfortunately, what the judge didn't have was the crucial letter written by Dr. Parkinson, my regular psychiatrist for five years when I was off all pills, in which he stated there was "no evidence" of bipolar disorder, and that I did "not require active psychiatric treatment."[21] However, this was not established as an exhibit in the trial.

The judge did acknowledge a causative link between my taking benzodiazepines and my behavioral problems, as well as the emotional distress I suffered during withdrawal, but still he did not rule in my favor, even on this issue. In reference to case law, the judge stated that physicians cannot be held liable for errors in judgment: "Where a physician makes a mistake after having honestly applied his or her mind and falls within the standard of care, it is an 'error of judgment' which does not result in liability."[22] Other excerpts from case law cited include: "the law will take account of differences of opinion within the medical profession. There may therefore be more than one body of professional judgment which is regarded as accepted practice in the profession. Provided the conduct of the physician conforms with one of the standards established as being generally accepted, then he or she is not negligent."[23] Further, Judge Clancy said, there was "clearly a body of medical practitioners who believe benzodiazepines may be used in the long term." It would seem that if there are enough doctors harming people, even when they should know better, they cannot be held accountable.

Another case established that the law generally requires that the patient give an informed consent to proposed therapy: "The underlying principle is the right of a patient to decide what, if anything, should be done with his body … it follows, therefore, that a patient's consent, whether to surgery or to therapy, will give protection to his surgeon or physician only if the patient has been sufficiently informed to enable him to make a choice whether or not to submit to the surgery or therapy."[24] For over two decades, I never understood the risks and potential short- and long-term effects of taking benzodiazepines as prescribed to me. Nonetheless, because of Dr. MacGillivray's testimony, the judge claimed he was "not persuaded" of my claim that Dr. MacGillivray had failed to provide an adequate standard of care.

Despite his disappointing decision, the judge said he was nonetheless troubled by some of Dr. MacGillivray's testimony. "As a matter of common sense," he wrote, "a lay person might question the advisability of continuing to prescribe benzodiazepines following the incidents where Ms. Gadsby exhibited unusual behaviour and attempted suicide. Logically, it seems that a physician would seriously consider discontinuing the use of tranquilizers and sleeping pills following such behaviour. It is this aspect of the matter that has caused me the greatest concern." Unfortunately, this too could have been supported by Dr. Wright's report, had it been properly entered as evidence. The judgment did not touch upon Dr. MacGillivray's failure to prevent or acknowledge my chemical dependency, or to help me safely through withdrawal. These facts were altogether ignored.

In summary, Judge Clancy conceded that his "reasons for dismissing the claim will not be acceptable to Ms. Gadsby ... [but] litigation must be resolved on the evidence led in court. ..."[25] I could hardly disagree with him on that point. Much of the *extensive* evidence and research I had amassed on the subject of benzodiazepines, as well as evidence regarding the huge impact that twenty years of iatrogenic chemical dependency had on my life, my family, and my career, had indeed *not* been presented properly in court.

Regrettably, my fight for justice was still not over. I had no choice but to move quickly to find another lawyer to review the judge's written decision and Shirley Khan's handling of my case. After interviewing yet more lawyers, I concluded a contingency arrangement once again with another lawyer, James (Jay) Straith, who filed an appeal on my behalf within the thirty-day time frame for launching an appeal in the B.C. Court of Appeal.

Initially, Jay concluded that "there are significant errors in law and fact that could be overturned at appeal." These centered on advising on treatment, causation, and standard of care, in particular. He also told me that it might be necessary to take my appeal to the Supreme Court of Canada, which I was prepared to do, and expressed concern at Shirley Khan's lack of preparation and presentation of my case, and the fact that key evidence had not been entered. However, by June 1998, after reviewing the many volumes of transcripts from the trial that I had ordered, Jay changed his opinion and instead recommended filing a claim against Shirley Khan for professional negligence. Jay further concluded that, while the appeal might be successful in certain areas, it would be a long, convoluted legal battle.

I wanted to twin-track the appeal and the case against Shirley Khan, but he recommended proceeding directly against Shirley. This presented a major dilemma for me, since I felt Dr. MacGillivray had not been properly held accountable. In September 1998, Jay wrote a further letter to me stating that, while an action against a lawyer is "relatively unprecedented, it is quite winnable considering the outrageous manner in which she [Shirley Khan] failed to fulfill her legal duties" to me.[26] In October, my claim against Shirley Khan was filed and we waited to obtain another trial date. My legal hassles were still not over, and wouldn't be for several years to come.

In the meantime, I was quickly getting boxed in. When the lawsuit against Dr. MacGillivray was dismissed by Judge Clancy, the defense team for Dr. MacGillivray was awarded their court costs and legal fees, which originally totalled more than $80,000, and they were pressing me for payment. This sum was eventually reduced at a hearing to $62,000, but aside from my quickly diminishing financial resources, this was part of my claim against Shirley Khan, and I requested that my lawyer advise the defense to wait until it was resolved. However, in December that same year, the firm representing Dr. MacGillivray filed a lien against my personal residence for $62,000 (in Dr. MacGillivray's name), adding insult to injury. But this again illustrates very vividly how the average person with a claim for medical malpractice can be coerced into not pursuing it. Deb and Carrie were also very alarmed by this development. After all, the house has been our family home for thirty years.

In March 1999, Jay received an unsolicited letter from Dr. MacGillivray's defense firm, Harper Grey Easton, proposing that they would accept payment of $30,000 of these costs if I filed a notice of abandonment of my appeal in return for their client abandoning the remainder of the legal costs.[27] This was an unexpected and thought-provoking development, but I was certainly not prepared to abandon the appeal. (Currently it is on hold, pending resolution of my case against Shirley Khan.) After all that I have been through, nothing will stop me now in my fight for justice.

CHAPTER THIRTEEN

Call to Action

DESPITE TEMPORARY SETBACKS on the legal front, I recognized that I was in a very strong position to continue my fight for systemic change. The trial, though unsuccessful, had provided a blaze of publicity for the victims of benzodiazepine dependency. There is no doubt that the inappropriate prescribing of benzodiazepines costs the health care system millions of dollars and affects the quality of life of many people—not only in Canada but worldwide. My years of research and personal experience have shown that these drugs are prescribed all too liberally by physicians to unsuspecting patients, many of whom trust their doctors implicitly. Many of the prescriptions are repeated refills, which in all likelihood accounts for the disproportionate number of elderly people who have become chemically dependent on them. The devastation of these people's lives and the societal costs are horrific—loss of careers and individual earning power, loss of property, lost productivity to employers, falls, car accidents, related crime, police and legal costs, and personal and family dysfunction, to name only a few examples. Many people have even lost their lives from unintentional overdoses.

The ensuing costs to the health-care system include not only the drugs and physician fees, but also added hospital costs associated with emergency admissions, detoxification, and treatment centers, rehabilitation and for services of other health-care professionals.

How has this been allowed to happen? Simply, pharmaceutical companies, not only in Canada, but worldwide, have spent billions of dollars marketing and promoting these drugs (replacing older drugs with newer

218 CALL TO ACTION

ones) in pursuit of sales and profits. After three decades as a marketing professional, I am well aware that repeat purchases are the key to successful marketing programs. And doctors have bought into the hype, ignoring their Hippocratic oath to "do no harm." Many of these doctors have been negligent about upgrading their knowledge, education, and training, or have been resistant to change, remaining firmly entrenched in antiquated attitudes and beliefs.

What is needed is the political will and leadership to focus on action and to effect systemic change. The message has to reach all the key stakeholders—patients, doctors, medical regulatory bodies, pharmaceutical companies, pharmacists, researchers, and government regulators. As Dr. Reg Peart of the Victims of Tranquilizers group said in June 1999 in his presentation to the Health Committee Inquiry on Procedures Related to Adverse Clinical Incidents and Outcomes in Medical Care in the United Kingdom, "benzodiazepine dependency is the biggest medically induced health problem of the twentieth century."

While I realized that bringing about systemic change would be a major challenge and a lifetime commitment, I could not do it alone. I decided to form the Benzodiazepine Call to Action Group, an organization that quickly attracted a nucleus of other people similarly affected, their families, and some health-care professionals.

Our initial objectives were highly optimistic, encompassing the following:

1. To create a high level of awareness that will deter physicians from overprescribing benzodiazepines, and provide consumers with all the information necessary to make an informed choice regarding their use.

2. To advocate for systemic and legislative change that would hold physicians, drug manufacturers, pharmacists, and political decision makers to a higher standard of ethics and accountability.

3. To provide consumer-driven information, services, referrals, alternatives, and specific assistance to individuals and families affected by benzodiazepine dependency, and to prevent new cases of dependency through information and education.

4. To work with consumers, physicians, pharmaceutical companies, pharmacists, and government regulators in a solutions-oriented,

win/win manner in order to reduce the consumption of benzodiazepines.

5. To serve as a model for other groups and individuals who share a common concern regarding the improper use of these prescription drugs.

It soon became apparent to us that we needed a Benzodiazepine Call to Action Resource Center, with links to other worldwide centers, accessible to the thousands of people adversely affected by these drugs. This would require regular ongoing funding for an office and staff. I had spent thousands of dollars of my own money over the past eight years, creating a library of research studies, reference papers and books, making phone calls all over the world, traveling as much as I could throughout North America to interview stakeholders, and giving extensive personal time to the project. All of our dedicated members were volunteers, putting in long hours, doing work that should have been done by the doctors, pharmaceutical companies, government regulators, and pharmacists whom society had entrusted with the responsibility, but who were not motivated to see change—who were, in fact, threatened by change, and who in most cases had vested interests in the existing system that perpetuates the overprescribing of these drugs. Some genuine efforts were being made within the system, but without leadership or dedicated political will, they were poorly coordinated and suffered from a lack of communication and commitment.

We developed a proposal for a resource center, outlining its key functions as follows:

1. To establish an up-to-date research and resource library, including worldwide references, to make objective information (on effects, risks, signs of dependency, withdrawal, and cognitive impairment associated with benzodiazepines) accessible to consumers and professionals.

2. To offer a wide range of referral services, with links to knowledgeable addiction specialists, detox centers, and other community resources for people needing support and guidance in overcoming and withdrawing from benzodiazepine dependency.

3. To embody a centralized, interactive advocacy center where concerned individuals, professionals, and groups can pool ideas

and resources with the common purpose of encouraging the legislative and systemic change necessary to reduce the epidemic of benzodiazepine use and misuse.

4. To take part in ongoing fundraising endeavors to support action-oriented initiatives, and encourage financial contributions from a wide variety of public- and private-sector organizations and governments.
5. To organize and implement education drives, identifying opportunities to draw media attention to the widespread problems associated with the improper use of benzodiazepines.
6. To provide guidance and support for persons taking legal action against offending doctors, drug manufacturers, and government regulators of these potentially dangerous drugs.

Drawing on my experience in strategic planning both as a politician and as a marketing executive with four of Canada's largest companies, I mapped out an overview of (a) the extent of the benzo problem worldwide; (b) key international research over the previous two decades; (c) the four most serious, damaging side effects of benzo use; (d) the roles of doctors, pharmaceutical companies, consumers, pharmacists, and government; and (e) the socio-economic costs of benzo use and misuse. Out of this, I developed a specific action plan identifying obstacles to getting the benzo problem reduced, with solutions. I brought the plan to the nucleus of the Benzo Call to Action Group, and after several weeks of further brainstorming, we had a comprehensive action-plan summary (documented at the end of this chapter).

Our proposal for the resource center has been presented to a number of public- and private-sector organizations and to the provincial and federal ministries of health over the past few years. The Call to Action Group fully recognizes that funding must be an ongoing initiative, as it will take several years of concerted effort to raise the money required.

In the meantime, I am continuing my awareness building, research, and advocacy. I feel very strongly that the time for action is now, before any more lives and families are destroyed. To this end, I have continued to seek out more and more opportunities to meet, make presentations to, and become actively involved with the key stakeholders.

CALL TO ACTION 221

I took the initiative in seeking an alliance with the new Centre of Excellence in Women's Health located at B.C. Women's Hospital in Vancouver, funded through the federal Department of Health. Dr. Nancy Hall, who had done the controversial study on excessive benzo prescribing on the North Shore previously, had become Director of Community Health Promotion there. After serving on the center's initial planning committee, my company, Market Media International Corp., became a signatory partner to the Centre of Excellence in 1996. Soon after, I became chair of the center's newly formed policy/action group, which was to look at better policies for benzodiazepine prescribing. I felt encouraged by this development, since it provided a more formalized structure to publicly recognize the perils of iatrogenic chemical dependency on tranquilizers and sleeping pills, and could also potentially provide some much needed funding.

Eventually, our policy group received a disappointingly modest allocation of $5,000 from Health Canada, through the center, to assist our Call to Action Group in developing papers and making presentations to key policy leaders and stakeholders. But in many ways, our association with the Centre of Excellence only slowed us down: this was a major research facility at the very heart of the health-care system and consequently was somewhat reluctant to "rock the boat" with doctors or the government. Unfortunately, it became clear to me quite early on that those working with us from within the system were intent on softening our very direct approach in calling for medical accountability and systemic change. It was somewhat of a "Catch-22" situation for the center, in that, if it made too much noise about the benzodiazepine problem, there was a risk that the center's Health Canada funding would be cut off, since part of the problem we were addressing was the federal government's ongoing lack of action through the Health Protection Branch, despite its responsibility to ensure that drugs available in Canada are *safe*, effective, and of high quality. I had, in fact, spoken personally with Dann Michols, director general of the Therapeutics Directorate of the Health Protection Branch, over a year earlier, recommending that it would be in the best interests of Canadian consumers if he simply drafted a letter to doctors, fully apprising them of the serious side effects associated with benzodiazepines, and advising them that these drugs are only for short-term use. But to the best of my knowledge, this was not done.

Part of our original Call to Action plan was used to obtain funding by the Centre of Excellence for our policy/action group, but to our great annoyance *only* the portion of our document that listed the "obstacles to getting the benzodiazepine problem reduced" was used. The "solutions" column that originally appeared in our summary chart alongside them was omitted—I assume, in order to attract research dollars for the work of identifying these very solutions. Obviously, the whole process was turning into a vehicle for obtaining more research money for the center, when it was clear to us that action, not more research, was needed.

Dr. Nancy Hall, through the center, obtained a further $15,000 grant for a research project on benzodiazepine prescribing, which would analyze gender differences and the average duration of use, as well as differences in prescribing rates between community- and facility-based patients. Part of this money was to be used to conduct a detailed literature review on the side effects of long-term benzo use. Of course, I considered this to be entirely unnecessary, a blatant waste of time and taxpayers' money. There was *plenty* of research on benzodiazepines and their adverse effects, much of which I had already collected and given to the center. Nancy Hall, in fact, attended one of our earliest Benzo Call to Action Group meetings at my home and I supplied her with a number of relevant research papers.

Yet another plan, this one for a three-phase participatory research project on benzodiazepines focusing on senior women, received an additional grant of $149,000 from the B.C. Health Research Foundation, with Nancy Hall as the researcher. The first stage of the project was classified as "action research," wherein a group of women would develop knowledge about healthy coping by reflecting on their own experiences, and interviewing their peers and medical professionals. Phase two was to encompass "education resource development"—the women would develop educational tools and helpful tips to facilitate other women's inquiries into these issues. This would be followed by a "community implementation phase"—the women would take their educational program into the community with the help of the project facilitator.[1]

Originally, I felt this project was positive in that it emphasized consumer education, which was certainly necessary, and I endorsed it with a supporting letter to the B.C. Health Research Foundation in its initial planning stages. However, when I heard the particulars of the project, specifically its duration (two years) and the amount of funding it had received, I felt strongly that this grant money would have been better spent on education that was not gender- or age-specific, and on immediate consumer protection. I also realized that the project, although well intentioned, was carefully crafted not to offend the medical/political establishment, and did nothing to address the root of the problem. What about the doctors? What about a plan to ensure compliance to prescribing guidelines? What about help for people who were already chemically dependent? Although consumer education and dialogue are important, I again felt that action was needed to address the overprescribing of these drugs; not more studies, talk, and make-work programs.

Although I tried to remain active and diplomatic within the context of the Centre of Excellence and its roundabout approach to the problem, I soon saw that I could be much more effective continuing on my own, working outside the system, with the help of my colleagues in Call to Action. As a group, we had nothing to lose. Unlike those working within the medical/political establishment, we were not worried about protecting our jobs or maintaining the status quo.

Mike Corbeill, head of British Columbia's Pharmacare program in 1996, acknowledged the problems associated with benzodiazepines, and supported our efforts to create awareness and systemic change; he promised to contribute $50,000 toward a conference that would bring together all the stakeholders. This was encouraging, but unfortunately, when he became Assistant Deputy Minister of Health in 1997, his Pharmacare successor, Anne MacFarlane, put plans for the conference on the back burner. When we met with her, she told us that budget restraints made the grant impossible. To this day, I continue to lobby her regarding the need for such a conference. It's very frustrating to see costs to the health-care system associated with misprescribing steadily escalating, while opportunities for change that would save millions of dollars, and directly improve the lives of thousands of people, are ignored. This point was noted in the B.C. Auditor General's report entitled *Managing the Cost of Drug*

Therapies and Fostering Appropriate Drug Use released in August 1998. George Morfitt stated that the Pharmacare Branch of the Ministry of Health could do more to foster appropriate use of drugs and recommended that "policies need to be developed promoting appropriate drug use."[2]

Toward the end of the trial in my lawsuit against Dr. MacGillivray, I received word that I was accepted as a presenter at the Review on Substance Abuse Policies for the House of Commons Standing Committee on Health. Although the timing was awkward, and I was given very little notice, it turned out that the date I was given to appear would be during a scheduled court hiatus, and I flew to Ottawa on an overnight trip to attend. It was a bit of a scramble to pull everything together at that particular time, but to have my voice heard in this forum was an important opportunity, and I was not about to miss it.

The review was to include an overview of substance-abuse policy issues and specific substances, with a focus on affected individuals, families, and communities; an overview of international policy and program experience; and an assessment of provincial, territorial, and municipal policy, programs, and services. The committee was to also assess demand reduction measures implemented under Canada's Drug Strategy more than ten years before, and make recommendations for future policy directions, all by no later than June 1997.

In my presentation to the All Party Parliamentary Committee, I brought to the committee's attention that the terms of reference did not include tranquilizers and sleeping pills (or any other prescription drugs), listing only alcohol, heroin, cocaine, nicotine, cannabis, crack, and LSD. I wondered if this telling omission correlated in any way with the overall denial within the medical and political communities that a major problem exists with legal drugs.[3]

In addition to testifying to my own horrific experience with benzodiazepines, and giving a summary of information gathered in the hundreds of interviews I had conducted with the various key stakeholder groups, I also gave the committee a brief overview of the pertinent worldwide research. In addition, I provided a research folder three inches thick to the chairman and a thirty-five-page excerpt of our Call to Action proposal, including the "Obstacles and Solutions" section, which I discussed in great detail. My message was simple: there had been a lot of research undertaken showing the dangers of these drugs over the past three decades, but little action taken to discourage their use. Specifically, I drew attention to the stalled Canadian Medical Association guidelines that should have been put in place a long time ago, the dire need for systemic recognition of the problem to prevent a further increase in the number of victims, and the equally great need for an infrastructure of detox facilities with adequate medical supervision and trained counselors to help "accidental addicts" get off these drugs safely (without having to be told by the medical community that their suffering is "all in their mind"). I further recommended that pharmaceutical companies should be required to contribute a fixed percentage of their sales or profits from these drugs to be used toward setting up this infrastructure. I particularly stressed the need for education programs targeting both doctors and consumers and pointed out that for every dollar spent in prevention, intervention, and education, at least eight times that would be saved in treatment and other related costs to the health-care system.

In June 1997, I made a similar presentation to the North Shore Health Board, in which I commended the withdrawal-management program recently established at Lions Gate Hospital (which had developed out of our Detox Services Committee discussions earlier) and the "academic detailing" project on the North Shore, where a hired pharmacist met with doctors on an individual basis to educate them on specific drugs. These were important steps that needed to be acknowledged and encouraged. However, there was still no coordinated, integrated program to address the issue on the North Shore, where Nancy Hall's 1996 study had shown there to be a significant overprescribing problem, and where denial and minimization by many health-care professionals was still prevalent. I also made it very clear that I felt no more research was necessary. We needed strategies aimed at prevention and education, systemic accountability, and the increased availability of safe, multifaceted detox and recovery programs.

Part of my objective in addressing various health, medical, regulatory, and political bodies during the mid-1990s was also to solicit support and funding for my television documentary project, Our Pill Epidemic, which was by then well into development. I saw it as a strong awareness-building vehicle for getting the message out, and my passion kept driving me toward its realization. Hedy Fry, federal Secretary of State for the Status of Women, also a doctor and a former president of the B.C. Medical Association, was very supportive of the need for the documentary, and acknowledged in a letter to me that the overprescribing of benzos was a serious problem. While I had already written to David Dingwall, then federal Minister of Health, regarding federal funding for the documentary, Hedy Fry also sent him a letter of support on my behalf. I had also written to the federal Finance Minister, Paul Martin, Minister Sheila Copps, and Minister David Anderson regarding support and funding for the documentary. I discussed this with all of them personally and had traveled to Ottawa to attend the Liberal Party Convention with a colleague from the Benzodiazepine Call to Action Group to continue to lobby for funding. Disappointingly, no funding for the documentary was ever obtained from the federal government.

Senator Ray Perrault, who lives on the North Shore, also expressed interest in and support for the issue in September 1996 when I met with him, and suggested that Senate hearings into the subject might well be justified at the federal level to bring about action. The matter, I was told, later had been referred to the Standing Senate Committee on Social Affairs, Science and Technology, and a senator's or MP's private bill, or a senator-sponsored inquiry/special study would be required before any hearing could be initiated. Now, almost three years later, little has happened other than many frustrating phone calls to Senator Perrault's office and empty promises.

More recently, Senator Lucie Pepin—whom I met at the 1998 National Women's Retreat at Whistler (an event started by former prime minister Kim Campbell that brings together a group of leading Canadian women involved in business, politics, media, and academia)—expressed concern about the issue as well, and said she, too, would pursue the idea of Senate hearings, but to date I have not been informed of any progress she's made toward this end.

Early in 1999, I met with federal Reform MP John Reynolds of West Vancouver/Sunshine Coast on this issue, who shared my concern at the lack of action and follow-up. He has referred the matter to the Reform health critic, whom I intend to meet with soon to have the issue raised again in the House of Commons in Ottawa.

Clearly, federal government representatives willing to speak up on this issue and take action are few and far between. Plenty of them are willing to discuss other (illegal) drug and alcohol problems in society, but to acknowledge the harm associated with prescription drugs could open up a politically unpopular can of worms. There might very well be demands for compensation from people harmed by such drugs, and the federal government does not want a repeat of the highly publicized and investigated tainted-blood scandal over the past several years in Canada. Their fear is not groundless: my research shows that the federal Department of Health knew about the problems with tranquilizers and sleeping pills in the early 1970s but did little about it.

The hearings held in connection with the Review on Substance Abuse Policies cost taxpayers hundreds of thousands of dollars, and their stated purpose was to "examine the impact of drugs on the social behaviour and physical health of Canadians, and to assess demand reduction measures ... then make recommendations on future policy directions no later than June, 1997."[4] However, no reports or recommendations on the misuse of prescription drugs ever appeared. I was informed by the committee clerk that "the work of the Standing Committee on Health in the previous Parliament terminated when the election was called, and no reports were presented after that date. ..." What's more, there were "no plans to recommence any work undertaken in the previous Parliament."[5] To put it mildly, this was a big disappointment.

In April 1998, after numerous phone calls to his office, I finally received a response from Alan Rock, the newly appointed federal Health Minister, whom I had met on several occasions by that time. His letter said what I already knew, and conveniently passed the buck to provincial authorities. "Health Canada has revised the prescribing information for benzodiazepines," he wrote. "The Product Monograph for these drugs now states that treatment should usually not exceed 7–10 consecutive days." He was careful to say what I had heard before from the federal Health Protection Branch, that "the practice of medicine is a responsibility of the provinces and territories," and he suggested I take my concerns to the Minister of Health in B.C.,[6] Penny Priddy, whom he copied in his reply. But if the committee hearings had not been intended to effect change and set *national* standards, I wondered, why have them at all?

By that time, I had met with many representatives of four successive provincial health ministers in B.C.—Andrew Petter, Paul Ramsay, Joy McPhail, and Penny Priddy—and lobbied hard for attention to the systemic problem of overprescribing benzodiazepines. My efforts may have had some positive cumulative effect. B.C. Health Minister Joy McPhail had also publicly expressed her concerns, informing the Commons Industry Committee in April 1997 that, according to her information, the Canadian pharmaceutical industry spends $950 million on marketing annually—an average of $20,000 per doctor. She stressed how important it is for doctors to receive "accurate and unbiased information about drugs … free from marketing hype," and—taking direct aim at the drug companies—added that at present "drug-industry marketing is intended to encourage more drug use and not necessarily appropriate drug use."[7]

Unfortunately, though, despite her strong stance on the issue, McPhail then passed the buck straight back to Ottawa when it came to proposed solutions, calling for *federal* action to address the problem. Just as with drug prices, McPhail suggested, we need *national* standards and initiatives to address the issue. Her recommendations included federal drug-industry marketing regulations, and the implementation of two programs that would follow the lead of British Columbia: first, a national "therapeutics initiative" like the one at the University of British Columbia (headed by Dr. Jim Wright, one of our expert witnesses at trial), which provides objective evaluation of drug effectiveness and utilization, and receives no funding from pharmaceutical companies; and, second, national adoption of B.C.'s academic detailing project. Prohibition of direct advertising aimed at consumers was also recommended as were restrictions on drug company promotional activities.

The pharmaceutical lobby is one of the most powerful political bodies in the world; the great wealth amassed by the drug companies from the sale and consumption of their products allows them to wield enormous influence. And as government funding for medical research has decreased in recent years, universities have come to rely more and more heavily on pharmaceutical sales and profits. For example, more than half the Medical Research Council of Canada's $1.2-billion budget over a recent five-year period came from drug companies.[8] Accepting industry funding for research without well-thought-out guidelines, regulations, and ethical considerations is not only shortsighted, but risky to people's health. It is obviously in drug companies' best interests to encourage research initiatives and promote scientific findings that will result in the utilization and/or creation of ever more, and supposedly ever better, drugs that can be widely marketed. Certainly, the encouragement and initiation of research that might illustrate deleterious side effects of existing high-demand drugs, such as tranquilizers and sleeping pills, would receive little if any funding. There is big money to be made in promoting the long-term use of drugs and in treating chronic or doctor-induced illness. Preventative and curative measures will never be so lucrative. This is plainly a dangerous conflict of interest, which affects the very foundation of our health-care system.

As D. Gilbert and A. Chetley made clear in the 1996 *Consumer Policy Review*, the same problem exists in the United Kingdom, as the National Health Service moves toward evidence-based medicine and more rational prescribing. There the drug companies, in seeking new ways to promote their products, target even the National Health Service by "sponsoring conferences, publications and continuing education. Of equal concern is the promotion of the Internet, and other forms of patient information to consumer/patient groups. This is defended as promoting consumer choice, but by redefining illness and 'selling' the disease, they create new markets for themselves. A thorough review of self-regulation is required."[9]

The drug companies themselves are aware of the growing discontent with their marketing strategies, and the Pharmaceutical Manufacturers' Association of Canada (PMAC), an unlikely body to acknowledge or publicize the dangers of prescription drug products, ran a public-relations article in the *Globe and Mail* nationally in March 1997 entitled "Your Money or Your Life," in which they implied that doctors only are to blame for the problem, and referred to the "urgent need to educate the medical profession [about] problems occurring with well-established medications ... such as benzodiazepines. ..."[10] Needless to say, this was a welcome, if belated, public acknowledgement of the doctors' roles in misprescribing these drugs. PMAC's stand on the issue came about after Dr. Robert Coambs of the University of Toronto's Centre for Health

Promotion led medical research teams in a PMAC-commissioned study, which found that, by conservative estimates, the cost of inappropriate prescriptions in Canada exceeds *$2.56 billion.*

In a letter to me in May 1997, PMAC president Judy Erola, whom I had met with previously, and whom I contacted after I read the public-relations piece in the *Globe and Mail,* claimed that PMAC had "long recognized the need for action" regarding the use of benzodiazepines, and had "brought this issue to the attention of all governments. ..." She also informed me that the organization "was in the process of discussing PMAC participation in a national research project on benzodiazepine utilization which would involve all the faculties of Continuing Health Education in universities across Canada, the Federation of Medical Licensing Authorities of Canada, the College of Family Physicians of Canada, the Royal College of Physicians and Surgeons, the federal Ministry of Health and several provincial governments." The objective of the project would be to "review the strengths and weaknesses of benzodiazepine utilization guidelines, and to develop educational interventions to address inappropriate utilization of this medication."[11] Again, this was another step forward to systemic change. Remarkably.

PMAC even reversed itself on support for my documentary film project. In a letter sent to me two years earlier, following a meeting I had with him in Vancouver at a PMAC-sponsored conference entitled "Putting Patients First," Vic Ackermann, the then president of Hoffmann–La Roche—the original manufacturers of Valium and marketers of Librium and Dalmane—said the company had decided "against involvement of any kind" with my documentary project.[12] The film had been in development for some time, but I was still pursuing funding. Shoppers Drug Mart had also turned down my application for funding.

Now, however, my vision of a one-hour TV documentary was finally becoming a reality. In the fall of 1997 a license fee was granted by the Baton Television Network (Vancouver Television) for *Our Pill Epidemic.* I was delighted that my persistence and determination had finally produced results. In addition to approximately $50,000 worth of research, and the time I had personally put into the project, funding came from B.C. Film, Pharmacare (the B.C. Ministry of Health), the B.C. Ministry of Women's Equality, the Vancouver Foundation, the Community Care

Education Society, MacMillan Bloedel, Finning (Canada), the Knowledge
Network (Open Learning Agency), the Alcohol-Drug Education Service,
and, eventually, PMAC (even though they had refused involvement two
years earlier).

I had been in regular contact with Jack McGaw, an award-winning
documentary producer, for over a year. Jack, who was also the former
host of the popular consumer show "Live It Up," and an investigative
journalist, produced and hosted *Our Pill Epidemic*, which initially aired
in British Columbia in November 1997. In 1998, it was twice broadcast
nationally in Canada on Baton/CTV's television network, which includes
twenty-five stations across the country. Jack McGaw and I were co–
executive producers of this program, which was subtitled: "The Shocking
Story of a Society Hooked on Drugs."

Our Pill Epidemic exposed the walking wounded—the people who
trusted their doctors and wound up in the grip of an addiction that can
be more debilitating than addiction to heroin or cocaine. People who lost
their health, their jobs, their families, and years of their lives. The film
asked why and how this happened. The roles of doctors, pharmaceutical
companies, governments, pharmacists, and consumers were investigated,
and a strong call-to-action message was delivered: an indictment of the
market-driven system that uncaringly creates a society crippled by the
effects of mind- and mood-altering drugs.

Judy Erola of PMAC appeared in the documentary and stressed the
importance of educating doctors about benzodiazepines. However, she
was quick to absolve the Pharmaceutical Manufacturers' Association of
any responsibility for the current rampant misuse of tranquilizers and
sleeping pills—which until very recently PMAC members had aggressively promoted—by asserting that benzodiazepines had been a generic
product for many years and were no longer controlled or promoted by
the name-brand manufacturers PMAC represented.

This sort of public acknowledgement is certainly a step forward, but
it is unfortunate that it has only occurred now as an element of corporate
damage control, rather than as an initiative taken by the drug manufacturers themselves. (In a decade or so, if history repeats itself, the same
situation will happen with drugs that PMAC members are so widely
promoting and marketing today, such as Prozac and Ritalin.)

232 CALL TO ACTION

Response to the documentary from across Canada was overwhelming. We heard from many, many viewers who wanted to know where they could go for help with benzodiazepine addiction, and many who just wanted to comment that they had never known that tranquilizers and sleeping pills could have such effects. "My doctor never told me," we heard, over and over.

The film has been made available in broadcast and videocassette format to consumers, health authorities, medical facilities, libraries, universities, and addiction specialists worldwide.

I also participated in a Psychiatric Update Conference in Niagara-on-the-Lake, Ontario, in the summer of 1997, organized by a psychiatrist who conducts seminars to educate other doctors; this time discussions on benzodiazepines were included. This was a positive link with the medical community, of which I took full advantage. I also made a presentation on benzodiazepines to the Pacific Addiction Institute Conference held at the University of British Columbia (UBC) in 1997, attended and met with representatives of the Canadian Public Health Association at its annual conference in Vancouver, and attended a Drug Therapy Decision-Making Conference sponsored by UBC Continuing Medical Education in 1997.

Perhaps one of the most comprehensive conferences I have attended, which provided some real leadership in strategies for systemic change, was the Second National Conference on Cost Effective Drug Therapy in Toronto in the fall of 1997, sponsored by Dr. Michael Rachlis, author of the book *Strong Medicine*. This conference, considered to be Canada's premier forum for pharmaceutical policy issues, was attended by key government officials, pharmaceutical company representatives, health-care professionals, academic researchers, employee-assistance personnel, and consumers. Focus for the conference was on how to control the rising cost of prescription-drug programs, since these costs are rising faster than any other health expenditure. At the conference, I raised my concerns over the inappropriate prescribing of tranquilizers and sleeping pills, and gained further exposure for my documentary.

In 1998 I also attended a conference held in Vancouver entitled Addictive Disease Issues for the 21st Century, sponsored by the College of Physicians and Surgeons of British Columbia, the Oregon Health Sciences University, and the Foundation for Medical Excellence. This conference was promoted as featuring numerous leading experts in addiction medicine, yet nobody on the roster specifically addressed the addiction problems and long-term effects of using benzos—the leading drugs of dependency in the world. I challenged Dr. Robert Dupont, Clinical Professor of Psychiatry at Georgetown University School of Medicine in Washington, on this point, and he sounded like he was representing the pharmaceutical companies' interests. Not surprisingly, he seemed quite threatened by my questions, my research, and my personal experience, as did a number of the other doctors in attendance.

The broadcast of my documentary did not mean the end of my research and advocacy. I have continued to assemble and analyze hundreds of research reports on benzodiazepines supplied by the VOT; the Institute for Study of Drug Dependence in London, England; pharmaceutical companies; and numerous other worldwide sources. A bibliography of some of the more significant studies and research papers can be found in Appendix 1. It includes information on:

- Side Effects/Adverse Reactions
- Paradoxical Reactions
- Addictions/Dependency
- Withdrawal/Protracted withdrawal
- Deaths, Overdoses/Toxicity
- Accidents and Injuries
- Geriatric/Elderly
- Cognitive Impairment
- Pregnancy/Floppy Baby Syndrome
- Medico—Legal

In his 1992 book *Power and Dependence*, Charles Medawar wrote that "there is clearly scope for systematic parliamentary scrutiny of drug safety standards; but we avoid making specific recommendations. This is not to say that solutions do not exist, but to emphasize that there can never be solutions until a problem is recognized and defined for what it is."[13] I wholeheartedly agree.

The list of obstacles and solutions to getting the benzodiazepine problem reduced that appears below was prepared with the help of our

234 CALL TO ACTION

Benzodiazepine Call to Action Group. It is based on my more than nine years of worldwide research, and hundreds of interviews with people from the key stakeholder groups. It is the foundation for a comprehensive action plan, and for the development and implementation of strategies to address this serious health issue that costs our health-care system millions of dollars and affects the quality of life of thousands of people. It is based on the Canadian system, but can apply anywhere in the world, and to other prescription mood-altering drugs.

Obstacles to Getting the Benzodiazepine Problem Reduced	*Solutions*
1. Lots of studies, little action.	**Redirection of research funding toward action-oriented strategies,** including professional help and supervision for chemically dependent persons, public awareness and education campaigns targeting doctors and consumers; i.e., through media, conferences, brochures, product inserts, pill hotline.
2. Prescribing guidelines are not being followed; i.e., CPS, CMA, HPB, Drug Formulary, Therapeutics Initiative.	**Recognition and acknowledgment of established guidelines** by doctors, their regulatory bodies, the Health Protection Branch (HPB). Enforcement of guidelines through mandatory monitoring of doctors' prescribing practices by the provincial Colleges of Physicians and Surgeons. Disciplinary measures and mandatory education for doctors who do not follow guidelines. Use of independent, objective health watchdog organizations (i.e., Therapeutics Initiative). Maximum utilization of PharmaNet program and warning letters from the HPB to doctors.
3. Doctors' lack of ongoing education.	**Compulsory educational upgrading of doctors** (including testing) based on research findings replacing outdated drug treatments. Better education strategies from the Colleges of Physicians and Surgeons, the Canadian Medical Association, and Pharmacare to encourage awareness and compliance; i.e., academic detailing.

Obstacles	*Solutions*
4. Lack of legal accountability.	**The development of government policy to assist those seeking restitution** for medical malpractice associated with inappropriate prescribing; i.e., specific legal action fund with mandatory contributions by pharmaceutical companies and doctors—also utilizing fines levied against offending doctors. Legislation to ensure that health-care practitioners are held accountable for improper prescribing.
5. Lack of objective information provided the consumer.	**Mandatory product labeling and package inserts for prescription drugs** with full disclosure of all potential side effects, dangers of long-term use, the intense withdrawal reactions associated, and cognitive impairment with benzos; i.e., the system followed in Europe. Awareness building and educational initiatives; i.e., use of media, brochures. Government regulations on pharmaceutical advertising targeting doctors and consumers. Expansion of drug-store role re: warnings with prescriptions; e.g., Shoppers Drug Mart model.
6. Incentive for pharmacists to follow up questionable prescriptions.	**Incentive-oriented government initiatives** that reward the implementation of flagging systems in pharmacies; e.g., B.C. Pharmacare program doubling pharmacists' dispensing fee for successful prescription intervention (after contacting the prescribing doctor).
7. High demand for the drugs due to doctor-induced chemical dependency; lack of alternatives for patients.	**Provide health-care coverage for psychologists (not just drug-oriented psychiatrists).** Multifaceted educational process encouraging doctors to counsel re: whole health factors—lifestyle/diet/exercise; provide information, support and referrals to addiction specialists, detox facilities, naturopathic physicians, and community support and activity programs.

Obstacles	*Solutions*
8. Lack of infrastructure, skill, and knowledge surrounding safe withdrawal.	**Education drives targeting doctors geared to better identification and recognition of benzodiazepine dependency,** short- and long-term withdrawal syndrome, the dangers of sudden withdrawal. Need for well-trained doctors to provide medical supervision. Explore U.K. model: doctors sending letters and information to patients at risk. **Create accessible infrastructure for safe, supervised withdrawal;** e.g., insured detox centers (percentage of pharmaceutical sales/profits to be allocated to set up infrastructure); systemic acknowledgment.
9. Minimization and denial of the problem by government, drug companies, doctors.	**Create awareness of socio-economic costs of drug-dependent patients** to the health-care system, justice system, productivity and safety in the workplace, and road safety; i.e., car accidents. Encourage transition toward redirection of monies supporting current chemical dependency and its complications to strategies addressing and alleviating the problem.
10. Industry education is often led by those who will profit from excessive prescribing—drug manufacturers.	**Provide and require issue of continually updated, objective prescribing guidelines** from impartial regulatory bodies not profiting from the promotion of prescription drugs; e.g., CMA, Health Protection Branch, Therapeutics Initiative. Strict controls and independent approval of advertising, product literature. Expand B.C.'s "academic detailing" program nationally.
11. Conflicting relationship between profit-motivated drug companies and research and development funding.	**People before profit.** Guidelines, conflict-of-interest regulations, and code of ethics set for allocating drug manufacturers' contributions to research at universities and for clinical trials to protect the public's health. Independent body directing research dollars. Well-publicized and audited clinical trials fully accessible to the public.

Obstacles	*Solutions*
12. Government's reliance on drug profits encourages drug-based health care—resulting in lack of insured alternatives not producing profit.	Acknowledge falsely economical "quick-fix" of drug treatments for normal emotional responses. **Progressive systemic change encouraging human approach to wellness with long-term benefits. Provide insured alternatives:** e.g., psychologists—allowing patients to avoid unnecessary, damaging drug therapies promoted by drug companies and doctors. Investigation of alternatives offered by naturopathic doctors and other holistic practitioners.
13. Lack of financial resources to rectify the problem.	**Expose the waste of money** linked to long-term benzo dependency; e.g., doctor's-office visits, emergency services, versus the short-term cost of assisting in recovery. **Initiate the redirection of money by reducing consumption.** Prevention equals savings.
14. Lack of coordinated, integrated effort by key stakeholders: doctors, pharmacists, pharmaceutical companies, academia, consumers. Lack of leadership and commitment.	**Legislative, regulatory acknowledgment encouraging open communication** between stakeholder groups focusing on prevention education and consumer protection. **A central information/advocacy center with an integrated approach to positive solutions. Leadership and commitment.**

Why Again, God?

FROM THE MID-1990s ON, while I was becoming more and more involved with my continuing international research and advocacy work, my two beloved daughters, Deb and Carrie, were busy developing their careers and pursuing their active personal lives.

I loved them both very much and I was very proud of them. They shared a concerned and caring attitude for others. Both had strong work ethics, working hard at whatever they did, had good sound values, were real "doers," took up new challenges with "gusto" and were dedicated to helping others and trying to make the world a better place. I thanked God every day that they turned out so well in spite of our difficult and dysfunctional home life. The three of us were closer as a family than we had ever been before.

After graduating from the University of British Columbia, Deb had chosen to work in the vocational-rehabilitation and disability-management field, with a strong grassroots, client-centered focus. A very natural, mature young woman, wise in the ways of the world and with a great deal of common sense, she learned and adapted to everything very quickly. Initially, she worked for North Shore Mental Health Association, developing a therapeutic work program, including a variety of prevocational training programs to assist in clients' integration into the workforce. From there, she became vocational program supervisor at Coast Foundation Society, providing vocational training, pre-employment counseling and placement services. In December 1988, she assumed the position of area coordinator with the I.A.M. Cares program, a pilot project in Canada uniting the interests and concerns of labor, industry, and rehab organizations to provide specialized employment-placement services to people with disabilities.

Having developed many innovative rehab programs to help men and women with various disabilities, she was recognized early on for her efforts, receiving a number of awards provincially and nationally, though she never sought such recognition but simply moved through her work in a quiet, unassuming manner, helping others. She was eventually approached by a headhunter for the position of director of vocational rehabilitation with the Workers' Compensation Board (WCB) of British Columbia. Her acceptance of the offer made her one of the board's youngest directors and one of the few women in management. Viewed as a "change agent," she was instrumental in rewriting the manual for vocational rehabilitation services and developing a case-management program for the WCB. She also presented frequently at conferences, traveling to Toronto and New York, and to Australia on occasion. One year she was selected to participate in the month-long executive management program at the University of Western Ontario (my old alma mater), and I was really pleased for her to be given this opportunity. She deserved it! She later moved to the operational side of WCB as director of client services and was responsible for ten area offices throughout British Columbia, traveling extensively. Later on, she was approached about her interest in an even more senior position in government relations and policy, which she declined because she preferred working at the grassroots level. She was also a founding member of the National Institute of Disability Management and Research.

Deb's marriage to Martin was very happy; he was now an entrepreneur running his own successful business, and together they enjoyed all kinds of sports—sailing, skiing, golfing, and jogging in particular.

One year she did the triathlon, and I recall very vividly the determination and speed with which she cycled the grueling route. They adopted two beautiful white wolf-husky dogs—Nootka and Shylo—who became their "boys." They loved nature, and lived in a unique log home surrounded by tall fir trees on a large lot, also in North Vancouver. They were very environmentally conscious. Deb had inherited my love of cars and soon acquired a white Jaguar convertible as a second vehicle, and later a

Stealth sports car. Deb, Martin, and I all loved music and occasionally went to concerts together to see Elton John, Kenny G., Rod Stewart, and Michael Bolton. As a young couple, they had done exceptionally well and were fulfilling their hopes and dreams.

Carrie, on the other hand—a kind, giving, sensitive, and bright young woman who had graduated from Simon Fraser University in communications—pursued a career in the film industry in Vancouver. She had decided to work in the creative end, in development, with plans to become a producer. She wanted to learn the ropes for producing films with a substantive message. In the first few years, her work as director of development with a film production and distribution company took her to Nice and the Cannes Film Festival twice, as well as to Milan and to the company's production facility in Prague; it was a great learning experience for her and gave her invaluable exposure to the industry.

In the summer of 1997, she decided she would have to work in Los Angeles for a few years to further her career. That would be a real change from living in Vancouver, and it was a big step, moving away from home. Her boyfriend, David, whom she met through the film industry and who was from New York, was also planning to move there, so that they could be closer to each other. In August that year, she and her dad drove to Los Angeles in her white Rabbit convertible, with me behind them in my Le Baron convertible, down the scenic coastal route to California. It was as though her dad and I were united again in our efforts to escort our grown-up daughter (who was now twenty-seven) to her new and (we hoped!) temporary home. We would miss her greatly, but we knew she had her own life to lead. It was our first real family trip together since Alan and I separated in 1977, a most enjoyable, yet heart-wrenching experience. After several months of looking for the right opportunity, she landed a position as a trainee with Oliver Stone's film company, Illusion.

This was a big change in all our lives. We had become accustomed—Deb, Martin, Carrie, Alan, and I—to getting together as frequently as possible, but particularly for birthdays, Christmas, and other special occasions. We had always had a lot of love in our family that somehow got submerged in the murkiness of my chemical dependency on prescription drugs. Since I was off all the pills, we had all made a concerted effort to get to know each other and understand each other better and rebuild our lives toward being a family again, even though Alan and I chose to live our separate lives. Both Deb and Carrie were pleased that Alan and I got along so well as friends. This was very important to me, and I was very happy with the results after so many years of estrangement. Both of our daughters had indeed carved out meaningful niches for themselves, both in their careers and in their personal lives. We all recognized that we had a lot of time and living to catch up on.

And we were just beginning. Which made what happened next all the more tragic.

One night in late January 1998, I received a chilling, devastating phone call from Deb. In her typically positive, stoic manner, she told me that four weeks earlier (only two days after our happy family Christmas dinner at my home), while showering, she had discovered a lump in her left breast. She was calling me now with the news that she was scheduled to have the lump removed the next morning. She hadn't wanted to worry me by telling me sooner. Tests would be done over the next few days to indicate the extent of the lump and the prognosis. I was badly shaken by this news, which instantly catapulted me back to that afternoon in July 1964 when I received the concerned phone call from Auntie about Derek. My son's subsequent two-and-a-half-year battle with a brain tumor, and his tragic death, were only too real. Nevertheless, I think I managed to match Deb's optimistic tone that night, saying that I was sure the results would be all right, and affectionately chastising her for not telling me earlier. She replied that she had also kept the news from Martin for a week.

The next day seemed endless. I prayed to God repeatedly that she would be all right as I waited patiently for good news. Later in the day, Deb called to say the lump was removed along with some lymph nodes under her left arm. She was sore, but doing well. That was my Deb!

Two days later, the day Deb and Martin were meeting with her surgeon to go over the pathology report, I was at home alone. When I saw their car pull into my driveway, I hurried to the front door, repeating my silent prayer. When I opened the door, she and Martin were walking down the driveway; it was one of the few times in my life I saw Deb in tears. I'll never forget her words as I approached her. "Mom, the news wasn't as good as we hoped." My heart sank. We went into the living room and we both sat in front of the fireplace on the slate ledge. I had my arms firmly around her and I held her hand, both of us in tears. Martin sat by quietly. The pathology report revealed the heartbreaking news: her tumor was 2 centimeters (3/4 inch) wide and indeed malignant, and all of the eight lymph nodes removed were positive. Her cancer was one of the more aggressive types (as is often the case in young women) and she was told that the most aggressive form of chemotherapy—high-dose chemotherapy with blood stem-cell transplant—was her only chance to survive. All of this was hard to accept, but I refused to feel defeated. "We're going to lick this," I assured her, and I meant it.

When I was on my own later, I kept asking myself: How could this be? Deb had seldom been sick a day in her life; she was the epitome of health; had always taken excellent care of herself and had been active physically in every sport activity imaginable, all her life. She had never ever been in a hospital overnight. I just couldn't understand why this insidious disease attacked her, of all people, and how, once again, one of my children had developed cancer.

Both Deb and I immediately began to research breast cancer. She was also very research-oriented. Over the ensuing weeks and months, we found out all we could about her type of cancer, treatment options, and clinical-trial results. I met with her oncologist, Dr. Paul Klimo, whom I knew from sitting on the board at Lions Gate Hospital, and whom I respected greatly. I asked him whether, if she were his daughter, he would let her go through the high-dose chemo with blood stem-cell transplant, with its inherent risks, including, possibly, death, and he said yes, it was Deb's best chance if he wanted to see her sitting across from him five years later. He would let her do it. He seemed very knowledgeable about the one-month procedure, including its risks, and had recommended that Deb go to Edmonton to interview the head oncologist and visit firsthand the Cross Cancer Clinic, where she would eventually undergo treatment. Unfortunately, she could not be assured of getting the same treatment in Vancouver at the B.C. Cancer Agency, which only offered it as part of a clinical trial where she would have a 50 percent chance of participating. This was a major disappointment but we just couldn't take the chance. Her life was at stake. As a preliminary, all three of us flew to Edmonton to meet the head oncologist.

In February, as part of our research into high-dose chemotherapy and Deb's particular type of breast cancer, Deb and I drove down to Seattle to the University of Washington Medical Center and the Swedish Tumor Institute to seek out two more expert opinions on treatment. Both doctors there, who were world renowned, concurred that her cancer warranted the maximum treatment available.

Despite my concerns, Deb kept right on working throughout this period, most days from her home, which made it a little easier. I continually reminded her that her health was all that was important right now. Since she and Martin lived only three miles from my home in North Vancouver, I was able to visit her regularly. She showed remarkable courage and a great sense of humor, in spite of such adversity. After two treatments of high-dose chemotherapy at Lions Gate Hospital preliminary to going to Edmonton, she and Martin flew to Edmonton in early May for the recommended treatment. She told me then that if she didn't go she might die. Nobody wanted to live more, or had more to live for, than Deb. She had lost all her hair from the treatment by this time, but that didn't seem to bother her; we had had a wig made that looked very natural. I drove to Edmonton with Alan, and stayed in a bed-and-breakfast guest house for the whole month, to be close to her and to support her in every way I could. Martin stayed with her in her hospital room every day and night, and was a first-class loving husband all the way. I was thankful for that and that they could be together. It was a very trying time.

Deb seemed to handle the intense dose of chemo remarkably well, largely as a result of her exceptionally good health otherwise; she even took being in complete isolation in her stride. She would tire and lose her appetite, and was monitored very closely to ensure that her white blood count did not slip too low. Her sense of humor throughout never faltered, nor did her courage and positive attitude. We were so excited when her doctor said she could finally come home to Vancouver in early June. But her treatment was not over. Daily radiation treatments followed her high-dose chemo a little more than a month later. They continued for over a month.

By July she was back at work at her office, golfing again and looking great—her hair had all come back, in thick tight brown curls. I thanked God every day and prayed that the cancer had been beaten. During my early morning runs I would visualize her completely well again, able to live a normal life. Carrie flew up to Vancouver from Los Angeles on a regular basis to see Deb, and we would all get together for meals as before. She and Martin had so much to live for, and so much of their lives ahead of them.

Approximately ten months earlier, before the appearance of the lump, on one of Deb's business trips to the Okanagan Valley in the interior of British Columbia, she had found a beautiful, spacious, three-level log home on a two-acre country estate nestled on the side of a mountain overlooking Kelowna and Lake Okanagan, close to one of the valley's finest golf courses. She and Martin fell in love with the property, which they had bought for their dream home in anticipation of moving there in a year's time. The lot had many large ponderosa pines, lots of fruit trees, and plenty of running room for their dogs, and offered complete privacy and tranquility. They both had decided they would prefer a country-oriented lifestyle; a warmer, dryer climate in summer; and a move away from Vancouver's denser population, traffic, and rain. During the summer, and on completion of Deb's radiation treatments, they decided to move to Kelowna on September 1, and they were busy for weeks cleaning out their home in North Vancouver, which they decided to rent out for a while. Deb's energy level had remained amazingly high throughout her treatment and she appeared to be back in full swing now. They eagerly looked forward to their move and I saw them off as planned, bright and early the morning of September 1. Deb had received a transfer to the Kelowna office of WCB, where her traveling would be less extensive. She could now drive to most of the offices for which she was responsible. Martin could operate his business from his home office, traveling back to Vancouver whenever necessary.

They both enjoyed their new home immensely and they settled in quickly. Deb would phone me early in the morning most days, raving about the nearby rooster crowing, the horses, the birds in her bird feeders on their expansive deck, and the freshness of the air. At night, it was the clear skies, the moon, and the stars that got her attention, and the solitude of it all. She had always loved nature and the outdoors. For my birthday in October she insisted that all the family drive up to celebrate. It was only a four-hour drive, mostly on the scenic Coquihalla highway.

Carrie and David flew up for the occasion, and once more we were all happily together as a family in an idyllic setting. It was like a dream come true, and everything I could have hoped for as a mother. But soon our lives were to be torn apart once again.

In November, Deb flew to Vancouver—for her regular weekly directors' meeting, I thought, but instead she saw her oncologist, Dr. Klimo. Deb's cancer was back—a recurrence in the scar tissue of her left breast with outwardly visible nodules. She also had a slight cough that I was concerned about. Deb had come to my home to tell me the news personally. The next morning I drove her to the airport to catch her flight back to Kelowna and her parting words to me were "Mom, you have to be strong." I was strong, but I cried all the way home. I couldn't help it. It was very tough to deal with this terrifying disease attacking my daughter again. I knew I had to focus on not giving in to the fear. Soon after, I came across the book by Dr. Bernie Siegel, *Love, Medicine and Miracles*, describing his experience with seriously ill cancer patients and the power of the mind to heal the body.

Once more I placed on my fridge door the affirming words "We are strong together because we love." Love, medicine, miracles, and a positive strong mind and a faith and trust in God, would see Deb through this horrible nightmare, I had to believe. Just above these words were pictures of Deb, Carrie, and me smiling so happily, taken just the Christmas before (two days before Deb found the lump). I also taped on the fridge one of my favorite pictures of Deb and Carrie fully dressed in Deb's huge Jacuzzi bathtub as a fun thing, smiling broadly. It was taken when we were all in Kelowna for my birthday the previous month, and they both looked so well and happy.

Deb soon started chemotherapy again, this time with a drug call Taxotere, and I flew up for her first two treatments, and to be with her and Martin.

Christmas was fast approaching, and once more Deb invited our whole family and Martin's parents for Christmas dinner and to spend a few days of the holidays with them. This was very important to her and to us all since Christmas was always a difficult time and a constant sad reminder of Derek's death thirty-two years before. Martin had put hundreds of multicolored Christmas lights outside, outlining their home, and on a perfectly shaped ponderosa pine tree at the end of their driveway. It was a beautiful scene, particularly with all the snow that had fallen.

Deb and he had picked out a ten-foot Christmas tree two weeks earlier, which they had decorated beautifully and placed just inside the French doors leading to their front deck. Deb was thrilled with it, and would sit and enjoy its bright lights for hours. The warm glow of the lights reflected off the warmth of the cedar inside their spacious living room, and nearby the roaring fireplace gave off its healing and soothing heat. Sadly, in years gone by, we never did have a real Christmas tree at home.

Christmas that year was what I always thought Christmas should be —thanks to Deb and Martin. It was picture-perfect—lots of love, family, and good food. Outside, the falling snow added to the mood of the festive season. Alan and I took many candid shots of the family cooking meals, playing games, opening presents, the snow, the tree, and their beautiful home and the panoramic views. Deb looked really well and was in great spirits. She was wearing her wig again, as she had once more lost all her hair. This was a very happy and contented time for us all, and we thanked God that we were able to be together. The uncertainty and sadness of Deb's cancer was ever-present in our minds, but we had faith and hope for the future. It all seemed so unfair, and to some extent unreal, that she should be going through such agony and anguish.

Deb's chemo treatments continued after Christmas, and in late January she and Martin flew to Vancouver for a consultation with six doctors at the B.C. Cancer Agency. The doctors were very pleased with the dramatic results from the Taxotere and decided against performing a mastectomy, indicating that the cancer might reappear in the scar if they did. Deb phoned me—she was excited that, come April, she would be back in her golf game again. She cautioned me, though, saying "There are no guarantees. That's the reality, the cancer might come back." It was something we all had to learn to live with.

In March, she and Martin flew to Vancouver—Deb for her regular directors' meeting and Martin for his business—and we celebrated Martin's forty-second birthday at my home on March 23. Deb's cough had worsened, which was of great concern to me, but her spirits were high as usual. That same weekend, however, I received a call from Martin that Deb was back in the Kelowna hospital with breathing problems, on oxygen. The news was what I had dreaded: the cancer had spread to her lungs. I immediately drove to Kelowna and stayed for over a week. She underwent an operation on Good Friday. Tubes were placed on both sides of her rib cage to drain out the fluid from her lungs. She stayed on oxygen full time. It was hard to believe that her cancer was aggressive enough to withstand all the chemotherapy that she had received by now. I was also becoming very concerned about the toxic effects the treatment was having on her immune system. But Deb was strong physically, mentally, and emotionally, and she rallied again after the operation and went home once more. Oxygen was installed in her home and she continued working, in spite of my concerns. It was obvious she preferred to keep busy and active instead of sitting around worrying and wondering what was going to happen next. That was not her style. She had always been such a conscientious and dedicated person in everything she did.

Both of us continued our research into the other cancer drugs that were available, including experimental drugs and alternative treatments for breast cancer. We kept track of clinical trials that were under way throughout the world.

Initially Deb had added vitamins and supplements to counteract the side effects of the intensive chemotherapy, but she disliked taking pills and had difficulty swallowing them. She was somewhat skeptical of their benefits, whereas I was convinced that the integrated approach of conventional and complementary treatments was needed. I researched integrated cancer-treatment centers all over North America and in Europe, and encouraged her to consider going to one in Mexico in early April. Unfortunately, such centers normally operate outside of the United States, since they are only partially recognized as offering bona-fide treatment by conventional medicine. But we needed to pull out all stops to save her life. That was becoming critically clear. Her diet and appetite were good, and she managed to maintain her weight, but she could no longer do the exercises that had been so much a part of her life in previous years. She also developed serious lymphedema in her left arm, with all the swelling and pain associated with that condition, and started regular physiotherapy.

The doctors added more drugs—for pain, for nausea, for swelling, and to keep her white blood cells up and platelets stable. The quality of her life was constantly being affected. I struggled personally with the fact that she needed chemotherapy in the first place, with all its side effects and all the other drugs to counteract these side effects (given my experience with tranquilizers and sleeping pills), but I recognized that everything possible had to be done to lick the cancer. It was sadly ironic.

Carrie, who was still living in Los Angeles, decided to fly home and spend a few days with Deb in Kelowna. She was making arrangements to move back to Vancouver after deciding she no longer wanted to be involved in the film industry, and naturally wanted to be close to Deb on a regular basis. David was also making plans to immigrate to Canada as soon as he could. Deb's situation was becoming all the more unpredictable and of increasing concern to all of us, and there was no doubt we had to stop this disease and stop it fast.

She and her big sister had always been close when they were young, and Deb, being nine years older, was like a second mother to Carrie. Now, as young women, they spent a lot of time discussing and sharing many things on a regular basis. There was much love between them. Carrie told me later that, one morning when she was staying with Deb and Martin, Deb climbed into bed with her the way she used to when they were children. I was so pleased that their sisterly bonds were still so strong. The horrors of what Deb was going through and the ongoing uncertainty had pulled them both even closer.

I had withdrawn from almost all my business, political activities, and advocacy efforts regarding benzos during this crucial time, but I had been selected several months earlier as a delegate to the B.C. Liberal convention, and I decided to attend, because it was being held in Kelowna this year and it gave me another reason to be close to Deb. On the weekend of April 16, I arrived at Deb and Martin's home on the Friday around noon, and when I walked in there was Deb in tears once again. She had just received a phone call from Dr. Klimo advising her that there was "nothing more they could do." He was recommending "no more chemotherapy." He told Deb, "If it was my wife, I would do no more." The news was devastating. I hugged and kissed Deb and held her hands; I still could not give up hope that we would together find an answer. That evening the oncologist from the Swedish Tumor Institute called from Seattle, and he told Deb there were still other chemotherapy drugs that could be tried—some of the ones Deb and I had been researching—and new experimental drugs as well.

That night, Deb, Martin, and I had a feast, with fresh oysters flown in from Vancouver Island, from one of the oyster farms Deb and Martin had invested in. This was to be a big treat for us all.

The next afternoon, when I came back after being at the Liberal convention for several hours, I found Deb sitting on her front deck in shorts, reading the Bible. It was a gloriously warm, sunny day, with a magnificent unobstructed view of the lake and the nearby mountains. Colorful birds were flitting around everywhere in the trees and around her feeders. Deb had been searching out the spiritual side of her life over the previous few weeks. She and Martin had attended the Celebration of Life church and had taken part in a healing circle, where everyone prayed together for Deb's recovery. Her search for and understanding of God had become a very meaningful part of her life, and of Martin's. She had music versions of the Psalms that she listened to over and over at night when she couldn't sleep. She bought a book, and a copy for me, entitled *Something More—Excavating Your Authentic Self*. It was all part of her reaching for answers and searching to understand what was happening in her life.

I returned to Vancouver, and a week passed. On Tuesday, April 22, Deb phoned and asked me to take care of some additional arrangements for their passports to go to Germany to an integrated cancer center that I had brought to their attention several weeks earlier. She had been in contact with the center and had sent her clinical records in anticipation of going. I was very encouraged by this development. It was one of our remaining areas of hope that Deb could be helped.

The next day her condition changed dramatically. Deb's nose began to bleed. It wouldn't stop, and so Martin took her back to the hospital, where she required five units of blood. Her platelets had bottomed out and she was put on oxygen. Her breathing had become very difficult. The oral chemotherapy drug (Xeloda) was discontinued that afternoon. Each day I talked to Martin on the phone. I planned to drive up to Kelowna on Saturday, if not before, and on Friday night Martin phoned to say that Deb might be able to come home on Saturday. I felt a little more encouraged again.

When I arrived at the Kelowna hospital on Saturday, Deb was in really bad shape—in obvious pain, getting morphine, and still on full-time oxygen, but with a full nose mask now. Martin told me she might not live through the day. I was in shock. How could her situation have changed so quickly? I didn't want to believe any of this was happening and I told her doctor in front of Deb that I was not giving up hope. Deb said to me again, "This is the reality." She had given instructions to the doctor not to resuscitate but not to turn off the oxygen either. Deb said to me, "You have to accept this," and I replied, "I can't."

She was surprisingly mentally alert all through Saturday, even with the increasing levels of morphine for the pain. She kept monitoring her heartbeat (which was exceeding 140 beats) and her oxygen intake. I sat beside her bed, holding her hand and rubbing her legs and feet. I didn't know what else to do to help. As a mother, I am supposed to be able to make my children better, and now in the immediacy of Deb's critical condition, I felt overwhelmed with helplessness, frustration, sadness, and some anger. Surely someone could do something! I left the room and cried. I returned to her room and tried to be reassuring and hopeful, but I couldn't stop my tears. I referred to the planned trip to Germany and Deb with her good sense of humor, and her love of cars replied, "Don't forget the Porsche for the Autobahn." Martin was continually placing cold compresses on Deb's forehead. She showed so much courage and was very much in control of what was happening, as she had been all her life.

When I left the hospital around nine that evening, I told Martin to call me if he needed anything or if Deb's situation changed. While it was hard for me to leave, I kissed Deb goodbye and told her I loved her and would see her in the morning. She said, "I love you too, Mom."

The phone rang about twenty minutes to midnight. It was Martin calling to say that Deb was not doing well at all. I rushed back to the hospital to find him sitting on the floor in the hallway not far from her room, holding his head in his hands and sobbing uncontrollably. I put my arms around him and started to cry too. At that point, the nurse came out of Deb's room and said she thought Deb was still breathing. I went back into her room, but that was no longer my Deb. Her spirit had left her body and her hands were cold. Deb had died.

I was numb; I was in shock. I tried my best to comfort Martin, who had lost his beloved wife of eighteen years. They had always been so much in love, so close, and had done so much together. They had reached for their dreams and had realized only some of them.

In a daze, I phoned my sister, Pat, and my two brothers, Bill and Bob, back east in Ontario to let them know that Deb had died. Carrie was already flying home to Vancouver from Los Angeles. I found out Deb had asked Martin to phone her earlier in the day to ask her to come home. Similarly, Martin had called her dad, and Alan was to pick Carrie and David up at the airport. When I spoke to Carrie, she was devastated, crying, and upset that she had not made it home in time to see Deb before she died. She had always thought Deb would be there as they grew older together. She had lost her big sister, whom she described as "one of the wisest people I ever met." Carrie, David, and Alan all stayed that night together at my home in North Vancouver, before the difficult and lonely trip up to Kelowna.

I drove back to Deb and Martin's home, sobbing in total disbelief. I felt so much despair and sorrow. I felt empty, as though someone had pulled out my heart and the real essence of my being. I had lost my beloved first child, my daughter, my friend, at the age of thirty-seven, after a seventeen-month battle with the cruelest and most unforgiving of diseases. It was May 1, 1999. She was my second child to die of this insidious disease. After Derek died on Christmas Day, 1966, I never for one moment thought that I would have to face losing another child, another young life taken so mercilessly. It was a mother's worst nightmare. I thought over and over again, life has not been kind to our family, and I asked, Why? I had no answers.

I prayed to God to surround me and my whole family with his guidance, wisdom, his love, and to keep us all strong together. We had to be strong. I could not blame God for causing Deb's cancer or for not saving her life, but my faith was severely tested. I thought God was love, and was all-powerful. At least, that is what I was brought up to believe. And we had prayed desperately for a miracle to save Deb's life. It didn't happen. Why? I had no answers.

Why did Deb get cancer in the first place? I didn't know. Her lifestyle was always healthy. Was it the birth control pills she had been on for eighteen years? Was it a genetic problem or an inherited predisposition to cancer? Was it our dysfunctional home life? Was it bad luck? What was it? I had no answers.

Why was my life spared with my last unintentional overdose from the pills Dr. MacGillivray had prescribed so freely and for so long after Derek had died? I had concluded that it was in part so that I could carry the message about tranquilizers and sleeping pills to help others and change a system that didn't work.

But why Deb? Throughout her life, she had dedicated herself to helping others, being sensitive to their needs and trying to make the world a better place, one day and one person at a time. And she had so much left to do with her life, including work in the area of cancer—we had talked about it many times. It was all so cruel and unfair.

These thoughts and questions kept running through my mind as I approached their home. As I pulled into the driveway, I could not accept the fact that she would no longer be coming home to this place she had loved so much, in which she and Martin had lived for only eight short months. All of their hours of hard work and determination and their hopes and dreams of a normal happy life together were gone.

Martin and his dad, who also drove up to Kelowna on Saturday, stayed up all night to watch the sunrise, hear the early morning rooster, and see the birds flitting about Deb's feeders. It was such an important part of her life in Kelowna—the simple things and the beauty of nature.

Carrie, David, and Alan arrived the next morning, and the whole family remained cloistered for the week at Deb and Martin's home grieving. Each of us was trying to come to grips with this incredible tragedy. We needed to comfort and support each other, and we felt Deb's presence all around us. Carrie and Martin made all the arrangements for two separate Celebration of Life services for Deb, one later that week in Kelowna, and the other the following Monday at Highlands United Church in North Vancouver, where Deb was baptized. Both services were attended by hundreds of Deb's family, friends, and colleagues from work over the years. The service was unconventional and simple, and included some of Deb's favorite psalms and songs, as well as eulogies and tributes by family, friends, and co-workers. One of Deb's favorite songs in recent years was played: "Angel," by Sarah McLachlan, from the film *City of Angels*, which Deb had found so comforting and meaningful. Over and over again we heard of Deb's compassion, her kindness, and the legacy she had left with everyone she had met—how she had changed their lives, the shared memories and the respect she earned. We had also put together a large photo montage of her life from early pictures of her with Derek, with Carrie, and with Martin; pictures of work colleagues; her, golfing, fishing, skiing; family pictures from Christmas; her cars; their sailboats.

Deb's body was buried in Lakeview Memorial Gardens North of Kelowna, beside a tree overlooking the lake, close to the mountains and surrounded by fruit trees.

After Deb died, Martin told me that her last words to him were, "Oh my God, here they come"—referring to the angels. At last, I thought, she is out of pain and in peace, and she will be joining her brother Derek in Heaven. I vividly recalled her sorrow in losing him when she was only five, and took comfort in the knowledge that they would be reunited. I had to believe that.

I was glad that I had been right there with her during her battle with breast cancer, to love, support, and encourage her. The hope that we all shared for her recovery was not to be realized, sadly, but her positive attitude and bravery even in her most difficult and darkest moments were truly indicative of the great personal strength she had shown all her life.

One of her key messages to Carrie when she had visited her in early April was to live each day and not to postpone doing things that are important in her life.

One of Deb's final messages for me conveyed through Martin after she died was to get my book out, produce a movie of the week, and keep up my running. And these I am committed to.

It has been a long and difficult struggle to rebuild my life and my family over the past nine years since I have been off all pills, and Deb's tragic death so young causes me incredible sadness that she is not here on this earth to continue to experience and share the rest of our lives together as we had hoped and planned.

What is significant, too, is that there were no pills necessary for me to cope with living with her disease on a daily basis, nor any pills prescribed for me to cope with the incredible grief of losing my beloved daughter. To have lost two children to cancer causes me great pain and anguish, but I realize that I must carry on with my life and my mission to help others and continue to work toward making the world a better place. I know Deb would want that.

In spite of the fact that my faith has been so severely shaken by Deb's death, and Derek's before her, I still believe God watches over all of us, providing guidance, wisdom, and love. This belief is reaffirmed every day through nature, as I know no human could have created the beauty all around us.

But the question remains: Why again, God?

I hope one day I will have an answer.

Conclusion

W HEN I FIRST CONFIDED in my doctor about my personal struggle to deal with the pain of Derek's illness and death, back in the mid-1960s, I believed I was doing the right thing. Naturally, the anguish I was experiencing at that time was affecting my overall health, and I discussed it openly with him. I know now, in hindsight, that as soon as I did so, I put myself in a very vulnerable position. I regret to say that this scenario is still playing itself out in doctors' offices today, not only in Canada but throughout the world. Many physicians still erroneously believe that troubled times and crises call for drug treatment, which can cause far more harm than good. In my case, the medical response to my grief and unavoidable emotional circumstances led me on a path that altered the course of my life forever, not only affecting me personally, but taking its toll on my whole family. It also cost the health-care system many dollars that need never have been spent.

There are numerous new mind and mood-altering drugs on the market now, and pharmaceutical companies are not likely to stop introducing them any time soon. Convincing millions of healthy people that they need tranquilizers and sleeping pills to cope with life's daily challenges, or that they have "chemical imbalances," ambiguous "mood disorders," or alleged psychiatric illnesses that must be treated with medication, is an insidious marketing ploy. As Dr. Robert Rangno, a spokesperson from Therapeutics Initiative at the University of British Columbia, put it in our documentary: "If you've got a cure, you have to sell the disease."

Today, one of the newest "diseases" is social anxiety disorder, for which Paxil, an anti-depressant, is being marketed.

Clearly, the trend continues, with benzodiazepines still being prescribed at alarming rates. They have often been called the most widely prescribed group of drugs in the world, and they are the biggest-selling drugs in the history of medicine. Current estimates place worldwide sales of benzodiazepines in excess of $21 billion. U.S. sales exceed an estimated $1.2 billion, and the most recent figure for Canada is an estimated $104 million.[1]

In the United Kingdom, Dr. Reg Peart of Victims of Tranquilizers reports that, in 1997, 7 percent of the population, or 4 million people, were prescribed benzodiazepines, with at least 1 million dependant on the drugs (Valium use increased an estimated 15 percent between 1994 and 1997).

In British Columbia, a report released in May 1999, entitled *B.C. Provincial Profile of Women's Health*,[2] revealed that, in 1997, benzodiazepine prescriptions surpassed all other Pharmacare prescriptions for women, exceeding cardiac drugs, antidepressants, and estrogen. Sixty-five percent of prescriptions issued went to women. Clearly, the lessons of history have not been learned, and there is an ongoing dependency epidemic being created. This in spite of all the warnings and research.

At the same time, there is a booming market for antidepressant medications, such as Prozac, Paxil, Zoloft, and Luvox and their sales have also reached billions of dollars worldwide. According to a 1997 magazine article, Prozac—the world's best-selling antidepressant—had reported sales of more than $2 billion, with more than 24 million users.[3]

In the recent B.C. study referred to earlier, results showed that 70 percent of all antidepressant prescriptions were prescribed for women, with a ratio of six prescriptions filled for every female user in 1997, indicating that these drugs are every bit as habit-forming as benzos. While statistics are not available on the numbers of people cross-addicted to benzodiazepines and antidepressants, my research and interviews strongly support the belief that many people are in fact being prescribed both.

As Dr. Sidney Wolfe of the Health Research Group in Washington, D.C., told me several years ago, "the anti-depressant Prozac is simply the follow-up to Valium, only twenty-five years later."[4] And just as with benzodiazepines, multinational drug companies, concerned above all with increased sales and bottom-line profits, continue to pump millions of marketing and promotional dollars into drugs whose side effects are every bit as hazardous to health as benzodiazepines are.

One ad for Prozac that I saw three years ago depicted a middle-aged couple smiling and gazing at flowers, with a caption that claimed: "Seldom has one drug helped change so many lives—Prozac as your first line of action." The obvious inference here is that you, too, can be happy once you're on Prozac. The ad listed potential side effects in small print, the most "commonly observed" being "headaches, nervousness, insomnia, drowsiness, fatigue, anxiety, tremor and dizziness." Should patients suffering from the side effects of Prozac, such as insomnia and anxiety, then be put on sleeping pills and tranquilizers? Drugs to treat the side effects of other drugs, as was done with me? I was particularly concerned to see this expensive, full-page color ad purchased by the manufacturers of Prozac, on the back of the *Canadian Medical Association (CMA) Journal*, which is distributed primarily to doctors. I contacted the CMA and told them that accepting such advertising was unethical and put them in a conflict of interest. I was told they needed the advertising revenue. There is clearly a need for a government regulatory body or an independent body to step in and control this blatantly irresponsible and inappropriate advertising. Even more alarming is the fact that Prozac is now available in a mint-flavored syrup for kids! It's just like the tobacco industry—if you hook them young, they're customers for life.

The drugging of our children continues with increasing regularity and controversy with the prescribing of Ritalin (a highly addictive central nervous system stimulant) for children diagnosed with attention-deficit disorder—another ambiguously labeled and contrived "psychiatric" condition. Two *Vancouver Province* articles, on August 8 and 9, 1999, had headlines that read "Why haven't they banned this drug?" "We're giving our kids a pill that can kill" and "Boys will be boys—that's why we've got them popping pills."[5]

The articles referred to shocking new findings about the overprescribing of drugs to children with attention or behavioral problems, revealing that "Canada is nearing a world record, with Ritalin use having increased 50 percent last year alone. It further reports that "only the United States has a higher rate of increase—up approximately *700 percent* between 1990 and 1998."

Eight- to thirteen-year-old boys made up almost half the British Columbia patients under nineteen years of age on Ritalin. In some communities, one of every four young boys is receiving this drug for hyperactivity and inattentiveness. Recent additions to the list of drugs for children include dexedrine, a former diet drug that fell out of favor but is reportedly making a big comeback to control kids, and Cylert, a controversial drug that can cause liver failure and death.

The newspaper articles appeared following the tragic death of a healthy fourteen-year-old boy who was put on Cylert for eighteen months and developed liver failure. According to the article, Abbot Laboratories, which manufactures Cylert, has ceased actively promoting it, although it is still available by prescription. U.S. authorities have issued a "Dear Doctor" letter to physicians (as I recommended to the Health Protection Branch for benzos, years ago) and, in Canada, the Health Department launched an investigation into the drug in December 1998 but has made no decision on whether to advise doctors in Canada to stop using the drug. Why the delay?

Side effects of these drugs are every bit as deleterious as those of benzodiazepines. Ritalin can cause appetite loss, insomnia, headaches, delayed growth, tics, depression, and possible psychosis. Long-term users who have become dependent on dexedrine may also become "mentally unstable and suffer severe depression and suicide associated with withdrawal," according to the CMA guidebook on prescription drugs.[6]

Regarding the huge increase in the prescribing of Ritalin, Health Canada is reportedly currently conducting a national survey of doctors to determine "whether attention deficit disorder is being properly diagnosed, but quickly points out that" it is virtually powerless to restrict its use since it is a "practice of medicine issue," and that it's up to the doctors to be monitored by their provincial organizations—the Colleges of Physicians and Surgeons.[7]

In early 1998, doctors in British Columbia, where Ritalin use has reached all-time highs, promised to review prescribing practices at the urging of the provincial Health Minister, Penny Priddy, but the investigation is still not complete. And it won't be made public, according to the article. Why is there so much secrecy? To protect doctors?

Many of the children on these drugs grow up to be involuntary addicts, psychologically and physically dependent on the effects of these pills and other pills to live their lives. This is unconscionable. It is imperative that consumers question their doctors very carefully regarding drugs prescribed for them and/or their children, and that they have all the facts before accepting a pharmacological approach to their problems.

The similarity between benzos and these drugs overprescribed to children is readily apparent, as is the slowness with which doctors' regulatory bodies and the federal Health Protection Branch respond to justified concerns. And many more lives continue needlessly to be affected and to be seriously put in jeopardy.

Another aspect of the benzodiazepine problem has arisen with the emergence of Rohypnol, the so-called date-rape drug, which is also a tranquilizer and is used to control and force victims into compliance.

By favoring the pharmacological approach, and denigrating any sort of alternative or complementary approach—such as services offered by psychologists, community support organizations, and naturopathic physicians (who look at whole health, including nutrition, exercise habits, and overall lifestyle) and a myriad of other holistic approaches to wellness— the conventional medical system (based on a disease model) has only encouraged treatment that predominantly facilitates drug-induced and chronic illness.

Revealing research undertaken at the University of Toronto in 1998 analyzed statistics from thirty-nine studies done in U.S. hospitals, spanning four decades. This significant study found that 2.2 million serious injuries and more than 100,000 deaths were attributed to prescription drugs taken as instructed! Even within these narrow criteria (which do not include injuries and deaths associated with unintentional overdoses and deaths resulting from suicidal ideation created as a side effect of drugs), the ingestion of prescription drugs was found to be one of the four leading causes of death, along with heart disease, cancer, and stroke.[8]

While advocating for change can be a lengthy, frustrating process, I do believe and have been told that my countless meetings and interviews with key organizations such as the PMAC, with drug company representatives, with federal and provincial government politicians and bureaucrats, with pharmacists, with researchers, and with the CMA and the College of Physicians and Surgeons, and others over the past nine years have helped to foster a dialogue and movement toward systemic

change. A letter I received from British Columbia's Deputy Health Minister in 1996 acknowledged that "the Ministry of Health concurs that
prescription drug abuse is a genuine and serious problem," and that "better information, particularly consumer and professional information, is
an important component in combating this problem."[9]

The collective "don't rock the boat" or status quo attitude toward
prescription drugs, and the multibillion-dollar industry behind them, is
undoubtedly linked to the lack of infrastructure (detox and treatment
facilities) and knowledge (trained medical supervision and counselors)
on how to address the issue of the thousands of already chemically dependent women and men. More likely, though, the cause is an overriding
fear of legal action from consumers who trusted their doctors in the first
place. But, I ask, how many more lives have to be destroyed, and how
many people have to die before something is done?

Many federal ministers, members of Parliament, and members of the
Legislative Assembly I have met with are well aware of the problems
associated with the overprescribing of benzodiazepines and other prescription drugs, but they have chosen to bury them, ignore them, or stall
concrete initiatives that could help, lacking the political will and leadership to take a stand. One of the top issues I discussed with Federal Health
Minister Alan Rock when we met was the incidence of impaired driving
and car accidents associated with benzodiazepine use resulting in injuries
and deaths. But to date he has done little about it.

Recently, I met with a senior vice-president at the Insurance Corporation of B.C. (ICBC) to offer my assistance in the development of a drug-
impaired-driving strategy, and an awareness program for the public.
This strategy would parallel the work of Mothers Against Drunk Drivers
(MADD), a group that promotes awareness of the dangers of drinking
and driving. The difference is that many benzo users are unaware of the
effects these drugs have on their concentration, coordination, and psychomotor abilities; they don't know that when they get behind the wheel
they endanger not only themselves, but other people on the road. I was
told that an impaired-driving program directed at prescription drugs
was "not the priority" of the corporation, and that the program was on
hold. (I had previously attended three meetings with ICBC officials on
the subject.)

Similarly, there is a significant need for public- and private-sector corporations, Workers' Compensation Boards, and employers and employee representative groups and associations to be made aware of the effects impairments caused by benzodiazepines and other mind-altering prescription drugs have on workplace safety, decision making, and productivity. The cost is millions of dollars to companies, organizations, and the economy as a whole. While illegal drugs and alcohol in the workplace receive attention, tranquilizers and sleeping pills do not.

Unfortunately, one of the best incentives for change is likely to lie with the upsurge of medical-malpractice cases being brought through the courts. As public awareness increases, use of the justice system for compensation by benzodiazepine survivors will only continue to grow. The *Medical Post* ran an article in June 1998 that reported that the number of legal actions brought by patients against their doctors continue to rise at a rate of 15 percent a year. And it is no surprise that the Medical Defence Union (MDU), representing doctors globally except in North America, listed the top reason for these medical malpractice claims as "medication errors; e.g., incorrect dosage, contraindicated medication, wrong drug."[10] In the United Kingdom, the legal proceedings launched by the thousands of former benzo users against their doctors, pharmaceutical manufacturers, and health authorities was "the largest civil action ever"[11] and drew much-needed public attention to the issue.

As part of its mandate to regulate and control the marketing requirements and standards for psychotropic substances, the federal Health Protection Branch's Therapeutic Products Directorate finally conducted a review and update of hypnotic agents in 1997. This review body worked in consultation with an expert advisory panel and revised the prescribing information (product monographs) for benzodiazepines and benzodiazepine-like drugs indicated in the treatment of insomnia. After so many years, the new draft product monograph now states, in part, that "a variety of abnormal thinking and behavioral changes may occur when you use benzodiazepine sleeping pills ... changes may include aggressiveness and extroversion which seem out of character" as well as "confusion, strange behaviour, restlessness, hallucinations ... and worsening depression, including suicidal thinking." It also recommends that "treatment should not exceed seven to ten consecutive days."[12] However, very little is being done by the Health Protection Branch to communicate this important information directly to doctors. An additional problem is that the marketing of these drugs has already been highly successful, and many people are hooked and have been for years.

On one of my trips to Ottawa, I met Dr. Michele Brill Edwards, a physician and specialist in federal drug regulation who worked for fifteen years with Canada's Health Protection Branch as the senior physician responsible for the regulation of prescription drugs in Canada. In her role to protect the public from health hazards in the sale and use of drugs, she became aware of repeated abuses and illegality within the drug-regulatory process to bow to political and industry pressure that led to jeopardizing lives. In 1992, Dr. Brill Edwards joined a successful federal court challenge to Health Canada's safety abuses within the drug-approval process. A month later, her senior medical position was declared redundant.

In January 1996, Dr. Brill Edwards, as a matter of principle, resigned from her newly assigned position to protest publicly the deficiencies of Canada's drug-safety systems. Her resignation prompted the formation of a new public-interest group, the Alliance for Public Accountability. Early in 1997 the group spearheaded a call for investigation of Health Canada's abuses of the drug-safety laws. Since that time, a host of citizens' groups have banded together to challenge Health Canada's uneven and illegal manipulation of the Food and Drugs Act for a variety of regulated products, including prescription drugs.

In her resignation letter,[13] Dr. Brill Edwards stated: "It is clear that our system for the evaluation of the safety and efficacy of drugs lacks the capacity to render reliable, informed decisions in the public interest." She further outlined that it was her "paramount concern that the Department must not continue to place the interests of pharmaceutical manufacturers ahead of the protection of public safety," pointing out that the Department of National Health and Welfare Act confers upon the Minister the duty to uphold the Food and Drug Act and its regulations "to protect the public against health hazards in the sale and use of drugs. ..."

What has happened with the CMA guidelines for benzos drafted in 1996? Disappointingly, nothing yet. They have still not been released, with the latest reason given that publication of the guidelines is "dependent on a background paper that has yet to be published by Dr. Anne

Holbrooke of the Centre for Evaluation of Medicines in Hamilton. Although the Centre receives its funding from a variety of sources including pharmaceutical companies, its purpose is to function as an independent and objective arbiter of therapeutic outcomes and to conduct research assessing the economic impact of drug therapies."[14] I look forward with great anticipation to publication of these much-delayed guidelines. Clearly, though, fear of litigation continues to be one of the reasons for delaying their release.

Understandably so. Dr. Anne Carter, former Director of Health Programs for the CMA, when giving evidence to the House of Commons Standing Committee on Health in 1997, stated that, "by law, when a physician prescribes for a patient, the physician is required to make sure the patient is fully informed about the risks and the benefits of the therapy prescribed, and consents, actually, to that therapy with full informed knowledge. ..."[15]

Unfortunately, talk is cheap, and while the CMA and other federal bodies may produce guidelines, and warn of legal requirements, a letter I received from the Director General of the Health Protection Branch discussing the new product monographs for benzodiazepines pointed out that "control over benzodiazepines in the context of the practice of medicine is the responsibility of provincial/territorial governments and their relevant organizations."[16] The problem is that, while provincial bodies pass on information filtered down from federal agencies, until very recently there has literally been no enforcement or compliance monitoring in place. Consumers already harmed by these drugs are left to address their complaints after the damage is done—lives lost and health destroyed—through the Colleges of Physicians and Surgeons.

And protection of patients' interests and rights is too often subordinated to the colleges' protection of doctors. There is an obvious conflict of interest in doctors' own professional associations investigating such complaints. An independent investigative and disciplinary body is called for.

It is also my intention to place the Benzodiazepine Call to Action Group into a university-based foundation, where ongoing funding can be raised to carry on vital work in the area of advocacy, research, and education. There is a pressing need for strong consumer advocates to sit on government advisory boards addressing this issue, both federally and provincially. The Benzo Policy Action Research Group in B.C. evolved from, but now excludes, consumer representation. Why? Discussions I have had with both Dr. John Anderson, medical advisor, and Dr. Rick Hudson, director, Clinical Support Unit for the B.C. Ministry of Health, have provided no answers.

In April 2000, I presented at a Canadian conference entitled "Building Bridges: An Integrated Approach to Women's Health" on the subject "Benzodiazepines—Time for Action!" My presentation focused on our action plan for an integrated approach linking *policy, practice,* and *research* for positive strategic partnership solutions among the key stakeholders. Other speakers at the conference included Dr. Nancy Olivieri, Professor of Pediatrics at the University of Toronto, a very forthright and courageous "whistle-blower" who publicly attacked the undue influence of the pharmaceutical manufacturers in attempting to suppress research she had done indicating potentially harmful effects of certain medications.

I will also be working closely with BAN, VOT's Reg Peart, and Geraldine Burns of Boston (another benzo survivor with a proactive approach) to coordinate the international conference in Boston in the spring of 2001 that will bring together all the key stakeholders to discuss strategies toward resolving the benzodiazepine problem. Our intention is to raise the profile of the issue with both the United Nations and the World Health Organization, and organize a conference that will stand in sharp contrast to the recent United Nations conference on drugs that excluded the topic of legal prescription drugs. It is our hope that the thirty other benzodiazepine advocacy and support groups from around the world will be able to attend this important conference. These groups are currently located in Great Britain, Continental Europe, Australia, New Zealand, South Africa, the United States, and Canada, and continue to grow in numbers and locations every day.

Dr. Reg Peart of the VOT group recently sent me a copy of his very effective presentation to the Government Health Committee Inquiry in Great Britain, which he made in June 1999. In his lengthy, thoroughly researched submission, Reg describes the nature and causes of forty years of benzodiazepine dependency, outlining in considerable detail the chronological events, circumstances, and consequences, with recommendations to improve the current situation and prevent such a problem in the future. Reg identifies that there are three root causes of the benzodiazepine epidemic "misprescribing, misdiagnosis and mistreatment, which have cost the United Kingdom billions of pounds."[17]

One of the key documents he included was the Erice Declaration on Communicating Drug Safety Information that was drawn up at the International Conference on Developing Effective Communications in Pharmacovigilance in Erice, Sicily, September 24–27, 1997, which was attended by health professionals, researchers, academics, media writers, representatives of the pharmaceutical industry, drug regulators, patients, lawyers, consumers, and international health organizations from thirty-four countries. The World Health Organization was one of the sponsors of the conference, which stressed the importance of drug safety, information, education, evidence on risks and benefits, the need for a system with independent expertise (non-partisan funding), and drug-safety monitoring. Dr. Peart has called for a separate government inquiry into benzodiazepines because of the "nature, magnitude and consequence of this serious health problem."[18] A public inquiry is also what I have called for in Canada and will continue to lobby for.

The continuing problem of misdiagnosis, misprescribing, and mistreatment surrounding tranquilizers and sleeping pills and other mood-altering drugs is essentially the same throughout the world. It is my objective to raise funding to produce an expanded, international version of our television documentary *Our Pill Epidemic*, which would include interviews with experts from the United States, Europe (particularly Sweden), Australia, and Britain, as well as survivors who belong to the international VOT organization BAN and other benzodiazepine organizations around the world. I plan to produce and distribute it internationally for other television markets, and in video format through my company, Market-Media International Corp., to health-care professionals, organizations, and consumers worldwide. (As a result of budget constraints, the first version of the documentary included predominantly Canadian data, experts, and patient profiles.)

My own fight for justice in the courts has been a lengthy and costly battle, but it is not over yet. As stated earlier, I am still moving toward an appeal in my case, which I am prepared to take to the Supreme Court of Canada if necessary. When I first initiated legal action against Dr. MacGillivray in 1992, I certainly had no idea of the extent of the David and Goliath battle I would be facing nor the exorbitant legal costs I would incur—some $115,000 to date. As a result, a Legal Action Fund in my name has been set up to encourage contributions to carry on the fight for justice through the court system. Following the trial, I was interviewed for an article in *Chatelaine* magazine, eventually titled "Tranquilizers: handle with care," which ran in their December 1997 issue. In addition a 1998 episode of the CBC television show "Alive" featured our Benzodiazepine Call to Action Group. This has since been broadcast outside of Canada.

Sadly, recent high-profile, widely publicized incidents like the murder-suicide of Phil Hartman and his wife will also continue to bring the public's attention to the devastating effects these drugs can have—*People* magazine pointed out that Hartman's wife, Brynn, who murdered him before committing suicide, had been taking an antidepressant "that can cause violent outbursts if mixed with alcohol or drugs."[19] Hartman's tragic death was, of course, only one of the last in a long line of prescription-pill–related celebrity deaths, including those of Judy Garland, Marilyn Monroe, and Elvis Presley.

In June 1999, I attended an excellent multidisciplinary conference in Bethesda, Maryland, that focused on "Psychotherapy and Counseling without Psychiatric Drugs"; it was sponsored by the International Center for the Study of Psychiatry and Psychology, and was attended by more than 200 professionals (including psychiatrists) working in medicine, psychology, social work, community organizations, law, and consumer advocacy from throughout North America and the world. The center, which is often referred to as "the conscience of psychiatry," was founded in the early 1970s by Dr. Peter Breggin, author of *Toxic Psychiatry*, *Talking Back to Prozac*, and *Talking Back to Ritalin*. Dr. Breggin is one of the world's foremost critics of biological psychiatry, including psychiatric drugs, and is a strong advocate for psychological and social human services.

Conference highlights included: "Why Discourage the Use of Psychiatric Drugs?" "Helping Clients to Stop Taking Psychiatric Drugs," and "Malpractice and Product Liability Issues in Psychiatry." It was particularly satisfying to connect with other like-minded, knowledgeable people, including health-care practitioners, who were not "pill pushers" and whose focus was on holistic methods, spirituality, healing, and teaching people how to be survivor personalities by being in tune with their minds, bodies, and spirits.

One of Dr. Breggin's most recent books is *Brain Disabling Treatments in Psychiatry: Drugs, Electroshock and the Role of the FDA*,[20] which provides up-to-date information on new findings that Prozac-like drugs, including benzodiazepines, can cause violence, suicide, psychoses, as well as damage to the brain. Dr. Breggin elaborates on the "brain disabling and toxic effects of benzodiazepines, the impairment of executive and cognitive function, the probability of permanent brain damage and brain atrophy caused by long-term use of benzodiazepines."[21]

His ongoing dedication to change the outdated medical system of drugging is highly commendable, but he too has been faced with many obstacles, including criticism and ostracism by his peers—other medical doctors threatened by his actions and who resist change.

One of Dr. Breggin's most recent advocacy efforts on behalf of patients is his letter in 1998 to the American Medical Association and the Food and Drug Administration in Washington, co-authored with three other doctors (Physicians for Responsible Medicine), calling attention to the "Crisis in Prescribing of Benzodiazepine Medications." In it, the doctors refer to withdrawal syndromes as having the potential for lasting months to many years (up to ten reported) and that chronic use is associated with structural changes in the brain that may not be reversible. The doctors call for "a concise review of the volumes of information documented in the medical journals ... to prevent further iatrogenic [doctor-induced] patient harm."[22]

Dr. Breggin also acts as a forensic medical expert in the courts and testified in a recent medical malpractice case of product liability and negligence in Baton Rouge, Louisiana, against Bristol Myers Squibb and a psychiatrist in which the plaintiff was awarded $1.3 million by a jury for damages caused by the side effects of a psychiatric drug.

I also received some encouraging news in recent months regarding the issue of benzodiazepine use with the release of *Benzodiazepines and Other Targeted Substances Regulations* by Health Canada's Bureau of Drug Surveillance. These proposed regulations call for the control of forty-four psychotropic substances, including more than thirty benzodiazepines,

(Valium, Dalmane, Restoril, Serax, and Ativan, among others), and link these controls to decisions agreed upon at two prior United Nations conventions, one held in 1971 and another in 1988. These regulations will restrict the international distribution of psychotropic substances, including benzodiazepines. Psychotropic substances are defined in the regulations as substances that have the capacity to produce a state of dependence and central nervous system stimulation or depression, resulting in hallucinations or disturbances in motor function, thinking, behavior, perception, or mood. There must be sufficient evidence that the substance is being or is likely to be abused so as to constitute a public health or social problem warranting the placing of the substance under international control. These conventions called for, among other things, control of the import and export of these drugs, the maintenance of strict records on quantities manufactured, and the provision of information to the United Nations on "domestic activities related to the Conventions as requested."

Despite the fact that Canada signed and ratified both conventions, the United Nations International Control Board (INCB) has "publicly brought attention to Canada's failure to implement requirements for some of the substances listed in ... the 1971 Convention."[23] Letters were written by the INCB to the Prime Minister, the Minister of Health, and the Minister of Foreign Affairs regarding Canada's noncompliance with these conventions, and pointed out that Canada faces severe sanctions as the result of such noncompliance. It's encouraging to see international attention being brought to the use and misuse of benzodiazepines, and even more encouraging to see that a typically inert federal government is finally being forced to move to enact greater control of these drugs. It's about time!

Another recent update is that the B.C. College of Physicians and Surgeons has begun to regularly monitor doctors' prescriptions for benzodiazepines through the triplicate prescription program. If the monitoring indicates a problem with any particular doctor's prescribing habits, that doctor is required to attend an educational session on the detrimental effects such overprescribing can have on patients. This practice is long overdue.

In August 1999 more than 2,000 of the world's leading scientists and mental-health professionals gathered in Vancouver at the Ninth Biennial Congress of the International Psychogeriatric Association, an organization concerned with challenges related to mental health and aging. The congress included topics on anxiety disorders, psychosis, depression, and suicide among the elderly and, although it discussed the role of benzodiazepines as treatment, there was not much discussion of the possibility of these drugs *causing* these very conditions, including dementia, in the elderly.

That is probably not surprising, considering that no fewer than nine drug manufacturers were sponsors of the congress, including Eli Lilly, which manufactures and sells Prozac, and Hoffmann–La Roche, which manufactures and sells Valium, Librium, and Dalmane. Drug companies' educational and public relations programs directed at doctors need to be carefully evaluated and monitored since their prime goal is to promote the sale and use of more and more drugs to enhance their bottom-line profits. The serious results of misprescribing and misdiagnosis by doctors and the long-term side effects of drugs they market also require drug companies' critical attention and funding.

In spite of my anticlimactic legal experience, I still feel it is imperative for victims and survivors of the overprescribing and misprescribing habits of doctors to pursue legal recourse, or join together in class-action suits whenever possible, just as was done in the highly publicized Red Cross blood scandal. When large numbers of people join together to seek compensation through the courts, they can send out a strong message. In some of the U.K. benzodiazepine cases, complainants are suing not only drug manufacturers such as Roche, Wyeth, and Upjohn, but also health authorities and other regulatory bodies for not fulfilling their mandate to protect the public's health.

It is legally significant, too, that there are more and more cases worldwide of people being charged with crimes such as shoplifting, criminal negligence in vehicular accidents, assault, manslaughter, and murder, and using what is termed the "benzo defence" in court. Under the influence of these drugs, defendants claim, they simply had no idea what they were doing, could not recall or did not know the role of drug effects in precipitating their aggressive, hostile, antisocial, and violent behavior. Research going back decades supports this.

There is little doubt that people become disabled from these drugs— both when they are on them and during withdrawal—and that they can suffer cognitive impairment for years following discontinuance. Many of these people have their long-term disability insurance wrongfully cut off and face financial ruin when they are still being affected by the drugs and cannot return to work. In a large number of these cases, doctors protect other doctors, and often the reports provided to insurance companies by extremely knowledgeable health-care professionals who are "non-medical"—such as psychologists, neuropsychologists, and psychopharmacologists—are not taken into consideration. Bringing better awareness and accountability to disability insurance companies is also a vital area that needs to be addressed.

I have been fortunate; I survived many situations that might have killed me during my twenty-three years on benzodiazepines, although I have certainly suffered in terms of my health, my career, my financial security, and my family life. I never understood the pills' insidious side effects. I trusted my doctor.

Although the quality of my life is ten times today what it was while I was on the drugs, I still live with many of their long-term and residual effects, including sensitivity to light, some problems with coordination, some emotional flatness, and some cognitive-related difficulties. I estimate that, after nine-and-a-half years off the pills, my cognitive functioning is about 90 percent of what it should be, and I am still working at this with great determination and diligence.

I am determined to live a meaningful and productive life—a life as it should always have been. I will continue pursuing research in the area of long-term cognitive impairment and brain damage caused by benzodiazepines, and plan to meet with researchers and doctors in the United States, Great Britain, Sweden (at the Karolinska Institute), and elsewhere who have been, for the past two decades, at the forefront in exposing this aspect of benzo usage experienced by former long-term therapeutic users of tranquilizers and sleeping pills. More "no strings attached" funding is vitally needed to advance research in this area.

I thank God every day that there are no more paradoxical reactions, no more overdoses, no more suicidal thoughts, no more depression, no more police, no more emergency-department admissions, and no more irrational anxieties in my life since I have been off all the pills.

What of my future career? Through my company, Market-Media International Corp., associates and I will continue to provide a range of consulting services to private- and public-sector clients in the field of strategic marketing and planning, corporate communications, issues management, ethics, and public and government relations. I have a growing enthusiasm for and interest in organic and natural foods, holistic health, promotion of wellness and prevention in the health-care field, and environmental issues.

In March 1999, I attended the first-ever Los Angeles Trade Mission for Canadian Women Entrepreneurs, which led to my election to the national board of directors for Women Entrepreneurs of Canada (WEC). In my career, I have moved away from the larger, bureaucratic corporate structure that was my workplace for twenty-eight years, and have adopted an "out of the box" philosophy that includes a more creative and visionary approach to business, politics, and advocacy. I have also considered the possibility of working on my PhD in public health (wellness and health promotion) at some point in the future. I may also consider running for public office, ideally to work toward becoming provincial Minister of Health and to effect long-overdue systemic changes in the health-care system, directly moving it toward a more "tuned-in" model of wellness and health promotion. I also continue to maintain a keen interest in politics at the local, municipal level, which is closest to the people. Since Deb's tragic death in May 1999, I have begun to look at becoming more involved again with the cancer cause. I find it incredible that there are still so few answers to conquering this insidious disease.

To my delight, Carrie, who is now twenty-nine, has recently moved back to Vancouver after working in the film industry in Los Angeles. Her fiancé, David, has moved to Vancouver with her, and they plan to be married in August 2000, on the North Shore, in a "sea to sky" ceremony that will begin on the seawall in West Vancouver with a reception following at the top of Grouse Mountain. Carrie has chosen to leave the film industry and is pursuing a career with a non-profit organization where she can use her communications skills and background. I know that whatever she does in the future she will do it with integrity, purpose, and determination. Most of all, I am so happy to have her home again, and I love her with all my heart.

I miss Deb every day and in so many ways, especially her guidance, wisdom, and love that I had come to rely on, her "can do anything" attitude, her confidence, her enthusiasm, her great sense of humor, and her warm infectious smile. I know she desperately wanted to be given that second chance at life but for some reason it was not given to her. Why was God's agenda so different from her own hopes and dreams? Why were we as a family not given more time to rebuild our relationships after I came off the pills? I am pleased to say that a scholarship in her name has been set up by the BC Federation of Labour, a golf tournament "the Hope Classic" was held in her memory with proceeds to the Cancer Society, and proceeds of a music concert in her name have gone to Breast Cancer Research. Alan, Martin, and I all ran the Kelowna Hot Sands Marathon three weeks after Deb died, raising funds for the Cancer Society. Also this year Martin has become the President Elect of the Kelowna Cancer Society. I still have Deb closeby all the time—running beside me every day and encouraging me to do my very best. Her words "Be strong, mom" and "live life to the fullest each day" keep adding more and more meaning to my life as I recognize there are no guarantees and no certainties.

I cry often about losing Deb, something I had great difficulty with after Derek died. The pills that were prescribed for me suppressed my emotions, as I later came to understand. However, I required no pills to face the fear and uncertainty of Deb's illness; nor were any pills prescribed for me to cope with my grief at her death. Nor were they ever required before or after Derek died.

I would like to end this book with one of my favorite poems.

New Day
This is the beginning of a new day
I have been given this day to use as I will
I can waste it, or use it for good
What I do today is important because I am
Exchanging a day of my life for it
When tomorrow comes, this day will be gone forever,
Leaving in its place whatever I have traded for it
I pledge to myself that it shall be: gain, not loss;

Good, not evil; Success, not failure—in order that I
shall not regret the price I have paid for this day.
—*Author Unknown*

It is my sincere hope that this book will be an important catalyst for
much-delayed systemic change. The quality of life of hundreds of thousands of people throughout the world is at stake, and many millions of
dollars in our embattled and dwindling health-care system can be saved.
What is needed is the political will, leadership, and commitment to effect
this change with positive solutions and concrete actions. And most of
all, *people working together to make a difference.*

To all of the doctors and psychiatrists who told me I *needed* the pills,
or that I would need them again, I can unequivocally say, "The proof is
in the pudding." My life since discontinuing these insidious, damaging
drugs has improved tenfold. Although my life following Deb's death will
never be the same, today I am full of energy, enthusiasm, and a "joie de
vivre." I am thankful to be alive, and plan to continue working with a
passion for the rest of my life, sharing my experience, my knowledge, my
research, and my message.

Notes

Acknowledgments

1. Not his real name.

Preface

1. Barbara Gordon, *I'm Dancing as Fast as I Can*, (New York: Harper & Row, 1979).
2. The Hippocratic Oath.

Chapter 4: Aftermath

1. Dr. MacGillivray's general chronological records, February 17 and March 3, 1966.
2. Ibid., January 5, 1967.
3. Summarized history written by Dr. Norman B. Hirt, psychiatrist, and provided to Mr. George Poulos, family court counselor, November 29, 1978.
4. Ibid.
5. Charles Medawar, *Power and Dependence: Social Audit on the Safety of Medicines* (London, UK: Social Audit Ltd., 1992), p. 85.
6. Dr. MacGillivray's general chronological records, December 8, 1967.
7. *Women, Drugs and Alcohol* video supplied by Alternatives, North Vancouver, produced 1980.
8. Peter Breggin, *Toxic Psychiatry* (New York: St. Martin's Press, 1991), p. 16, 53, 56.
9. "Librium," *Compendium of Pharmaceuticals and Specialties* (CPS) (Canadian Pharmaceutical Association, Product monograph, 1970).
10. R.J. Rowlatt, Effects of Maternal Diazepam, *British Medical Journal* 1 (1978): 985.
11. Health and Welfare Canada, *It's Just Your Nerves: A Resource on Women's Use of Minor Tranquilizers and Alcohol* (Health and Welfare Canada, 1981), p. 10.
12. Dr. Mark Berner, Benzodiazepines: An Overview, *Ontario Medical Review*, April 1982: 233–242.

Chapter 5: Front-Page News

1. Dr. MacGillivray's general chronological records, April 8, 1971.
2. Ibid., November 19, 1972.
3. "Librium," *Compendium of Pharmaceuticals and Specialties* (CPS) (Canadian Pharmaceutical Association, Product Monograph, 1971).
4. James R. Milam and Katherine Ketcham, *Under the Influence* (Seattle, WA: Bantam Books/Madrona Publishers Inc., 1981), p. 171.
5. Dr. MacGillivray's general chronological records, December 27 and 28, 1972.
6. Dr. Allan Adler, psychiatrist, report written to Dr. MacGillivray, March 30, 1973.
7. Medawar, p. 200.
8. "Librium."

Chapter 6: More Pills—More Trouble

1. Letter to F. Allan Taylor from Dr. Norman B. Hirt, March 4, 1976.
2. Letter to Joan Gadsby from Alan G. Clews, former chairman of the BCMA Alcohol and Drug Committee, April 17, 1995.
3. H. Ashton, "Anything for a Quiet Life," *New Scientist,* 1989; vol. 6, pp. 34–37.
4. From police statements and report received by Crown Counsel in North Vancouver on October 29, 1975, regarding the incident of October 19, 1975, involving Joan Gadsby.
5. Not his real name.
6. From police statements and report received by Crown Counsel in North Vancouver on October 29, 1975, regarding the incident of October 19, 1975, involving Joan Gadsby.
7. Joel Lexchin, M.D. *The Real Pushers: A Critical Analysis of the Canadian Drug Industry* (Vancouver: New Star Books, 1984), p. 213.
8. Letter to Malcolm A. MacDonald, legal counsel to Joan Gadsby from Dr. Norman B. Hirt, October 23, 1975.
9. Letter to Mrs. L. Spurr, legal counsel to Joan Gadsby, from Dr. Norman B. Hirt, May 14, 1970.
10. Letter to Dr. Norman B. Hirt from F. Allan Taylor, November 19, 1975.
11. Letter to F. Allan Taylor from Dr. Norman B. Hirt, November 20, 1975.
12. Ibid.

Chapter 7: A Dangerous Mix

1. Benzodiazepines, Memory and Mood: a Review, the Department of Psychiatry, De Crespigny Park Institute of Psychiatry; London, England; 1991.
2. "Dalmane," *Compendium of Pharmaceuticals and Specialties* (CPS) (Canadian Pharmaceutical Association, Product Monograph, 1977).
3. Berner, 234–235.
4. From letter written to Dr. MacGillivray from a family court counsellor with the Ministry of the Attorney General, November 24th, 1978.
5. Summarized history written by Dr. Norman B. Hirt, psychiatrist, to Mr. George Poulos, family court counsellor, November 29, 1978.
6. Milam and Ketcham, p. 180.
7. Summarized history written by Dr. Norman B. Hirt, psychiatrist to George Poulos, family court counsellor, November 29, 1978.
8. From an affidavit written by Carrie Gadsby, February 5, 1997.
9. Dr. MacGillivray's general chronological records, July 17, 1979.
10. Dr. Norman Hirt's chronological records, 1977–80.
11. Dr. MacGillivray's general chronological records, 1982.
12. Berner.

Chapter 8: Turning Point

1. Not his real name.
2. From an affidavit written by Carrie Gadsby, February 5, 1997.
3. Shirley Trickett, *Coming Off Tranquillizers: A Withdrawal Plan that Really Works* (Wellingborough, New York: Thorsons Publishing Group, 1986).
4. Dr. MacGillivray's general chronological records, 1983 and 1984.

5. Ibid.
6. Ibid.
7. From an affidavit written by Carrie Gadsby, February 5, 1997.
8. Dr. Pankratz' general chronological records, January, 1987 to June 1990.
9. Dr. MacGillivray's general chronological records, 1985 to 1990.
10. Not his real name.
11. From report written by Dr. Peter Hotz, M.A., Ph.D., December 11, 1986.
12. Examination for Discovery in the Supreme Court of British Columbia. No. C923152., Vancouver Registry, p. 58.
13. Dr. MacGillivray's chronological records, March 1987.
14. Breggin, p. 243.

Chapter 9: Withdrawal

1. Restoril, *Compendium of Pharmaceuticals and Specialties* (CPS), 1990.
2. Dr. MacGillivray's general chronological records, February and March, 1990.
3. Dr. Pankratz' general chronological records, 1990.
4. Testimony in the Supreme Court of British Columbia, Dr. MacGillivray's cross-examination by Ms. Khan, Volume VI Transcript, No. CA023568.
5. Medical Claims History Report obtained from MSP Claims Division, September 12, 1995.
6. See footnote four.
7. Dr. MacGillivray's general chronological records, May 25, 1990.
8. Anne Geller, M.D., "Management of Protracted Withdrawal," American Society of Addiction Medicine, 1994.
9. Summarized from Public Citizen activity summary, in *Worst Pills, Best Pills*, Sidney M. Wolfe, M.D. and Rose-Ellen Hope, R. Ph., Washington, DC.: Public Citizen Health Research Group, 1994.
10. From North American Life insurance forms completed by Dr. MacGillivray, June 26, 1990.
11. Ibid.
12. Dalmane, *Compendium of Pharmaceuticals and Specialties* (CPS) (Canadian Pharmaceutical Association, Product Monograph 1979, 1982, 1987, 1990; "Restoril," "Serax," CPS 1990).
13. Ibid.
14. Ibid.
15. Gadsby v. MacGillivray Trial Transcripts (Collected excerpts from Research References). In the Supreme Court of British Columbia, No. CA023568, Volume VI, pp. 856 through 863.
16. Letter from North American Life to the British Columbia Health Association, September 28, 1990.
17. Letter from Joan Gadsby to Dr. MacGillivray, kept in his records, October 15, 1990.
18. Letter written to Joan Gadsby by Katherine Manchuk, North American Life, November 16, 1990.
19. Letter written by Dr. Edward Margetts to Dr. MacGillivray, December 14, 1990.
20. Benzodiazepine Dependence, Department of Psychiatry, Charing Cross Hospital, London, England, 1993.

21. Terence T. Gorski, MA, "Post Acute Withdrawal," *Professional Counsellor*, August, 1993.
22. Ibid.
23. Letter to North American Life from Dr. Margetts, December 3, 1990.
24. See note 19.

Chapter 10: Systemic Denial
1. *DSM-IV* listing for Cyclothymic Disorder, section 301.13.
2. Letter by Dr. MacGillivray to North American Life LTD Claims Examiner, January 21, 1991.
3. From Dr. Kennedy's clinical records, May 9, 1991.
4. R. Greenberg, "Dream Interruption Insomnia," *Journal of Nervous and Mental Disease* 1967, 144: 18–21.
5. Lydia Dotto, *Asleep in the Fast Lane* (Toronto: Stoddart Publishing Co. Ltd., 1990), p. 124.
6. Letter written to Dr. Trebell by Jonathan A.E. Fleming, University Hospital (U.B.C.) Sleep Disorders Clinic, February 5, 1991.
7. AC Higgitt, MH Lader and P. Fonagy, "Clinical Management of Benzodiazepine Dependence," *British Medical Journal* 1985, 291: 688–690.
8. H. Ashton, "Protracted Withdrawal Syndromes from Benzodiazepines," *Journal of Substance Abuse Treatment* 1991, 8: 19–28.
9. JS Huff and HG Plunkett, "Autograde Amnesia Following Triazolam Use in Two Emergency Physicians," *Journal of Emergency Medicine* 1989, 7: 153–155.
10. Letter written to North American Life by Dr. Mary Stewart-Moore, August 24, 1991.
11. Letter by Dr. Hirt to Dr. Parkinson, June 24, 1991.
12. Letter by Dr. Klonoff, Psychologist and Neuropsychologist, December 7, 1992.
13. Report (re: test results) by Dr. Ursula Wild, May 21, 1993.
14. Forms completed by Dr. Ursula Wild, November 2, 1994.
15. Letter by Dr. James H. Brown, Psychiatrist, to North American Life, June 7, 1993.
16. Joel Lexchin, M.D., *The Real Pushers: A Critical Analysis of the Canadian Drug Industry* (Vancouver: New Star Books, 1984), pp. 9, 23.
17. Ibid., p. 22, 23.
18. Benzodiazepines, Memory and Mood: a Review, the Department of Psychiatry, De Crespigny Park Institute of Psychiatry, London, England, 1991.
19. Chronic Use of Benzodiazepines and Psychomotor and Cognitive Test Performance, Department of Psychiatry, University of Pennsylvania School of Medicine, 1986.
20. "Benzodiazepine Dependence and Memory Impairment," *Mayo Clinic Proceedings*, August 1993, Volume 68.
21. Letter by Dr. MacGillivray to Dr. A.W. Askey, Deputy Registrar of the College of Physicians and Surgeons, April 21, 1992.
22. Letter, College of Physicians and Surgeons to Joan Gadsby, May 25, 1992.
23. From an affidavit written by Carrie Gadsby, February 5, 1997.
24. Statement of Claim filed June 26, 1992, Vancouver Registry, No. C923152 in the Supreme Court of British Columbia.

Chapter 11: Mounting Evidence

1. B.C. Press Council Release, October 4, 1994, Vancouver.
2. Fax to Joan Gadsby from Tokuo Yoshida, Programme on Substance Abuse, World Health Organization, Geneva, Switzerland, June 1995.
3. Medawar, p. 5.
4. Dr. Michael Rachlis and Carol Kushner, *Strong Medicine* (Toronto: HarperCollins 1994), p. 125.
5. Eve Bargmann, MD, Sidney Wolfe, MD, Joan Levin, and the Public Citizen Health Research Group, *Stopping Valium* (Washington, DC: Public Citizen Health Research Group, 1982).
6. Wolfe and Hope, p. 5.
7. *Sainsbury Report,* quoted by Medawar, *Power and Dependence,* pp. 74–75.
8. *British Journal of Addiction* 1990. Quoted in *Power and Dependence.*
9. Malcolm Lader, M.D. "History of Benzodiazepine Dependence," *Journal of Substance Abuse Treatment* 1991 8: 53–59.
10. Victims of Tranquilizers home-page (B.A. Merchant). Supplied by North Shore Health, April 24, 1996.
11. VOT Support Group *Newsletter,* B.A. Merchant, 12D Worbeck Road, Anerly, London. SE 207SW, August 1995.
12. Sandy Zisook, M.D., and Richard A. De Vaul, M.D., "Adverse Behavioural Effects of Benzodiazepines." *Journal of Family Practice,* vol. 5, no. 6, 1977.
13. Ibid.
14. Editorial, Over-Medicated Society? *CMA Journal* vol. 112 (February 22, 1975): p. 413
15. Martin J. Bass, M.D., and Jon C. Baskerville, Ph.D., "Prescribing of Minor Tranquilizers for Emotional Problems in a Family Practice," *CMA Journal* vol. 125 (December 1, 1981): p. 1225.
16. Sharon Kerr, Detoxification Procedures for Tranquilizers and Sedative Hypnotics, College of Pharmacists of B.C., September 1987 Newsletter.
17. "Benzodiazepine Usage," *The Drug Usage Review* (Victoria: B.C. Drug and Poison Information Centre, B.C. Ministry of Health, 1991).
18. Dr. Alan G. Clews, Chair, BCMA Committee on Alcohol and Other Drugs, "Resolved: 'That Physicians Use Great Caution ...'," *B.C. Medical Journal,* Vol. 30 Number 10 (October 1992) and 1991–1992 *BCMA Annual Report.*
19. To Sleep Or Not to Sleep, *Therapeutics Newsletter,* Vancouver: Therapeutics Initiative Evidence-Based Drug Therapy Program, University of British Columbia, November/ December 1995.
20. Copy of Draft Guidelines on Benzodiazepines from Canadian Medical Association, October 4, 1996.
21. Fax to Joan Gadsby from CPG Database Manager, Canadian Medical Association, June 11, 1998.
22. Dr. Nancy Hall, Prescribing Benzodiazepines to North Shore Seniors: Time for Reappraisal, North Shore Health Department, 1995.
23. Dr. Ray Ancill, Tranquillity in a Bottle? *Your Better Health Magazine* vol. 2, issue 4, B.C. Ministry of Health (1991).

24. Larson, E.B. et al., Adverse Drug Reactions Associated with Global Cognitive Impairment in Elderly Persons, American College of Physicians *Annals of Internal Medicine* 107 (1987): pp. 169–73.

25. B.C. Ministry of Health, *B.C. Provincial Health Officer's Annual Report* (Victoria: 1995), pp. 105–7.

26. *Sociology of Health and Illness* vol. 1, No. 3 (1970).

27. Walter W. Rosser, M.D., Women and Tranquilizers, *Modern Medicine of Canada*, September 1987.

28. Current Estimates from the Health Interview Survey: United States, 1975–1977, *U.S. Department of Health, Education and Welfare, National Health Series* 10 (1978): 115.

29. Ibid.

30. Berner, 239.

31. R. Gundlach et al., "A Double-Blind Outpatient Study of Diazepam (Valium) and Placebo," *Psychopharmacologia*, Berlin, vol. 9, 1966: 81–92.

32. H.F. Ryan et al., "Increase in Suicidal Thoughts and Tendancies Associated with Diazapam Therapy," *Journal of American Medical Association*, vol. 203, 1968, pp. 1137–39.

33. R.C.W. Hall, Joffe J.R., "Aberrant Response to Diazapam: A New Syndrome," *American Journal of Psychiatry*, vol. 129, 1972, pp. 738–42.

34. Benzodiazepines: An Overview.

35. L.F. Prescott, "Benzodiazepines, From Molecular Biology to Clinical Practice," (New York: Raven Press), 1983, pp. 253–65.

36. R.G. Priest and S.A. Montgomery, "Benzodiazepines and Dependence: A College Statement," Royal College of Psychiatrists, Great Britain, vol. 12, 1988: 107–9.

37. H. Ashton, "Anything for a Quiet Life," *New Scientist*, vol. 6, 1989, pp. 34–37.

38. A. Herxheimer, "Driving under the Influence of Oxazepam (Serax): Guilt without Responsibility?" *Lancet* 1982, ii p. 223.

39. Susan Golombok, P. Moodley, and M. Lader, "Cognitive Impairment in Long Term Benzodiazepine Users," *Psychological Medicine* 18: 365–74, United Kingdom.

40. Ibid.

41. Margaret Munro, "Sleeping Pills Tied to Many Accidents," *Vancouver Sun*, January 11, 1996.

42. Alert for the Elderly, BCTV News Highlights Newsfax, July 2, 1997, referring to findings published in the *Journal of the American Medical Association*.

43. "Tranquilizer Terror," and "$1 Million Claimed for Drugs Addiction," *New Zealand Herald*, May 19, 1994, and June 17, 1995.

44. Ibid.

45. Dr. Malcolm Lader, "Benzodiazepine Problems," *British Journal of Addiction*, 1991, 86: 823–28.

46. Dr. Malcolm Lader, "Anxiety or Depression During Withdrawal of Hypnotic Treatments," *Journal of Psychosomatic Research* 1994, 38 ('supp'): 113–23.

47. J. Landry, et al. "Benzodiazepine Dependence and Withdrawal: Identification and Medical Management." *Journal of the American Board Family Practitioners*, March-April 1992, vol. 5, no. 2: 167–74.

48. Dr. Anne Geller, "Management of Protracted Withdrawal," *American Society of Addiction Medicine Journal*, 1994, chapter 2, 1–6.

49. *Tranquilizer Users Recovery Network (TURN) Newsletter*, 228 B. South Cedros Ave., Solono Beach, CA, 92075.

50. H.A. McClelland, "The Forensic Implications of Benzodiazepine Use," in *Benzodiazepines: Current Concepts, Biological, Clinical and Social Perspectives* (New York: John Wiley & Sons, 1990), pp. 227–249.

51. Ibid., pp. 241, 242, 246.

52. "Legal Aid for Mass Litigation," *The Lancet*, January 23, 1993, 233.

53. Fax to Joan Gadsby from Dr. H.A. McClelland, March 29, 1996.

54. Not her real name.

55. Molly Thomson, Ph.D., "Prescribing Benzodiazepines for Noninstitutionalized Elderly." *Canadian Family Physician*, vol. 41, May 1995.

56. Letter from Dr. Ursula Wild, psychologist and neuropsychologist, to Shirley Khan, lawyer, December 10, 1996.

Chapter 12: Lawsuit in the News
NOTE: Much of the information found in this chapter related to the 16 day trial February 24, 1997, to April 29, 1997, B.C. Supreme Court No. CA023568 Gadsby v. MacGillivray is taken from Vols. I-VI of Court Transcripts.

1. Report written by Dr. Schmidt, neuropsychologist, January 4, 1996.

2. Letter from Dr. Parkinson to Shirley Khan, December 13, 1996.

3. Figure obtained by Joan Gadsby from the Communications Department of the B.C. Ministry of Health.

4. *Victims of Tranquilizers (VOT) Newsletter*, Issue 1, August 1995; B A Merchant, 12D Worbeck Road, Anerley, London SE20 7SW.

5. Not his real name.

6. Letter from trial lawyer to Joan Gadsby, October 19, 1996.

7. Court transcript, March 3, 1997, testimony of Alan Gadsby.

8. Court transcript, March 4, 1997, testimony of Carrie Gadsby.

9. Court transcripts, March 24–27, 1997, testimony of Dr. MacGillivray.

10. Ibid.

11. Ibid.

12. Court transcripts, March 26, 1997, testimony of Dr. Pankratz.

13. Court transcripts, March 3, 1997, testimony of Dr. U. Wild.

14. Court transcript, March 6, 1997, of Dr. Barry Beyerstein and Dr. Beyerstein's Expert Report December 6, 1996.

15. Ibid.

16. Deposition of Dr. Raymond Parkinson, March 5, 1997.

17. Letter to Shirley Khan from Dr. Jim Wright, December 10, 1996.

18. Expert Report sent to Shirley Khan, by Dr. Jim Wright, March 5, 1997.

19. Reasons for Judgment of the Honorable Mr. Justice Clancy at Vancouver, British Columbia, June 30, 1997.

20. Ibid.

21. Report of Dr. Raymond Parkinson to Shirley Khan, December 13, 1996.

22. Gilbert Sharpe, *The Law and Medicine in Canada* 2nd ed. (Toronto and Vancouver: Butterworths).
23. Qureshi v. Nickerson (5 April 1988) Vancouver C843290 (B.C.S.C.)
24. Hopp v. Lepp (1980), 112 D.L.R. (3d) 67 (S.C.C.) p. 71
25. Reasons for Judgment of the Honourable Mr. Justice Clancy at Vancouver, British Columbia, June 30, 1997.
26. Letter, James L. Straith, lawyer, to Joan Gadsby, September 9, 1998.

Chapter 13: Call to Action
1. Project Summary/Proposal for a participatory action research process, applicant: Nancy Hall. (1997).
2. BC Auditor General Report. August 1998, p. 10.
3. Presentation to House of Commons Standing Committee on Health, April 22, 1997.
4. Alcohol and Drug Education Service Newsletter, September 1996.
5. Letter to Joan Gadsby from Ellen Savage, Clerk of the Committee for the House of Commons Standing Committee on Health, November 17, 1997.
6. Letter to Joan Gadsby from Allan Rock, Federal Minister of Health, April 30, 1998.
7. "For the Record: Minister Wants Marketing by Drug Firms Curbed." *Vancouver Sun*, April 1997.
8. "Drug Firms' Research Possible Health Risk," *Vancouver Sun*, September 1996.
9. Gilbert D, Chetley A. *New Trends in Drug Promotion, Consumer Policy Review* 1996, 6: 162–167.
10. "The New Frontiers of Medicine" sponsored by the Pharmaceutical Manufacturers Association of Canada, *Globe and Mail*, March 1997.
11. Letter to Joan Gadsby from Judy Erola, PMAC President, May 7, 1997.
12. Letter to Joan Gadsby from Vic Ackermann, President Hoffmann-La Roche, May 28, 1996.
13. Medawar, pp. 5–6.

Conclusion
1. IMS Health fax to Joan Gadsby September 9, 1999.
2. *Provincial Profile of Women's Health*, BC Women's Health Bureau, May 1999.
3. Rosa Harris-Adler, Prozac's very, very happy birthday, *En Route*, October 1997, pp. 46–54.
4. Conversation with Dr. S. Wolfe, 1994.
5. *Vancouver Province* August 8, 1999, p. 1, August 9, 1999, pp. 14–17.
6. Ibid.
7. Ibid.
8. "Drugs Doing Damage?" *The Medical Post*, April 28, 1998, reported in the *Journal of the American Medical Association*, April 15, 1998.
9. Letter from B.C. Deputy Minister of Health, June 18, 1996.
10. "World's Largest Medical Defence Group Sees Claims Rise 15% a Year." *The Medical Post*, June 30, 1998.
11. Lader, 53–59.
12. Summarized in a letter from M. Michols, Director General, Federal Health Protection Branch Therapeutic Products Directorate, May 1997.

13. Letter from Dr. Brill Edwards to Deputy Minister, Health Canada, Michel Jean, January 19, 1996.
14. Fax to Joan Gadsby from Centre, August 4, 1999.
15. Evidence by Dr. Anne Carter, Director of Health Programs for the CMA to the Standing Committee on Health, House of Commons of Canada, 35th Parliament, 2nd Session, Meeting No. 31, March 4, 1997.
16. Summarized in a letter to Joan Gadsby from Dann. M. Michols, Director General, Federal Health Protection Branch Therapeutics Products Directorate, May 1997.
17. Dr. Reg Peart of VOT, presentation June 1999 to Government Health Committee Inquiry in Great Britain.
18. Ibid.
19. *People Magazine*, 1999.
20. Peter Breggin. M.D. *Brain Disabling Treatment in Psychiatry.* New York, Springer Publishing, 1997.
21. Ibid.
22. Peter Breggin M.D. et al., Letter to the AMA and the FDA June 1998 from Physicians for Responsible Medicine.
23. Proposed Benzodiazepines and other Targeted Substances Regulations, sent to Joan Gadsby from Health Canada's Bureau of Drug Surveillance by Julie Gervais, August 10, 1999.

Appendix 1

Ashton H.
Anything for a Quiet Life?
New Scientist 1989; 6: 34-37.

"Valium, Librium and Mogadon once seemed to provide the perfect answer to stress. We now know how this group of drugs alters the chemistry of the brain; no wonder they create more problems than they solve." [SUMMARY p. 52]

"The problems begin with chronic use; that is, regular use for more than a week or two. Harmful effects fall into two categories that may coexist; the drugs may begin to have powerful but unwanted side effects, and also to become less effective. The individual taking them may develop tolerance, dependence and the symptoms of withdrawal.

Unwanted effects can be pronounced. Many benzodiazepines are eliminated from the body only slowly and may accumulate, causing drowsiness, a lack of coordination, impairment of memory and concentration, and confusion. These effects are most marked in the elderly, making them more likely to suffer falls and fractures. Benzodiazepines taken as sleeping pills often give rise to a "hangover", impairing performance the following day. Benzodiazepines may contribute to traffic and industrial accidents and worsen the effects of other depressant drugs, including alcohol.

Taking benzodiazepines over the long term can cause both depression and "emotional anaesthesia", an apathetic state in which people are unable to feel pleasure or pain. The drugs can aggravate depressive illness and provoke suicide. On the other hand, benzodiazepines sometimes produce apparently paradoxical stimulant effects. Patients may commit uncharacteristic antisocial acts such as shoplifting or sexual offences, or becoming aggressive with outbursts of rage and violence. Some researchers have suggested that chronic use of benzodiazepines may contribute to "baby-battering", "wife-beating" or "grandma-bashing." [p. 54]

Ashton H.
Protracted Withdrawal Syndromes from Benzodiazepines.
Journal of Substance Abuse Treatment 1991; 8: 19-28.

"Depression can be caused or aggravated by chronic benzodiazepine use, yet it also appears to be a feature of the withdrawal syndrome. It may be severe enough to qualify as a major depressive disorder and may persist for some months. (...)

It is not clear whether protracted depressive symptoms are more common in patients with a previous history of depression or whether it recurs in subsequent years after withdrawal." [p. 25]

"Tinnitus is a common symptom of benzodiazepine withdrawal and may initially result from the characteristic general hypersensitivity to sensory stimuli. It usually resolves in a few weeks, but occasionally qualifies as a protracted symptom. Busto et al. (1988) describe two cases in which tinnitus persisted for 6 and 12 months after withdrawal and mention a third patient who was unable to withdraw from benzodiazepines because of severe tinnitus at each attempt. Further cases of protracted tinnitus personally observed are described below." [p. 25]

"Tinnitus is fairly common in the general population, and the apparent relation to benzodiazepine use may be incidental, but these cases raise the suspicion that benzodiazepines may occasionally cause permanent or only slowly reversible brain damage." [p. 25]

"Formication is also common during benzodiazepine withdrawal, and many patients temporarily complain of a feeling of insects crawling on the skin or of lice or nits in the hair. Occasionally, more bizarre sensations are reported, such as a feeling of slime or water running over the body, a sense of inner vibration, or a feeling of "trembling inside", and these symptoms may be protracted." [p. 26]

"Occasionally muscle jerking persists for a year or more after withdrawal and the clinical picture may suggest myoclonus, tics, or exaggerated startle reactions. (...) Restless legs syndrome may also be protracted." [p. 26]

"Gastrointestinal symptoms are extremely common during chronic benzodiazepine use and in withdrawal. Many chronic benzodiazepine users have been investigated by gastroenterologists and found to have "irritable bowel syndrome." [p. 26]

Byrne A.
Benzodiazepines: The End of a Dream.
Australian Family Physician 1994; 23: 1584-1585.

"Benzodiazepine tranquillisers were introduced in 1960 after brief clinical tests at the University of Texas in 1959. Controlled trials were not required for evaluation and "efficacy" was demonstrated by anecdotes and testimonials. If introduced today they would probably only be approved for limited indications." [p. 1584]

"Some critical authors have suggested that the medical profession and drug companies have been guilty of knowingly ignoring the dangers of tranquillisers." [p. 1584]

"Side-effects, including instability and falls in the elderly, memory disturbance, abnormal sleep patterns, sexual disturbance, depression, fatigue and habituation are all well documented." [p. 1584]

"Use of these drugs for minor complaints, or as first line of management is no longer justified." [p. 1584]

"Some patients can withdraw from these drugs rapidly without great trouble. For others, it is a long, harrowing experience." [p. 1585]

Cochran PW.
Drugs for Anxiety.
JAMA 1974; 229: 521.

"Your editorial, "Drugs for Anxiety" (228: 875, 1974) prompts an uneasy feeling that has been growing on me for some time. Diazepam is cited as a safe drug not particularly subject to abuse when prescribed on an as-needed basis with a cover statement that some psychic distress should not be alarming. This is floridly at variance with my uncollated experience; in fact, so much so that I regard it as virtually a "once on, never off" preparation.

I have long prescribed it only for stressful circumstances of clearly brief duration. Despite this precaution, I never prescribe it without a heartfelt sigh, knowing how frequently the initial prescription will be followed not by the requested visits for discussion, but by calls from the pharmacist relaying ever more frequent requests for refills, and then psychotherapy-by-telephone as the patient attempts to justify his need for the drug in three minutes rather than come in to discuss problems."

Golombok S, Moodley P, Lader M.
Cognitive Impairment in Long-Term Benzodiazepine Users.
Psychological Medicine 1988; 18: 365-374.

"The finding that patients taking high doses of benzodiazepines for long periods of time perform poorly on tasks involving visual-spatial ability and sustained attention, implies that these patients are not functioning well in everyday life. Furthermore, the lack of relationship between benzodiazepine intake and the cognitive Failures Questionnaire, a subjective measure of impairment, suggests that they are not aware of their reduced ability. This is in line with clinical evidence that patients who withdraw from their medication often report improved concentration and increased sensory appreciation, and that only after withdrawal do they realize that they have been functioning below par." [p. 373]

Benzodiazepine Withdrawal Syndromes.
New Zealand Medical Journal 1980; 92: 94-96.

"We report eight cases of benzodiazepine withdrawal syndromes seen in a general psychiatric hospital. These consisted of acute organic brain syndrome, grand mal convulsions and abstinence syndromes. All of the cases were using benzodiazepines in prescribed therapeutic doses. These problems appear to be more common than are generally acknowledged." [SUMMARY p. 94]

All of the reported cases were using benzodiazepines in therapeutic doses and were documented within a short period of time in a relatively small population, alarming us regarding the true incidence of these problems. (...)

"Amongst the group who manifested the abstinence syndrome certain common features were discerned. These were women who had been prescribed a benzodiazepine in therapeutic doses over a minimum of three years for persisting anxiety and/or depression. On withdrawal they uniformly suffered from insomnia, panic attacks, agitation, depersonalisation and an increase in depression. Their suffering was obvious and they all described it as being the worst experience of their lifes." [p. 96]

Lader M.
History of Benzodiazepine Dependence.
Journal of Substance Abuse Treatment 1991; 8: 53-59.

"The widespread usage of the benzodiazepines has inevitably led to thousands of people becoming dependent, perhaps 500,000 in the U.K. and twice that number in the U.S.A. where long-term use is less common. Patients who have become dependent and have either been unable to withdraw or have only done so with great symptomatic distress justifiably feel aggrieved against their doctors and the benzodiazepine manufacturers for not warning them about the risk. In the U.K. about 2000 people have started legal proceedings, coordinated by about 300 firms of lawyers. It is the largest civil action ever." [p. 58]

Lader M.
Benzodiazepine Problems.
British Journal of Addiction 1991; 86: 823-828.

Benzodiazepine present problems related to both unwanted and withdrawal effects. Dosage adjustments usually obviate unwanted effects except for paradoxical reactions such as hostility. Patients with apparent benzodiazepine dependence need careful assessment with respect to personality, social situation and psychiatric disorder. The patient must be motivated and carefully prepared for withdrawal and taught anxiety management techniques. Withdrawal must always be gradual over at least 6 weeks but very prolonged schedules are counter-productive. Substituting a long-acting for a medium-acting benzodiazepine may be helpful in the more intractable cases. An antidepressant may be needed if a depressive disorder supervenes, but other adjunctive therapies are usually helpful. [ABSTRACT p. 823]

"Most withdrawal symptoms have subsided by 3 months after final discontinuation. In a few unfortunate patients symptoms may persist and include feelings of unsteadiness, neck tension, a "bursting" head, perceptual distortions and muscle spasm. The strange nature of these symptoms distresses the patient, perplexes the doctor and may lead to the patient being regarded as a hopeless neurotic or even a malingerer. We believe this to be a genuine part of a protracted withdrawal syndrome as the symptoms are identical with those seen earlier in withdrawal." [p. 828]

Peet M, Moonie L.
Abuse of Benzodiazepines.
BMJ 1977; 1: 714.

"There is increasing evidence that benzodiazepines are widely abused and that withdrawal effects are much more common than was previously supposed. In a recent survey of 2500 patients seen in hospitals suffering from drug-induced lethargy, drowsiness, or coma, diazepam was second only to alcohol as the most common drug of abuse. In another recent study of 50 patients prescribed diazepam strong evidence was found of tolerance to the drug leading to increasing dosage and of withdrawal effects, including anxiety and insomnia. A panel of physicians, while blind to the type of drug, rated 40% of the subjects as being at least moderately addicted. However, they changed their opinion to one markedly more favourable to the drug after they learnt that it was diazepam. (...)

We suggest that clinicians have become convinced that benzodiazepines do not cause
dependence or withdrawal symptoms and that this has led them to overlook the available
evidence."

Prescott LF.
Safety of the Benzodiazepines.
In: Costa E, ed. *The Benzodiazepines. From Molecular Biology to Clinical Practice.* New
York: Raven Press, 1983; 253-265.

"The most common and most important adverse effects of the benzodiazepines are those
affecting the central nervous system. These effects usually represent exaggerated pharmacological actions and include drowsiness, lethargy, retardation, depression, dysarthria, ataxia,
confusion, disorientation, and, in the elderly, dementia. These drugs also have subtle effects
on mood, mentation, and behavior, reducing activity, drive and initiative to the extent that
patients may fail to react appropriately to adverse or dangerous situations and be unable to
face and cope with their problems. In addition they may blunt discretion and precipitate
the taking of an overdose.

The elderly are particularly susceptible to the central effects of benzodiazepines, and they
are also least able to compensate for cerebral functional impairment." [p. 254]

"The benzodiazepines are often prescribed as a panacea for the pressures and problems of
life in people who are disappointed, unhappy, or frustrated. Although some undoubtedly
obtain benefit, there is evidence that others are made worse and have more difficulty in
coping with adverse circumstances.

More worrisome is the possibility that these drugs might cause or aggravate depression
and predispose to self-poisoning. Certainly, in my experience, many patients admitted to
hospital with self-poisoning admit that the benzodiazepines prescribed previously for their
personal problems actually made them worse, making them feel more "depressed" and less
able to cope." [p. 255]

"The adverse effects of drugs on psychomotor function may be subtle and unrecognized
by the patient. The risks again are likely to be greatest with the cumulative long-acting
benzodiazepines since effects may persist for many hours or days after the last dose. The
patient who takes nitrazepam at night will still have about 85% of the dose in his body as
he drives his car to work the following morning." [p. 256]

"It is the prescribing doctor's clear responsibility to warn patients accordingly. Unfortunately
many patients who had been prescribed these drugs do not seem to have been warned of
the possible risks by their doctors. I have encountered drivers of double-decker buses, heavy
goods vehicles, and even the operator of a very large dockside crane who stated they had
been prescribed benzodiazepines without any warnings or restrictions." [p. 256]

Priest RG, Montgomery SA.
Benzodiazepines and Dependence: A College Statement.
Bulletin of the Royal College of Psychiatrists 1988; 12: 107-109.

"Amnesia is frequently a real side effect of the use of benzodiazepines and not just a figment of the individual's imagination or a coincident symptom of emotional disorder.

It is often inadvisable to prescribe benzodiazepines to a patient in an acute crisis as the amnesic property of these compounds may not allow patient to make an optimum response to the situation which they are facing. In cases of loss or bereavement, the psychological adjustment to this trauma may be severely inhibited by benzodiazepines and any tendency to denial could be reinforced." [p. 107]

"It is recognised that the use of benzodiazepines has been (and is still) far too widespread and they are frequently prescribed for trivial and imprecise indications. This has arisen from the belief that benzodiazepines were safe compounds.

It is now acknowledged that the risks of benzodiazepines far outweigh the benefits in many cases and we would recommend that benzodiazepines should not be used in general for vague or mild disorders and should be prescribed for short-term relief when the problem is (i) disabling (ii) severe or (iii) subjecting the individual to unacceptable distress and even then should ideally be prescribed for no more than one month." [p. 108]

"The prescribing of benzodiazepines in cases of depression may have serious consequences and many precipitate suicide. Withdrawal from benzodiazepines in many cases may precipitate depression." [p. 108]

Rowlatt RJ.
Effects of Maternal Diazepam.
BMJ 1978; 1: 985.

"High doses (30 mg or more) of diazepam administered during labour cause, in the infant, failure to start breathing, shallow, inadequate respirations, periodic cessations of respiration, floppiness, subnormal temperature, and poor sucking. These effects last several days and significant plasma levels of diazepam and of its active metabolites persist for up to eight days. Diazepam accumulates in tissue of the fetus, and is metabolised and excreted slowly by the newborn baby."

"The depressant effects of pethidine and other drugs given during labour would be made worse by diazepam."

"Diazepam is excreted in breast milk, which may sedate the baby and cause feeding difficulty. Finally, there is the fear of impairing future intellectual development by exposing the developing brain to the influence of tranquillizers."

Tata PR, Rollings J, Collins M, Pickering A, Jacobson RR.
Lack of Cognitive Recovery Following Withdrawal from Long-Term Benzodiazepine Use.
Psychological Medicine 1994; 24: 203-213.

Twenty-one patients with significant long-term therapeutic benzodiazepines (BZ) use, who remained abstinent at 6 months follow-up after successfully completing a standardized inpatient BZ withdrawal regime, and 21 normal controls matched for age and IQ but not for anxiety, were repeatedly tested on a simple battery of routine psychometric tests of cognitive function, pre- and post-withdrawal and at 6 months follow-up. The results demonstrated significant impairment in patients in verbal learning and memory, psycho-motor, visuo-motor and visuo-conceptual abilities, compared with controls, at all three time points. Despite practice effects, no evidence of immediate recovery of cognitive function following BZ withdrawal was found. Modest recovery of certain deficits emerged at 6 months follow-up in the BZ group, but this remained significantly below the equivalent control performance. The implications of persisting cognitive deficits after withdrawal from long-term BZ use are discussed. [SUMMARY p. 203]

"The main cognitive functions assessed in this study including working memory, verbal learning and memory, visuo-motor and visuo-conceptual skills. The lack of evidence for clinically significant cognitive recovery raises concern about the severity and reversibility of any underlying BZ-induced organic impairment." [p. 211]

"The adverse effects of acute diazepam administration on memory and arousal in man are well known (Lister & File, 1984; Lister, 1985), and have been linked to the high density of BZ receptors in the hippocampus and reticular formation (Wolkowitz et al. 1985), although the neurochemical basis of chronic post-withdrawal deficits has yet to be demonstrated." [p. 212]

"Persisting neuropsychological deficits affecting psychomotor function and new verbal learning have occupational implications. Driving and safety at work with machinery may both be impaired (Skegg et al. 1979, Roy-Byrne & Cowley, 1990). Patients' impairment, following withdrawal from long-term BZ use, is likely to be less than that due to acute drug ingestion or the early withdrawal phase. Yet, one must be cautious in predicting either rapid or comprehensive cognitive recovery for those patients contemplating or undergoing a withdrawal regime, or in estimating the cognitive effects of mood dysfunction, which require further investigation." [p. 211]

Trickett S.
Withdrawal from Benzodiazepines.
Journal of the Royal College of General Practioners 1983; 33: 608

Thousands of people could not possibly invent the bizarre symptoms caused by the therapeutic use of benzodiazepines and reactions to their withdrawal. Many users have to cope, not only with a frightening range of symptoms, but also with the disbelief and hostility of their doctors and families. It is not uncommon for patients to be "struck off" if they continue to complain about withdrawal symptoms. Even when doctors are concerned and understanding about the problem, they often have little knowledge of withdrawal procedure, and even less about treatment. The drugs newsletter on benzodiazepines issued in this region will help them. Is anything being done elsewhere?

Appendix 2

COMMON BENZODIAZEPINES

Generic Name	Brand Name
Alprazolam	Xanax
Chlordiazepoxide	Rivotril
Clonazepam/Clorazepate	Tranxene
Diazepam	Valium
Estazolam	ProSom
Flunitrazepam	Rohypnol
Halazepam	Paxipam
Flurazepam	Dalmane
Lorazepam	Ativan
Nitrazepam	Mogadon
Oxazepam	Serax
Quazepam	Doral
Temazepam	Restoril
Triazolam	Halcion

Author's Note

CAUTION: Under no circumstances attempt to withdraw from any of the above drugs without proper, ongoing medical supervision such as a doctor well informed about addiction or chemical dependency.

Several excellent Web sites are dedicated to the problems associated with benzodiazepines.

www.benzodiazepines.net   *www.benzo-problems.org*

To join the benzodiazepine withdrawal e-mail support group, go to

www.onelist.com\subscribe\benzo.

Bibliography

The worldwide sources consulted in writing this book were many and diverse. Listed below are only selected references that I found to be most informative:

Books

Armstrong, Pam. *Back to Life*. Liverpool, England: Print Origination (NW) Ltd., 1992.

Bielovich, Felicity. *The Judas Window*. Vancouver: South Africa, Zoetic Inc. Publishers, West Vancouver, 1996.

Breggin, Peter. *Toxic Psychiatry*. New York: St. Martin's Press, 1991.

Breggin, Peter. *Brain Disabling Treatment in Psychiatry*. New York: Springer Publishing, 1997.

Breggin, Peter, and David Cohen. *Your Drug May Be Your Problem*. Reading, Massachusetts: Perseus Books, 1999.

Coleman, Vernon. *Life Without Tranquilizers*. London: Judy Piatkus Publishers Ltd., 1985.

Colvin, Rod. *Prescription Drug Abuse: The Hidden Epidemic*. [city?], Nebraska: Addicus Books, Inc., 1995.

de Jonge, Anna. *Resource Handbook: Drugs Patients Rights Advocacy*. Hamilton, New Zealand: Waikato Inc., 1999.

Dotto, Lydia. *Asleep in the Fast Lane*. Toronto: Stoddart Publishing Co. Ltd., 1990.

Drummond, Edward H. *Benzo Blues*. New York: Penguin Group Publishers, 1998.

Dukes, M.N.G., and B. Swartz. Responsibility for drug induced injury. Amsterdam, The Netherlands: Elsevier, 1988.

Faust, Beatrice. *Benzo Junkie*. Ringwood, Victoria, Australia: Penguin Books, 1993.

Gordon, Barbara. *I'm Dancing as Fast as I Can*. New York: Harper & Row, 1979.

Jones, Heather. *Prisoner on Prescription*. Heslington, England: Headway Books, 1990.

Lanctot, Guylaine. *The Medical Mafia*. Coaticook, Quebec: Here's the Key Inc., 1995.

Lexchin, Joel. *The Real Pushers*. Vancouver: New Star Books, 1984.

Medawar, Charles. *Power and Dependence*. London: Social Audit, 1992.

Milam, James R., and Katherine Ketcham. *Under the Influence*. Seattle: Bantam Book – Madrona Publishers, Inc., 1983.

Peluso, Emanuel, and Lucy Silvay Peluso. *Women and Drugs*. Minneapolis, Minnesota: CompCare Publishers, 1988.

Penfold, S., and G.A. Walker. *Women and the Psychiatric Paradox*. Vancouver: The Open University Press, 1984.

Physicians' Desk Reference, 41st ed. Oradell, N. J.: Medical Economics Company, 1987.

Porritt, Di, and Di Russell. *Accidental Addict*. Sydney, Australia: Pam Macmillan Publishers, 1994.

Rachlis, Michael, and Carol Kushner. *Strong Medicine*. Toronto: Harper Collins Publishers Ltd., 1994.

Ricketts, Max, with Edwin Bien. *The Great Anxiety Escape*. La Mesa, California: Matulungin Publishing, 1990.

Ritson, Peter. *Alive and Kicking*. Liverpool, England: Casa Publishing, 1989.

Sahley, Billie J., and Katherine M. Birkner. *Breaking Your Rx Addiction Habit*. San Antonio, Texas: Pain & Stress Publications, 1996.

Silverman, M., and P.R. Lee. *Pills, Profits and Politics*. Berkeley, California: University of California Press, 1974.

Trickett, Shirley. *Coming Off Tranquilizers*. New York: Thorsons Publishing Group, 1986.

Trickett, Shirley. *Free Yourself From Tranquilizers and Sleeping Pills*. Berkeley, California: Ulysses Press, 1997.

Wolfe, Sydney M., and Rose-Ellen Hope. *Worst Pills, Best Pills*. Washington: Public Citizens' Health Research Group, 1993.

York, Geoffery. *The High Price of Health*. Toronto: James Lorimer & Company, 1987.

Studies, Reports, Research Papers, and Articles

Allgulander, Christen, Stefan Borg and Britt Vikander. A 4-6 year follow up on 50 patients with primary dependence on sedative and hypnotic drugs. *American Journal of Psychiatry*, 141:12, 1984.

Anderson, John E. Prescribing of tranquilizers to women and men. *Canadian Medical Association Journal*, Vol. 125 (December 1), pp. 1229–1232, 1981.

Anderson, R.M. The use of repeatedly prescribed medicines. *College of General Practitioners*, Vol. 609 (October), p. 163, 1980.

Anxiolytics, minor tranquilizers. *Canadian Family Physician*, Vol. 22 (April), p. 91, 1976.

Ashton, H. Adverse effects of prolonged benzodiazepine use. *Adverse Drug Reaction Bulletin*, 118, pp. 440–443, 1986.

Ashton, H. Benzodiazepine withdrawal: An unfinished story. *British Medical Journal*, Vol. 288, 1984.

Ashton, H. Benzodiazepine withdrawal. *British Journal of Addiction*, Vol. 82, pp. 665–671, 1987.

Ashton, H. Anything for a quiet life. *New Scientist*, Vol. 6, pp. 34–37, 1989.

Ashton, H. Protracted withdrawal syndromes from benzodiazepines. *Journal of Substance Abuse Treatment*, Vol. 8, pp. 19–28, 1991.

Ashton, H., and J.F. Golding. Tranquilizers: Prevalence, predictors and possible consequences – a United Kingdom Survey. *British Journal of Addiction*, Vol. 84, pp. 541–546, 1989.

Baker, P.M. Drug-induced depression and attempted suicide. *Medical Journal of Australia*, Vol. 2, pp. 322–324, 1977.

Barton, R., and L. Hurst. Unnecessary use of tranquilizers in elderly patients. *British Journal of Psychiatry*, Vol. 112, pp. 989–90, 1966.

Bass, Martin J. Do physicians overprescribe for women with emotional problems? *Canadian Medical Association Journal*, Vol. 125 (December 1), p. 1211, 1981.

Bass, Martin J., and Jon C. Baskerville. Prescribing of minor tranquilizers for emotional problems in a family practice. *Canadian Medical Association Journal*, Vol. 125 (December 1), pp. 1225–1226, 1981.

Beeley, L. Benzodiazepine and tinnitus. *British Medical Journal*, Vol. 302, p. 1465, 1991.

Bell, R.W., and L. Osterman. The compendium of pharmaceuticals and specialties: A critical analysis. *International Journal of Health Services*, Vol. 13, pp. 107–118, 1983.

Benzodiazepine withdrawal syndrome. *New Zealand Medical Journal*, Vol. 92, pp. 94–96, 1980. Benzodiazepines – Current data and demographics – US emergency room admissions. Drug Abuse Warning Network, 1990.

Bergman, Hans, Stefan Borg and Lena Holm. Neuropsychological impairment and exclusive abuse of sedatives or hypnotics *American Journal of Psychiatry*, Vol. 137, No. 2 (February), 1980.

Borg, S. Dependence on hypnotic/sedative drugs. Pharmacological Treatment of Anxiety, National Board of Health and Welfare, Drug Information Committee, Sweden, Vol. 1, pp. 135–143, 1988. British Columbia Drug and Poison Information Centre. *Drug Usage Review Program-Benzodiazepines*. British Columbia College of Physicians and Surgeons, British Columbia Medical Association, College of Pharmacists of British Columbia, 1982.

Busto, U. et al. Protracted tinnitus after discontinuation of long term therapeutic use of benzodiazepines. *Journal of Clinical Psychopharmacology*, Vol. 8, pp. 359–362, 1988.

Busto, U., et al. Benzodiazepine use and abuse in Canada. *Canadian Medical Association Journal*, Vol. 141 (November 1), pp. 917–921, 1989.

Busto, U., et al. Withdrawal reaction after long-term therapeutic use of benzodiazepine. *New England Journal of Medicine*, Vol. 315, pp. 854–859, 1986.

Busto, Usoa. Withdrawal reaction after long term therapeutic use of benzodiazepines. *New England Journal of Medicine*, Vol. 315 (October 2), pp. 854–859, 1986.

Byrne, A. Benzodiazepines: The end of a dream. *Australian Family Physician*, Vol. 23, pp. 1584–1585, 1994.

Canadian government to launch campaign to warn public of abuse of tranquilizers. *Canadian Medical Association Journal*, Vol. 115 (October 23), p. 816, 1976.

Canadian Medical Association. Guidelines for review of use of stimulants and sedatives in medicine discussed by CMA committee. *Canadian Medical Association Journal*, Vol. 103 (August 15 and 29), pp. 428–429, 1970.

Carney, M. W. P., and P.F. Ellis. A policy on benzodiazepines. *Lancet*, Vol. II, pp. 1406, 1987.

Clare, A. W. Diazepam, alcohol and barbiturate abuse. *British Medical Journal*, Vol. 4, p. 340, 1971.

Clews, Alan G. *Benzodiazepines and substance use disorders*. Alcohol and Drug Committee, May, 1991.

Closser, M. H. Benzodiazepines and the elderly – A review of potential problems. *Journal of Substance Abuse Treatment*, Vol. 8, pp. 35–41, 1991.

Cockran, P.W. Drugs for anxiety. *Journal of American Medical Association*, 229: p. 521, 1974.

Committee on the Review of Medicines. Systematic review of the benzodiazepines. *British Medical Journal*, March 29, 1980.

Cooperstock, Ruth. Social aspects of the medical use of psychotropic drugs. *Canadian Family Physician*, Vol. 22 (January), p. 88, 1976.

Cooperstock, R. *The Effects of Tranquilization Benzodiazepine Use in Canada*. Health and Welfare Canada, 1982.

Cooperstock, R., and J. Sim. Mood modifying drugs prescribed in a Canadian city – hidden problems. *American Journal of Public Health*, Vol. 61, pp. 1007–1016, 1971.

Dangers and medico-legal aspects of benzodiazepines. *Journal of the Medical Defence Union,* Summer, pp. 6–8 (a), 1987.

Do MDs' prescribing habits contribute greatly to drug abuse? *Canadian Family Physician,* Vol. 22 (May), pp. 16, 17, 1976.

Drugged driving – Behind the wheel, Valium may kill. *Health Science Digest,* September, 1986.

Edwards, J. G. Adverse effects of antianxiety drugs. *Drugs,* Vol. 22, pp. 495–514, 1981.

Floyd, J.B., and C.M. Murphy. Hallucinations following withdrawal of Valium. *Journal of Kentucky Medical Association,* Vol. 74 (November), pp. 549–550, 1976.

Gabe, J., and S. Lipshitz-Phillips. Tranquilizers as social control? *Sociological Review,* Vol. 32, No. 3, pp. 524–546, 1984.

Gad, R. Addiction to benzodiazepines – How common? *Archives of Family Medicine,* Vol. 5, p. 384, 1996.

Gene-Bodia, J. et al. Risk factors in the use of benzodiazepines. *Family Practice,* Vol. 5, pp. 282–288, 1988.

Gillberg, C. Floppy Infant Syndrome and maternal diazepam. *Lancet,* Vol. II, p. 244, 1977.

Goski, Terence T. Post acute withdrawal. *Professional Counselor,* August, 1993.

Grant, I., et al. "Organic impairment in polydrug users; Risk factors. *American Journal of Psychiatry,* Vol. 135, pp. 178–184, 1978.

Greenberg, R. Dream interruption insomnia. *Journal of Nervous and Mental Disease,* Vol. 144, pp. 18–21, 1967.

Greenblatt, D.J., and R.I. Shader. Dependence, tolerance and addiction to benzodiazepines clinical and pharmacokinetic considerations. *Drug Metabolism Review,* Vol. 8, I, pp. 13–28, 1978.

Grimes, J.D. Drug-induced Parkinsonism and tardive dyskenisa in non psychiatric patients. *Canadian Medical Association Journal,* Vol. 126, p. 468, 1982.

Guidelines for the prevention and treatment of benzodiazepine dependence: Summary of a report from the Mental Health Foundation. *Addiction,* 88, pp. 1707–1708, 1993.

Guilleminault, C. Benzodiazepines, breathing and sleep. *American Journal of Medicine,* Vol. 88, suppl: 3A, pp. 3–25, 1990.

Hall, R.C.W. and J.R. Joffe. Aberrant response to diazepam – A new syndrome. *American Journal of Psychiatry,* Vol. 129, pp. 738–742, 1972.

Hallstrom, C. Benzodiazepines dependence: Who is responsible? *Journal of Forensic Psychiatry,* Vol. 2, No. [??]1, pp. 5–7, 1991.

Hallstrom, C., and M. Lader. Benzodiazepine withdrawal phenomena. *International Pharmacopsychiatry,* Vol. 16, pp. 235–244, 1981.

Harding, J. The pharmaceutical industry as a public health hazard and as institution of social control. In *Health and Canadian Society,* Toronto: Fitzhenry and Whiteside, 1981.

Health and Welfare Canada. *It's Just Your Nerves: A Resource on Women's Use of Minor Tranquilizers and Alcohol.* Ottawa, 1978.

Health Protection Branch, Dept. of National Health and Welfare. Therapeutic monograph on anxiolytic – sedative drugs. *Canadian Medical Association Journal,* Vol. 124, pp. 1439–1446, 1981.

Hecker, R. et al. Risk of benzodiazepine dependence resulting from hospital admission. *Drug and Alcohol Review,* Vol. II, pp. 131–135, 1992.

Hendler, N. et al. Comparison of cognitive impairment due to benzodiazepines and to narcotics. *American Journal of Psychiatry*, Vol. 137, pp. 828–830, 1980.

Higgitt, A. et al. The prolonged benzodiazepine withdrawal syndrome. *Acta Psychiatrica Scandinavica*, Vol. 82, pp. 165–168, 1990.

Hoffman, Brian F. and Gerald Shugar. Benzodiazepines: Uses and abuses. *Canadian Family Physician*, Vol. 28 (September), pp. 1630–1639, 1982.

Holtom, A., and P. Tyrer. Five year outcome in patients withdrawn from long-term treatment with diazepam. *British Medical Journal*, Vol. 300, pp. 1241–1242, 1990.

Informed consent: Ethical considerations for physicians and surgeons. Royal College of Physicians and Surgeons of Canada, Ottawa, 1987.

Krakowski, A.J. and L.M. Langlais. Acute psychiatric emergencies in a geriatric hospital. *Psychosomatics*, Vol. 15, pp. 72–75, 1974.

Kripke, D.F., and L. Garfinkel. Excess nocturnal deaths related to sleeping pill and tranquilizer use. *Lancet*, Vol. 1, p. 99, 1984.

Lader, M. Benzodiazepines – the opium of the masses? *Neuoscience*, Vol. 3, pp. 159–165, 1978.

Lader, M. Benzodiazepine problems. *British Journal of Addiction*, Vol. 86, pp. 823–828, 1991.

Lader, M. Benzos and memory loss: More than just old age. *Prescriber*, Vol. 3, p. 13, 1992.

Lader, M. Anxiety on depression during withdrawal of hypnotic treatments. *Journal of Psychosomatic Research*, Vol. 38: supplement, pp. 113–123, 1994.

Lader, M. Iatrogenic sedative dependence and abuse – have doctors learnt caution? *Addiction*, Vol. 93. No. 3, pp. 1133–1135, 1998.

Larson, E.B., et al. Adverse drug reactions associated with global cognitive impairment in elderly persons. *Annals of Internal Medicine*, Vol. 107, pp. 169–173, 1987.

Lennane, K.J. Treatment of benzodiazepine dependence. *Medical Journal of Australia*, Vol. 144, pp. 594–597, 1986.

Mallory, J.D. Diazepam (Valium) most commonly prescribed drug. *Canadian Family Physician*, p. 19, October, 1975.

McClelland, H.A. The forensic implications of benzodiazepine use. In *Benzodiazepine: Current Concepts, Biological, Clinical and Social Perspectives*, New York: John Wiley & Sons, 1990, pp. 227–249.

McGregor, Maurice M.B. Pharmaceutical generosity and the medical profession. *Annals Royal College of Physicians and Surgeons*, Vol. 21, No. 5 (July), 1988.

Mondanaro, Josette. Benzodiazepine dependency and detoxification – The consequences of misprescribing. In *Chemically Dependent Women* pp. 95–111, 1989.

Morgan, P.P. Pharmaceutical advertising in medical journals. *Canadian Medical Association Journal*, Vol. 130, p. 1412, 1984.

Nathan, R.G. Long term benzodiazepine use and depression. *American Journal of Psychiatry*, Vol. 142, pp. 144–145, 1985.

O'Bixler, Edward et al. Adverse reactions to benzodiazepine hypnotics: Spontaneous reporting system. *Pharmacology*, Vol. 35, pp. 286–300, 1987.

Olajide, D., and M. Lader. Depression following withdrawal from long term benzodiazepine use. *Psychological Medicine*, Vol. 14, pp. 937–940, 1984.

OMA [Ontario Medical Association] urges physicians to re-assess patients prescribed benzodiazepines. *Canadian Medical Association Journal*, Vol. 127 (September 1), p. 406, 1982.

Oster, G. Benzodiazepine, tranquilizers and the risk of accidental injury. *American Journal of Public Health*, Vol. 80, pp. 1467–1470, 1990.

Oster, G., et al. Accident and injury related health care utilization among benzodiazepine users and non users. *Journal of Clinical Psychiatry*, Vol. 48 (12 suppl.), pp. 17–21, 1987.

Overmedicated Society? (editorial). *Canadian Medical Association Journal*, Vol. 112 (February 22), p. 413, 1975.

Patch, V.D. The dangers of diazepam (Valium). *New England Journal of Medicine*, Vol. 290, p. 807, 1974.

Patten, S.B., and E.J. Love. Neuropsychiatric adverse drug reactions – Reports to Health and Welfare Canada. *International Journal of Psychiatry in Medicine*, Vol. 24, pp. 45–62, 1994.

Peet, M., and L. Moonie. Abuse of benzodiazepines. *British Medical Journal*, Vol. 1, pp. 714, 1977.

Pekkanen, J. The impact of promotion on physicians' prescribing patterns. *Journal of Drug Issues*, Vol. 6, pp. 1320, 1976.

Penfold, S. Are Mood Altering Drugs Overprescribed? Paper presented at annual meeting of Canadian Psychiatric Association, Vancouver, September 25, 1986.

Petursson, H., and M.H. Lader. Withdrawal from long-term benzodiazepine treatment. *British Medical Journal*, Vol. 283 (September), pp. 643–645, 1981.

Petursson, H., et al. Psychometric performance during withdrawal from long-term benzodiazepine treatment. *Psychopharmacology*, Vol. 81, pp. 345–349, 1983.

Phelan, H., et al. Night sedation in pregnancy – Inappropriate prescribing. *Irish Medical Journal*, Vol. 86, p. 107, 1993.

Pomara, N., et al. Increased sensitivity of the elderly to the central depressant effects of diazepam (Valium). *Journal of Clinical Psychiatry*, Vol. 46, pp. 185–187, 1985.

Poser, W. and S. Poser. Abuse of and dependence on benzodiazepines. *Internist*, Vol. 27, pp. 738–745, 1986.

Power, K.G., et al. Controlled study of withdrawal symptoms and rebound anxiety after six week course of diazepam for generalized anxiety. *British Medical Journal*, Vol. 290, pp. 1246–1248, 1985.

Prescott, L.F. Safety of the benzodiazepines. In E. Costa, ed., *The Benzodiazepines from Molecular Biology to Clinical Practice*. New York: Raven Press, 1983, pp. 253–265.

Priest, R.G., and S.A. Montgomery. Benzodiazepines and dependence. *Bulletin of the Royal College of Psychiatrists*, Vol. 12, pp. 107–109, 1988.

Ray, W.A. Prescribing patterns of drugs for the elderly. In *Pharmaceuticals for the Elderly*, Pharmaceutical Manufacturers Association, 1986.

Ray, W.A., et al. Psychotropic drug use and the risk of hip fracture. *New England Journal of Medicine*, Vol. 316, pp. 363–369, 1987.

Ray, W.A., et al. Psychoactive drugs and the risk of injurious motor vehicle crashes in elderly drivers. *American Journal of Epidemiology*, Vol. 136, pp. 873–883, 1992.

Ree, Elin. Beyond benzodiazepines. *Tranx Australia*, 1997.

Rigby J., et al. Mania precipitated by benzodiazepine withdrawal. *Acta Psychiatrica Scandinavica*, Vol. 79, pp. 406–407, 1989.

Romney, D.M., and W.R. Angus. A brief review of the effects of diazepam on memory. *Psychopharmacology Bulletin*, Vol. 20, pp. 313–316, 1984.

Rona, Zolton. Overprescription. *Canadian Medical Association Journal*, Vol. 120 (May 19), p. 1209, 1977.

Ross, M. Lozazepam (Ativan) associated drug dependence. *Journal of the Royal College of General Practitioners*, February, 1986.

Rossen, W.W., J.G. Simms, D.W. Patten, and J. Forster. Improving benzodiazepine prescribing in family practice through review and education. *Canadian Medical Association Journal*, Vol. 124, pp. 147–153, 1981.

Rowlatt, R.J. Effects of maternal diazepam. *British Medical Journal*, Vol. 1, p. 985, 1978.

Royal College of Physicians. The relationship between physicians and the pharmaceutical industry. *Journal Royal College Physicians*, Vol. 20, No. 4, pp. 235–240, 1986.

Ryan, H.F., et al. Increase in suicidal thoughts and tendencies associated with diazepam therapy. *Journal of American Medical Association*, Vol. 203, pp. 1137–1139, 1968.

Salzman, C., et al. Cognitive improvement following benzodiazepine discontinuation in elderly nursing home residents. *International Journal of Geriatric Psychiatry*, Vol. 7, pp. 89–93, 1992.

Saskatchewan Medical Association (SMA) warns of possible litigation involving use of benzodiazepines. *Canadian Medical Association Journal*, Vol. 139 (August 15), p. 324, 1988.

Scharf, M.B., and J.A. Jacoby. Lorazepam (Ativan) – Efficacy, side effects and rebound phenomena. *Clinical Pharmacology and Therapeutics*, Vol. 31, pp. 175–179, 1982.

Schiralli, Vanna and Marion McIntosh. Benzodiazepines: Are we overprescribing? *Canadian Family Physician*, Vol. 33 (April), pp. 927–934, 1980.

Schlicht, H.J., and H.P. Gelbke. Frequency of positive diazepam screening in post mortem examinations. *Zeitschrift fur Rechtsmedizin*, Vol. 82, pp. 271–277, 1979.

Schneider-Helmert, D. Why low dose benzodiazepine dependent insomniacs can't escape their sleeping pills. *Acta Psychiatrica Scandinavica*, Vol. 78, pp. 706–711, 1988.

Schweizer, E., et al. Improvement in anxiety and depression after withdrawal from benzodiazepines. *American Journal of Psychiatry*, Vol. 146, p. 1242, 1989.

Sellers, Edward M. Alcohol, barbiturate and benzodiazepine withdrawal syndromes: Clinical management. *Canadian Medical Association Journal*, Vol. 139 (July 15), pp. 113–120, 1988.

Sellers, Edward M. Clinical pharmacology and therapeutics of benzodiazepines. *Canadian Medical Association Journal*, Vol. 118 (June 24), pp. 1533–1538, 1978.

Shorr, R.I., et al. Failure to limit quantities of benzodiazepine hypnotic drugs for outpatients: Placing the elderly at risk. *American Journal of Medicine*, Vol. 89, pp. 725–731, 1990.

Sketris, Ingrid S., et al. Is there a problem with benzodiazepines prescribing in Maritime Canada? *Canadian Family Physician*, Vol. 31 (September), pp. 1591–1595, 1985.

Smith, David E., and Donald R. Wesson. The benzodiazepines: Two decades of research and clinical experience. *Journal of Psychoactive Drugs*, Vol. 15, No. 1-2, January–June 1983.

Snaith, R.P., and I. Hindmarch. Psychotropic drugs and road accidents. *British Medical Journal*, Vol. 2, p. 263, 1977.

Soloman, F., et al. Sleeping pills, insomnia and medical practice. *New England Journal of Medicine*, Vol. 300, p. 803–804, 1979.

Speight, A.N.P. Floppy Infant Syndrome and maternal diazepam. *Lancet*, Vol. II, p. 878, 1977.

Surendrakumar, D. Hospital admission and the start of benzodiazepine use. *British Medical Journal*, Vol. 304, p. 881, 1992.

The Medical Letter on Drugs and Therapeutics. New York, Vol. 28, pp. 99–106, 1986.

Trickett, S. Withdrawal from benzodiazepines. *Journal of the Royal College of General Practitioners*, Vol. 33, p. 608, 1983.

Tune, L.E., and F.W. Bylsma. Benzodiazepine induced delirium in the elderly. *International Psychogeriatrics*, Vol. 3, pp. 397–408, 1991.

Tyrer, P. The benzodiazepine bonanza. *Lancet*, Vol. I, pp. 709–710, 1974.

Tyrer, P. The benzodiazepine post-withdrawal syndrome. *Stress Medicine*, Vol. 7, pp. 1–2, 1991.

Use and misuse of benzodiazepines. Hearing before the Subcommittee on Health and Scientific Research of the Committee on Labor and Human Resources, United States Senate, September 10, 1979.

Varnam, Ken. Excessive drug use concerns committee. *British Columbia Medical Journal*, Vol. 22 (April), 1980.

Waldron, I. Increased prescribing of Valium, Librium and other drugs – an example of the influence of economic and social factors on the practice of medicine. *International Journal of Health Services*, Vol. 7, I, pp. 37–62, 1977.

Wallace, J.D. The moral duty of the profession in the tranquilizer-on-demand syndrome. *Canadian Medical Association Journal*, Vol. 113 (August 23), p. 317, 1975.

Wolfe, Sidney M., Eva Bargmann and Joan Levin. Stopping Valium and Ativan, Centax, Dalmane, Librium, Poxipam, Restoril, Serax, Tranxene, Xanax. Public Citizen Health Research Group, Washington, 1982.

Wolfe, Sydney M. Tranquilizers and sleeping pills – Two groups of dangerously over-prescribed drugs. *Public Citizen Health Research Group Health Letter*, Vol. 5 (May), 1989.

Zisook, Sidney, and Richard A. DeVaul. Adverse behavioral effects of benzodiazepines. *Journal of Family Practice*, Vol. 5, No. 6, pp. 963–966, 1977.

Index

North Shore Mental Health Association, 238
North Shore News, 162, 205
North Vancouver Chamber of Commerce,
  72, 162

Olivieri, Dr. Nancy, 264
Ontario Medical Journal, 66, 95, 169, 174
Ontario Addiction Research Foundation, 155
Oregon Health Sciences University, 282
osteoporosis, 79
*Our Pill Epidemic: The Shocking Story of a Society
  Hooked on Drugs*, 225-26, 230-31, 265
Oxazepam. *See* Serax

Pacific Addiction Institute Conference, 232
Pacific Medical Center, 166
Padwick, Dr., 40-41, 48
palpitations, 108
panic attack(s), 15, 107-8
Pankratz, Dr., 110, 112, 115, 121-23, 125, 128,
  132, 135, 137, 141, 152, 205, 212
paranoia, 15, 81, 144, 169, 197
Parkinson, Dr. Raymond, 150-52, 192-93,
  209, 213
Parroult, Ray, 226
Patient Rights Advocacy, 19
Patty Duke Canyon Springs Hospital, 154
Paxil, 256
Peart, Dr. Reg, 180-81, 182, 218, 256, 264-65
People, 266
Pepin, Lucie, 226
Pharmacare, 189, 223, 224, 230, 234-36
Pharmaceutical Manufacturers' Association of
  Canada (PMAC), 229-30, 231, 259
Pharmacological Treatment of Anxiety, 176
PharmaNet, 189-90, 234
Physicians for Responsible Medicine Program,
  267
*Power and Dependence: Social Audit on the
  Safety of Medicines*, 70, 233
prescription drugs, 16-18, 70, 105, 108, 113, 150,
  166, 186, 210, 227, 234, 236, 258-60, 261, 264
Priddy, Penny, 227-28, 258
Prisoner on Prescription, 20
Professional Advisory Committee of Pharma-
  care's Drug Usage Review Program, 172
Provincial Ministry of Social Services. *See* British
  Columbia
Prozac(-like), 129, 175, 231, 256-57, 266-67, 269
Psychiatric Update Conference, 232
psychoactive drugs, 138
Psychological Medicine, 175-76, 178
Psychopharmacologia, 174
Psychopharmacology, 95

psychotropic drugs, 88, 267-68
Public Citizen Health Research Group, 129,
  165, 256

Queen's University, 33

Rachlis, Dr. Michael, 164, 232
radium therapy, 45
Rangno, Dr. Robert, 255
*Real Pushers, The,: A Critical Analysis of the
  Canadian Drug Industry*, 85, 154
Red Cross, The, 269
Restoril, 15, 122, 128-29, 149, 198, 203, 268
Review on Substance Abuse Policies. *See* House
  of Commons
Reynolds, John, 226
Ritalin, 231, 257-58, 266
Roche, 269
Rock, Alan, 227, 260
Rohypnol, 259
Royal College of Physicians and Surgeons, 230
Royal College of Psychiatrists, 174

schizophrenia/-ic, 17, 187
Schmidt, Dr. James, 126, 192, 208, 212
Scott Paper, 15, 38-39, 41, 45, 46
sedative(s), 68, 98, 177, 178
Serax, (oxazepam), 15, 24, 25, 94-95, 103, 107,
  108, 114, 149, 168, 174, 176, 186, 203, 268
Shoppers Drug Mart, 230, 235
Siegel, Dr. Bernie, 245
Simon Fraser University, 160, 207, 240
sleeping pill(s), 18, 19, 28, 111, 124, 128, 140,
  190, 252; combination of, 199; continuing
  problems with, 265; Dalmane, 59, 114; Dept.
  of Health knowledge of, 227; Dr. Reg Baker
  and, 187; Dr. Roderick MacGillivray and,
  159, 204; Dr. Raymond Parkinson and, 150;
  effects of, 95, 203, 248; legal case on, 212-14;
  long-term effects, 270; marketing of, 255;
  numbers dispensed, 172; Parliamentary
  Committee presentation of, 224; perils of
  dependency on, 221; PMAC and misuse of,
  231; product monograph for, 261; Prozac
  and, 257; research funding, 229; response to
  documentary on, 232; withdrawal from, 126,
  129, 136
Sociology of Health and Illness, The, 173
*Something More—Excavating Your Authentic
  Self*, 249
Southam Newspaper Group, 163
Southland Canada Corporation, 15, 109
St. John's Convalescent Home, 36
St. Michael's Hospital, 31